The Rise, Fall, and Influence of the Tea Party Insurgency

Emerging in 2009, the Tea Party movement had an immediate and profound impact on American politics and society. This book draws on a decade's worth of original, extensive data collection to understand why the Tea Party emerged, where it was active, and why it disappeared so quickly. Patrick Rafail and John McCarthy link the Tea Party's rise to prominence following the economic collapse that came to be known as the Great Recession. Paying special attention to the importance of space and time in shaping the Tea Party's activities, the authors identify and explain the movement's disappearance from the political stage. Even though grassroots Tea Party activism largely ceased by 2014, they demonstrate the movement's effect on the Republican Party and American democracy that continues today.

PATRICK RAFAIL is Associate Professor in the Department of Sociology at Tulane University in Louisiana. His work focuses on social movements, collective behavior, social control, and computational social science.

JOHN D. MCCARTHY is Distinguished Professor Emeritus in the Department of Sociology and Criminology at the Pennsylvania State University. His diverse and extensive research began with resource mobilization, including numerous studies of social movement organizations. Notre Dame's Social Movement Lifetime Scholarly Achievement Award is named in his honor.

T0372711

Cambridge Studies in Contentious Politics

General Editor

David S. Meyer *University of California, Irvine*

Editors

Mark Beissinger *Princeton University*
Donatella della Porta *Scuola Normale Superiore*
Jack A. Goldstone *George Mason University*
Michael Hanagan *Vassar College*
Doug McAdam *Stanford University and Center for Advanced Study in the Behavioral Sciences*
Holly J. McCammon *Vanderbilt University*
Sarah Soule *Stanford University*
Suzanne Staggenborg *University of Pittsburgh*
Sidney Tarrow *Cornell University*
Charles Tilly (d. 2008) *Columbia University*
Elisabeth J. Wood *Yale University*
Deborah Yashar *Princeton University*

Manfred Elfstrom *Workers and Change in China: Resistance, Repression, Responsiveness*

Olivier Fillieule and Erik Neveu, editors, *Activists Forever? Long-Term Impacts of Political Activism*

Marcos E. Pérez *Proletarian Lives: Routines, Identity and Culture in Contentious Politics*

LaGina Gause *The Advantage of Disadvantage: Costly Protest and Political Representation for Marginalized Groups*

Corinna Jentzsch, *Violent Resistance: Militia Formation and Civil War in Mozambique*

Abel Bojar., *Contentious Episodes in the Age of Austerity: Studying the Dynamics of Government-Challenger Interactions*

Ches Thurber *Between Mao and Gandhi: The Social Roots of Civil Resistance*

Dana M. Moss *The Arab Spring Abroad: Diaspora Activism Against Authoritarian Regimes*

Sidney Tarrow, *Movements and Parties: Critical Connections in American Political Development*

Shivaji Mukherjee *Colonial Institutions and Civil War: Indirect Rule and Maoist Insurgency in India*

Teri L. Caraway and Michele Ford, *Labor and Politics in Indonesia*

Yao Li, *Playing by the Informal Rules*

Suzanne Staggenborg, *Grassroots Environmentalism*

Grzegorz Ekiert, Elizabeth J. Perry, and Yan Xiaojun editors, *Ruling by Other Means: State-Mobilized Movements*

Olena Nikolayenko, *Youth Movements and Elections in Eastern Europe*

The Rise, Fall, and Influence of the Tea Party Insurgency

PATRICK RAFAIL
Tulane University

JOHN D. MCCARTHY
Pennsylvania State University

CAMBRIDGE
UNIVERSITY PRESS

CAMBRIDGE
UNIVERSITY PRESS

Shaftesbury Road, Cambridge CB2 8EA, United Kingdom

One Liberty Plaza, 20th Floor, New York, NY 10006, USA

477 Williamstown Road, Port Melbourne, VIC 3207, Australia

314–321, 3rd Floor, Plot 3, Splendor Forum, Jasola District Centre, New Delhi – 110025, India

103 Penang Road, #05–06/07, Visioncrest Commercial, Singapore 238467

Cambridge University Press is part of Cambridge University Press & Assessment, a department of the University of Cambridge.

We share the University's mission to contribute to society through the pursuit of education, learning and research at the highest international levels of excellence.

www.cambridge.org
Information on this title: www.cambridge.org/9781009423779

DOI: 10.1017/9781009423724

First published 2024

A catalogue record for this publication is available from the British Library.

Library of Congress Cataloging-in-Publication Data
NAMES: Rafail, Patrick, 1980- author. | McCarthy, John D. (John David), 1940- author.
TITLE: The rise, fall, and influence of the Tea Party insurgency / Patrick Rafail, John D. McCarthy.
DESCRIPTION: Cambridge, United Kingdom ; New York, NY : Cambridge University Press, 2023. |
   Series: Cambridge studies in contentious politics | Includes bibliographical references and index.
IDENTIFIERS: LCCN 2023024346 (print) | LCCN 2023024347 (ebook) | ISBN 9781009423779
   (hardback) | ISBN 9781009423731 (paperback) | ISBN 9781009423724 (epub)
SUBJECTS: LCSH: Tea Party movement. | United States–Politics and government–2009-2017. |
   United States–Politics and government–2017-2021.
CLASSIFICATION: LCC JK2391.T43 R34 2023 (print) | LCC JK2391.T43 (ebook) |
   DDC 320.520973–dc23/eng/20230627
LC record available at https://lccn.loc.gov/2023024346
LC ebook record available at https://lccn.loc.gov/2023024347

ISBN 978-1-009-42377-9 Hardback
ISBN 978-1-009-42373-1 Paperback

Contents

Figures

Tables

Preface

This book began as an innocuous email conversation between the authors in early April of 2009. We had learned that a coordinated set of conservative protest events was planned for April 15, and they immediately caught our eye. After reviewing internet listings for the rallies, we decided to index and download the website that had appeared to assist local activists in staging events. At first, our goals were quite modest, and consisted of only writing a single study on the spatial distribution of the Tea Party's first major coordinated effort. The success of the rallies caught us off guard, and our instincts told us that we should try to capture the Tea Party phenomenon more thoroughly. We started a research project, finally culminating in this book, in the following days.

At the time Rafail was a graduate student and McCarthy was well along in his career. Rafail is now an Associate Professor on the cusp of promotion to Full Professor and McCarthy is retired. If the Tea Party had remained a vital insurgency, now well on course to becoming an established social movement, like the Pro-Life movement for instance, the story we have to tell would probably not have been anywhere near as interesting or as theoretically revealing as it has become. That it intersected with the emergence of the Trump phenomenon gave us the opportunity to nest it in what became substantially more interesting theoretical conversations. We never imagined we would take so long to tell the story in the granular detail we eventually achieved, or even that we would persevere in our commitment to capturing it.

We began by scraping newspaper databases for reports of Tax Day protests, quickly developing a codebook to systematically record the details of the protests. We had each separately (McCarthy, McPhail, and Smith 1996; Rafail 2010) and together (Martin, Rafail, and McCarthy 2017; Rafail,

Soule, and McCarthy 2012) used newspaper data to study protest, so we began with what we knew how to do, following Abraham Kaplan's (1998) dictum:

Give a small boy a hammer, and he will find that everything he encounters needs pounding. It comes as no particular surprise to discover that a scientist formulates problems in a way which requires for their solution just those techniques in which he himself is especially skilled. (p. 28)

The "Tea Party Project," as we called it, was not an immediate priority for either of us at the time. But we plugged away, keeping old web crawlers running, building new ones, and planning some new papers to assess the social and economic characteristics of communities that witnessed high rates of Tea Party activity. Given the scale of data that we were collecting, it became clear that we needed research assistant support. We wrote a successful National Science Foundation (NSF) proposal to extend the project and work with the hundreds of gigabytes of unstructured data that we had assembled (NSF awards SES-1322568 and SES-1321802).

By then enterprising colleagues employing the same well-worn methodology as we were using had begun publishing analyses of the social and structural variation across US communities that predicted variation in Tea Party strength (e.g., McVeigh and colleagues (2014) and Banerjee (2013)). For the most part, these studies seemed to have gotten the story right. So, we did not pursue publication of our parallel analysis of the Tea Party origin story since we didn't believe it made much of a theoretical or methodological contribution.

This was before we fully grasped how central the Great Recession was to the Tea Party's story as we began digging more deeply into our data. It was also before we appreciated the accuracy of Skocpol and Williamson's (2011) claims about the insurgency's mobilizing structures and that its local groups were by and large such modest affairs. We began to think about the entire trajectory of the Tea Party as a puzzle larger than just its emergence. By then our data collection efforts strongly indicated that the Tea Party was in rapid decline. Temporal variations within the Tea Party's decline as well as what kinds of effects it had on electoral political processes quickly came into focus as guiding questions as we continued our data collection and analyses. We dramatically widened our theoretical approach, coming into dialogue with scholars who began vigorously addressing how social movements and political parties interact, particularly the work of McAdam and Kloos (2014), Tarrow (2021), Blum (2020), and of course, the original work of Skocpol and Williamson (2011).

Many students and colleagues helped us in the more than a decade we pursued this project. At Penn State, Ashley Gromis heroically coded the original data on the 2009 Tax Day protests. Ashley went on to earn a PhD in sociology at UCLA and is currently employed at the RAND Corporation. Kevin Reuning and Hyun Woo Kim joined the team and led the construction of our web survey of Tea Party activists. Kevin received his PhD in Political Science at Penn State and is currently an Assistant Professor at Ohio University. Hyun Woo received his PhD in Sociology from Penn State and is currently an Assistant Professor at Chungbuk National University. Claire Kovach did much of the detective work on the Tea Party Caucus and the careers of its original members. Claire finished her PhD at Penn State and is now a Research Analyst at the Keystone Research Center in Harrisburg, PA. Finally, Kerby Geoff provided assistance with analyzing our web survey. Kerby received his PhD from the Sociology Department at Penn State and is currently Associate Director of Research for the Boniuk Institute for the Study and Advancement of Religious Tolerance at Rice University.

In 2012, Rafail took a position in the Sociology Department at Tulane University where he began extending the event database beyond the Tax Day rallies. His research team included Isaac Freitas, Cate Irvin, Victoria King, and Prisha Patel who worked for several years collecting newspaper data on Tea Party events, coding and annotating it, and creating coordinates for where events were occurring. Isaac is now a Senior Data Developer and Cate is Director of Economic Development in Pittsburgh. Victoria works for the New Orleans government and Prisha is attending medical school.

This work has benefited tremendously from the advice and criticism of several colleagues. We thank the two anonymous reviewers who gave us generous feedback both large and small. Their comments significantly strengthened this book. We are particularly indebted to Sidney Tarrow, who enthusiastically gave incredibly helpful feedback on nearly the entire manuscript, one piece at a time. His sharp insights and commentary significantly shaped our core arguments, broadened our theoretical scope, and helped us better conceptualize the importance of status threats. Participants in Penn State's Social Movements Reading Group gave helpful feedback on Chapters 3, 6, and 8. Doug McAdam's feedback on Chapter 8 allowed us to better locate and contextualize the Tea Party's political legacy. Our sincere thanks to Michael Haney, who shared his interview transcripts from his discussions with Tea Party activists. The interviews provided essential context that helped us connect the ecological patterns of Tea Party activism with the individuals who took part. We also thank Rachel Blaifeder and David Meyer at Cambridge University Press for their enthusiasm and for helping us see our project through.

This work would not have been possible without the support of our families. Pat thanks Katie, Una, and Miriam for their patience and support during the late nights and early mornings of writing, or more often, frantically fixing a web crawler. John cannot thank Pat enough for her unwavering moral and intellectual support for the project throughout.

The Tea Party

An Insurgent Social Movement

In the wake of what threatened to be a major economic depression, nearly one million frustrated citizens banded together in communities across the US in the spring of 2009, calling for a reduction in federal taxes and government spending. They were motivated, in part, by newly elected President Barack Obama's proposal for federal stimulus legislation to revive the deteriorating economy. The economic upheaval amounted to a deep recession, but one with profound, lasting effects. The activists met, they organized, and they protested. On April 15, 2009, the deadline for filing federal income taxes, adopting the mantle of the "Boston Tea Party" rebels, Tea Party activists rallied in more than a thousand communities. By 2010, the Tea Party had achieved a series of remarkable victories. The Tax Day rallies happened again in 2010, this time with over one million activists turning out. Local Tea Party chapters[1] were popping up across the country to sustain and support these efforts. The Tea Party had also made significant inroads in reshaping the Republican Party. By 2010 many Republicans aligned themselves with the Tea Party. Few episodes of contentious political activity in American history have been so consequential, especially considering how quickly the Tea Party came to dominate politics.

Multiple indicators show that grassroots Tea Party activism had almost completely disappeared less than a decade later. By 2015, the candidacy of Donald Trump remade the Republican Party in ways that deviated sharply from the core principles promulgated by the Tea Party. The hope of a more fiscally responsible Republican Party, a cornerstone of the original Tea Party

---

[1] We use the terms groups and chapters interchangeably throughout this book in reference to the local social movement organizations that were formed by Tea Party activists. We do not intend to imply any strong and stable relationship with an umbrella organization by our use of the term chapter.

orthodoxy, lay in ruins. Matt Kibbe, President of FreedomWorks, a major conservative advocacy group and organizing hub for the Tea Party, lamented in early 2018, "Republicans, now controlling both the legislative and executive branches, jammed through a 'CRomnibus' spending bill that strips any last vestiges of spending restraint from the budget process" (Kibbe 2018). The bill that had so disheartened Kibbe was the Trump administration's Tax Cuts and Jobs Act. It reduced tax rates for businesses and individuals, increased the standard deduction and family tax credits, reduced the alternative minimum tax for individuals, eliminating it for corporations, and more than doubled the taxable threshold for the estate tax. The Congressional Budget Office (CBO) estimated that implementing the Act would add an estimated \$2.289 trillion to the national debt over 10 years, or about \$1.891 trillion after taking into account macroeconomic feedback effects (Congressional Budget Office 2018). After regaining control of the levers of power, the Republican Party spent like the proverbial drunken sailor.

And it continued to do so. In the wake of the several trillion-dollar 2020 bipartisan federal legislative response to the raging COVID-19 pandemic, eventually signed by President Trump, a leader of another major Tea Party group vacillated in her support. Jenny Beth Martin, the founder and decade-long president of Tea Party Patriots sent the following appeal for guidance to the group's email list, asking supporters:

We need to know where you stand so that we can reflect your thoughts in our response to these policies. In light of the public health crisis that is occurring due to the Coronavirus, the federal government has been proposing many responses to try to relieve the American economy. However, many of these solutions are the very types of things that inspired the protests that launched the tea party movement. We would like to know your thoughts on these proposals as well as if you have any ideas on how the government can help in this time of crisis. We support President Trump and want to do everything we can to help him succeed, but many of these policies go against everything we've stood for since the beginning of our movement – i.e., bailouts, stimulus packages, and reckless government spending. (Martin 2020)

After this last halting nod toward fiscal restraint, Martin's appeals to her electronic mailing list wholeheartedly continued its support of the erratic trajectory of the Trump administration, despite her acknowledgment of its fiscal irresponsibility. A decade after the Tea Party had begun, one of its few remaining national leaders caved on its most cherished principle: fiscal responsibility.

What happened to the Tea Party, and why was its vision lost so quickly? Tracing the movement back to its beginnings, in this book we assess the trajectory of the Tea Party and its political consequences. Much of the earlier research on the Tea Party emphasized its initial phase of mobilization (DiMaggio 2011; McVeigh et al. 2014; Skocpol and Williamson 2011), its early maturation (Brown 2015; Westermeyer 2019, 2022), and its relationship to the Republican Party (Blum 2020; Gervais and Morris 2018). The best of the existing research record on the Tea Party is outstanding and robust, but, nevertheless, incomplete. Surprisingly, any systematic research examining the subsequent obvious signs of the Tea Party's decline is almost entirely absent, except for work by Berry (2017). The full story of the Tea Party movement has yet to be told, but its details are essential to understanding the current state of American democracy. It is a story we endeavor to tell in great detail in this book.

In the remainder of this chapter, we provide a general summary of the Tea Party, then outline the key components of the theoretical arguments we develop to explain its rise, fall, and political consequences. Next, we ask seven substantive research questions that together motivate our work, and briefly summarize our answers. We then highlight the unique body of evidence we accumulated for this book. The extent and quality of that body of evidence, we believe, establishes the credibility of our empirical claims. We conclude by summarizing each of the chapters and our major conclusions.

WHAT WAS THE TEA PARTY? AN OVERVIEW OF ITS DEFINING FEATURES

Since its origins, researchers and journalists have struggled to classify the Tea Party, which we characterize as an *insurgent social movement*. Some have suggested that the Tea Party was heavily dependent on the elite manipulation of conservative citizens (e.g., Fallin, Grana, and Glantz 2014), with some claiming that it was entirely driven by elite actors without any tangible grassroots base (DiMaggio 2011). Others have treated the Tea Party as a party–movement hybrid existing within the Republican Party. For example, Blum (2020) treats the Tea Party as an insurgency, as we do, but she emphasizes that it was an insurgent party faction within the Republican Party (or "Grand Old Party" [GOP]). Blum argues that the Tea Party aimed to take over the GOP from within by any means necessary. Another group of scholars have framed the Tea Party as a hodge-podge of mostly disconnected grassroots activists, elite conservative activists and media stars, GOP leaders, and billionaire financiers of a variety of conservative causes, the Koch brothers (Gervais and Morris 2018:3; Skocpol and Williamson 2011:11). We are most sympathetic with the latter group, though caveat that the grassroots activists who comprised the primary manifestation of the Tea Party generally maintained few sustained ties with the elite conservative facilitators.

We conceptualize the Tea Party movement as an *insurgency* rather than a social movement because it turned out to be so fragile. This is not to deny that the Tea Party was a social movement; it categorically was and emerged within a swelling of conservative grassroots enthusiasm. Certainly, the Tea Party was a vigorous insurgency while it lasted. Yet as we will demonstrate in the chapters that follow, the outburst of grassroots activism was short and by 2014 only a few local groups remained, those organizations having virtually no public protest presence. Durable organizations and the sustained and wide use of disruptive tactics are two of the most important characteristics of sustained social movements (della Porta and Diani 2020; Tarrow 2011).

The Tea Party emerged in early 2009 and substantially demobilized by the end of 2014. Its first actions occurred in February 2009, when leaders staged about 20 coordinated protests that expressed an anti-tax, anti-spending vision in response to the Great Recession that was ravaging the American economy. These events were organized by a coalition of conservative advocacy groups who had similarly tried to stoke a mass movement several times previously, with little to show for it. This attempt was different because it worked. The rest of this section will provide executive summary of the Tea Party's main features, including its origins, main actors, message, tactics, and eventual decline. We also introduce the distinctive conceptual language we use for the different factions of the Tea Party.

How Did the Tea Party Start?

The forceful opposition to Barack Obama, the newly elected Black president, and his economic policies resonated with conservatives during a time of widespread economic precarity and White animosity. Elite conservative groups were instrumental in launching the Tea Party. These included Americans for Prosperity and its spin-off, FreedomWorks, along with DontGo, Smart Girl Politics, and the American Liberty Alliance. The coalition of conservative groups seized the moment, setting up a website, taxdayteaparty.com, encouraging another set of rallies on April 15, 2009. Because it marks the final date for Americans to file their federal taxes with the Internal Revenue Service (IRS), April 15 is symbolically powerful. The groups provided primary messaging, set the tone of the rallies, and created the online infrastructure for local activists to stage events. The website was essential to the Tea Party's origins, as it provided the tools for disconnected activists nationwide to independently plan and stage a protest. More than 1,000 protests occurred on Tax Day, jump-starting the Tea Party into motion as a national force.

What Was the Tea Party About?

The Tea Party's primary claims focused on federal economic policies, taxation, and government spending, as already mentioned. Activists proposed a variety of policy solutions, including significant cuts to corporate tax rates, ending the estate tax, and reducing rarely specified bloat in government programs. These positions were far from novel, and indeed, a direct extension of decades of anti-tax mobilization funded by rich conservatives and elites. A main reason that the Tea Party became such an important political force was that its elite-driven claims were uniquely connected to a credible mass movement of grassroots activists.

Alongside the anti-spending and anti-tax rhetoric was a logic of racialized resentment animating the Tea Party, giving voice to White Christian trepidation about their perceived decline in social power. Though the Tea Party's economic arguments were on the face of it race neutral, they embedded a logic claiming that government spending disproportionately benefited "undeserving" minority groups, and that these groups were responsible for the Great Recession. Such views were rooted in a longstanding campaign by conservative politicians and activists linking government spending and the social safety net to racialized groups. The Tea Party adopted a form of exclusive patriotism, where they claimed to represent the silent majority of Americans whose livelihoods were threatened by reckless spending aimed at helping those responsible for the Great Recession.

Who Were the Main Actors in the Tea Party and What Did They Do?

After the 2009 Tax Day rallies, the three core constituencies of the Tea Party came into focus. First, the *elite facilitators of the Tea Party*, comprising several national Tea Party umbrella groups, emerged in 2009 and early 2010. They formed an elite-led "Astroturf movement" – so-called as participants were deemed to represent manufactured grievances rather than authentic ones emerging from aggrieved communities themselves. Tea Party umbrella groups emerged in 2009 and early 2010. They built and maintained the Tea Party's websites, created its core messaging of tax minimization and spending reduction, and provided logistical assistance in the first wave of protest events. These national groups each claimed to speak for the grassroots Tea Party and included the 1776 Tea Party, FreedomWorks, Patriot Action Network, Tea Party Nation, and Tea Party Patriots. With rare exceptions, the national groups subsequently provided no resources to local activists. Nor did they help link the local groups to each other, making sustained regional or national coordinated activity quite infrequent.

Second, *the Tea Party was a grassroots insurgency*, comprising somewhere between 140,000 and 310,000 dedicated activists, 1–2 million protest participants, and several thousand local chapters at its peak. These activists staged protests, organized town halls, held meetings, and mobilized for change. By the end of 2009, close to 1,000 local Tea Party groups had formed, a number ballooning to more than 2,000 by the end of 2011. Groups were forming and disbanding from the beginning of the insurgency in 2009 through 2014. We identified more than 3,500 groups that were active at some point between 2009 and 2014. Nearly all the groups were independently organized by local activists, exhibiting only loose ties with the national Tea Party umbrella groups.

Last, the Tea Party was an intraparty faction within the Republican Party (Blum 2020; Rubin 2017), which we refer to as the *institutionalized Tea Party*. Several political leaders loosely adopted the aggressive style and main policy agenda of the Tea Party. After the 2010 election Michelle Bachman, an incumbent Representative from Minnesota, helped found the Tea Party Caucus in the House of Representatives. We identified 71 Republicans who joined the Tea Party Caucus, only a small minority of whom were first elected in 2010. The Tea Party Caucus emphasized fiscal restraint, strict constitutionalism, and small government, making its rhetoric consistent with the other constituencies of the Tea Party. Members of the Caucus pursued a non-compromising and obstructionist, "take-no prisoners" legislative style. The Caucus was effectively defunct by 2014.

The three components of the Tea Party were loosely connected but operated largely as independent entities. The local chapters and activists used the web platforms created by the elite actors, but the ties between the two were quite thin. Similarly, the elite actors provided the main framing for Tea Party politicians but provided only marginal financial support of the insurgency's agenda in Congress. The politicians who adopted the Tea Party name had few strong ties to the grassroots activists who mobilized across the country.

What Did the Tea Party Do?

The Tea Party rose to prominence as a protest movement. After the successes of the 2009 Tax Day rallies, activists continued staging events maintaining the momentum of the movement. Between 2009 and 2014, we identified almost 20,000 protests, rallies, meetings, and other events staged by Tea Party groups. A notable example of such mobilization was the town hall protests that occurred in the summer of 2009. These were characterized by Tea Party activists attending and disrupting the gatherings staged by political leaders to oppose the health care reform legislation being drafted by the Obama administration. By 2010, activists staged a second set of Tax Day rallies. This time, 674 protests took place – a decline from 2009 – with over one million activists turning up to demonstrate. Over time, Tea Party activists concluded that protests were ineffective and were reluctant to stage future rallies or demonstrations. Instead, they focused on hosting meetings, book clubs, and discussion groups that were highly localized. This tactical decision further removed the Tea Party from the public eye, making it increasingly difficult to sustain mobilization.

As the protests staged by the grassroots Tea Party activists declined, the elite facilitators did little to restart mobilization or to actively expand the Tea Party's organizational network. While these umbrella groups maintained their websites for the local Tea Party groups, they otherwise remained at arm's length from the grassroots activists. Though the institutionalized Tea Party achieved little in terms of major legislative victories, affiliated politicians gladly took credit for obstructionist tactics aimed at slowing down or stopping the Obama administration's policy agenda.

Is the Tea Party Still Active?

The main period of Tea Party mobilization occurred between 2009 and 2014. After that, the insurgency effectively ceased to exist as a significant force in American politics. We use several related measures to make a case for the Tea Party demobilization. By 2014, fewer than 300 local chapters showed any signs of activity, and street-level protests had almost completely vanished. The annual Tax Day rallies that initially demonstrated the Tea Party's strength had dwindled to just 22 events nationwide by 2014. A similar trajectory was evident in the institutionalized Tea Party, which significantly declined in power and influence. By 2015, the Caucus officially dissolved, although it had been mostly inactive for several years preceding its formal demise.

Small remnants of the Tea Party's elite facilitators persist, maintaining websites, sending out emails, and serving as fundraising vehicles for the broader conservative movement. The mobilizing structures built by the facilitators have nearly entirely disappeared. To the degree that any grassroots Tea Party activism persisted, it was largely the result of the efforts of a small number of independent activists rather than any semblance of an active national coalition. Though the Tea Party now shows few signs of life, we argue that its political legacy altered the course of American democracy. The Tea Party's aggressive, uncompromising approach to politics has become mainstream in the Republican Party, further widening the divide between major political parties.

UNDERSTANDING THE TEA PARTY

Our theoretical approach to understanding the Tea Party draws heavily upon the *resource mobilization* (McCarthy and Zald 1977) and *framing* perspectives (Snow et al. 1986). We also emphasize more recent work on the role of social movements within *institutionalized politics and political parties* (McAdam and Tarrow 2010, 2013; Tarrow 2021). Our perspective is also grounded in the view that social movements are composed of citizens acting collectively in attempts to bring about social change. Accordingly, it is essential to emphasize the dual importance of *structure* and *agency* in generating social change (Sewell 1992). These ideas are central to our account of the timing, extent, and location of collective action. We distinguish theoretically between the Tea Party's emergence, maturation, and decline. Given these areas of focus, we concentrate on explaining the Tea Party's demands, the grievances that motivated activists, and the tactical and organizational decisions made by movement leaders.

The first theoretical building block to our analyses is *sentiment pools*, or concentrations of individuals supportive of a movement's goals but inactive in mobilization (McCarthy and Zald 2002). Movements that emerge with preexisting, widely available support for their goals are advantaged. Lacking such blessings, movements must accomplish the hard work of what Klandermans (1997) calls consensus mobilization. The goals of the Tea Party – lower taxes and reduced government spending – had already found wide support among conservatives ahead of the election of Barack Obama in 2008. Elite conservative groups and activists had done the hard work of consensus mobilization around these issues for several decades. Due to these efforts, broad swaths of American conservatives believed that government spending primarily benefited the "undeserving" poor, who were widely understood to be members of racial minority groups, and that White, middle-class economic hardship was primarily the result of high taxes and reckless spending.

The mobilization of citizens out of a preexisting sentiment pool rarely occurs without agency. Organizers, whether organic or elite, are often regularly trying to mobilize sentiment pools without success. This was true for the Tea Party too – elite actors had attempted to foment something like the Tea Party several times, none of which had been successful. Sometimes historical circumstances help organizers succeed in their mobilization efforts. Such historical opportunities are most impactful if they succeed in creating mass disruptions of the quotidian or "the threatened interruption of the taken-for-granted routines of everyday life" (Snow and Soule 2010:36). We treat such disruptions as *suddenly imposed grievances*, which were essential to understanding the Tea Party's emergence. We particularly emphasize the role of *material threats* and the *status threats* in shaping collective action. These threats were linked to two historical occurrences. First, we argue that the Great Recession created a looming sense of economic precarity as its effects spread. These material threats were powerful motivators of Tea Party activism. Second, we turn to the election of Barack Obama in November 2008, which hastened a growing sense of status threat for White, conservative Christians, as they became alarmed that their social power was in decline. This was further exacerbated by the Obama administration's call for a massive spending bill to blunt the effects of the Great Recession, legislation that was widely opposed by conservatives.

The third component of our theoretical argument emphasizes the role of the *organizational and mobilizing structures* activists choose, and the consequences of these decisions. For the Tea Party, elite facilitators disseminated an organizational template that was widely adopted by grassroots activists, resulting in the rapid proliferation of local groups. These efforts spawned a mass insurgency, but one where local chapters were not connected in any coherent way with one another, or to the elite facilitators that put the Tea Party into motion. The organizational and mobilizing structures chosen by activists laid the groundwork for the Tea Party's rapid decline. We draw from scholarship emphasizing the *tactical decisions* (Tilly 2006) made by activists and how movements *frame their grievances* (Snow et al. 1986). The decoupled mobilizing structures made it difficult for local activists to coordinate broadly when planning events or honing their political messaging. Over time, the Tea Party's message became increasingly unfocused, and activists became steadily more disconnected as local organizations ceased their activities.

Last, our theoretical account seeks to describe and explain the Tea Party's impact on electoral politics, and the Republican Party more generally. The Tea Party was not a political party, but a social movement linked to a *Republican intraparty faction* (Blum 2020). Grassroots Tea Party activists were quite hostile to Republicans, and GOP leadership particularly, who were derided as weak politicians who routinely caved to Democratic demands. The emergence of the Tea Party Caucus in the House by 2010 created what Tarrow (2021) calls a *blended hybrid* form of movement–party interaction. We extend Skocpol and Williamson's (2011) argument that the Tea Party served as a *watchdog* for congressional Republicans. Activists used a variety of tactics to pressure politicians to act in accordance with the movement's goals, including threatening to support primary challengers to incumbents and actively opposing any semblance of Republican compromise with the Democrats. The cumulative result of these activities, we argue, was that Tea Party activism hastened radicalization within the GOP.

RESEARCH QUESTIONS

Insurgencies occur unevenly across local communities (Smelser 1962), a pattern also true for the Tea Party. Community conditions become more or less conducive to generating activism, and in some cases help to sustain it (Cunningham and Phillips 2007; McVeigh 1999; Snyder 1979). For several decades, scholars deemphasized the role of grievances as precursors to collective action. More recently, grievances have received renewed attention (Simmons 2014). Our research questions build on these insights by emphasizing how local social structural characteristics enabled Tea Party mobilization by helping the movement's activists make their grievances more relevant to their immediate surroundings. The local contexts where a disproportionate segment of residents share the grievances articulated by a social movement should see heightened levels of activism. Importantly, we argue that the individuals most likely to become active, due to a perception of heightened risk, need not be personally affected by the social forces motivating their activism.

Seven questions shape the intellectual backbone of the chapters that follow. We emphasize the central importance of local community characteristics where Tea Party mobilization occurred, along with the significance of time in understanding evolving patterns of activism. This strategy affords us a unique ability to engage in a granular examination of the evolution of the Tea Party from its genesis, into its maturation, and through its eventual decline. No other research has examined both the spatial and temporal dynamics of the Tea Party, particularly over an extended period of time. As a result, our findings generate important new insights into existing questions about the Tea Party, and provide answers to new questions that remain unasked or unresolved. The research questions are: Why did the Tea Party emerge when it did? Who were the Tea Party activists and what were their motivations? Was the Tea Party an

Astroturf movement, a more organic grassroots insurgency, or something else? What tactics did the Tea Party use? What were the consequences of the Tea Party's mobilizing structures? What became of the Tea Party? What were the political consequences of the Tea Party? We now elaborate each question in more detail.

Question 1: Why Did the Tea Party Emerge When It Did?

Episodes of collective action do not appear randomly and are almost never completely spontaneous. Developing a comprehensive analysis of the Tea Party therefore requires consideration of the longer-run social, political, and economic developments along with the occurrence of any suddenly imposed conditions that together may have facilitated its mobilization. From its earliest moments, the role of elite conservative advocacy groups and activists in putting the Tea Party into motion was heavily scrutinized by both researchers and observers. The insurgency's elite facilitators, however, had been proselytizing a variety of conservative causes for decades. This importantly explains the substance of the Tea Party's anti-tax, anti-spending platform, but cannot account for its timing.

We argue that the timing of Tea Party insurgency requires deliberate attention to the local social, economic, and political contexts where mobilization occurred. National conservative elites had been attempting to spark credible grassroots mobilization like the Tea Party for some time, but with little success. Scholars have already noted that while elite facilitation of the Tea Party did take place, it was relatively thin and fleeting (Skocpol and Williamson 2011). We move beyond the Tea Party's elite facilitators and focus on areas where the Tea Party idea disproportionately resonated. These were communities that were more profoundly impacted by the economic upheaval of the Great Recession, and those areas where there were larger populations of would-be activists, especially White, conservative, evangelical Christians. Both factors are essential to understanding the spatiotemporal dynamics of Tea Party activism.

Question 2: Who Were the Tea Party Activists and What Were Their Motivations?

Many earlier studies on the Tea Party sympathizers suggest they were generally White, older, Christian, and quite conservative politically (Arceneaux and Nicholson 2012; Maxwell and Parent 2012; Perrin et al. 2014). Others have noted the importance of race and racism in motivating Tea Party support (Parker and Barreto 2014), which became particularly pronounced in the ferocious, sometimes explicitly racist rejection of Barack Obama that animated conservative opposition (Barreto et al. 2011). Supporters of a social movement, however, are not necessarily the same as a movement's activists. Some research using ethnographic methods to study Tea Party activists appears to affirm an initial overlap between the characteristics of supporters and activists (e.g., Hochschild 2016), but whether and how Tea Party activists differ from supporters largely remains an open question, particularly since there is still so little research on the activists themselves.

Many explanations about what particularly motivated participants in the Tea Party have been advanced. Some emphasized the role of distributive justice (McVeigh et al. 2014) while others have centered on the mobilizing impact of the conservative media ecosystem (Banerjee 2013; DiMaggio 2011). We agree with these scholars but distinctively expand our scope to include the outsized role of the Great Recession in motivating Tea Party activists. Scholars have not treated the Great Recession as a major catalyst of the Tea Party, despite the temporal coincidence of the two and the insurgency's categorical rejection of the Obama administration's plans to blunt the recession. We stress, therefore, the importance of considering the role of material threats resulting from the Great Recession as essential motivators of Tea Party activism. Our inclusion of both material and status threats as precursors to Tea Party activism both complements and extends earlier understandings of the insurgency.

Question 3: Was the Tea Party an Astroturf Movement, a More Organic Grassroots Insurgency, or Something Else?

A common strategy to delegitimize collective action is to claim that mobilization is a product of the hidden work of "outside agitators" who represent a "loud minority" (Gillion 2020). One manifestation of this strategy is to brand a movement as "Astroturf" and, as we noted above, the Tea Party was almost immediately accused of being an Astroturf movement that was manufactured by elite conservative groups. There is some truth to this claim, as the earliest wave of Tea Party mobilization was put into motion by well-funded and long-standing conservative groups. Given its origins, it is well worth directly asking: Was the Tea Party wholly or in part an Astroturf movement?

We provide a nuanced answer to this question. Yes, the Tea Party began as an Astroturf movement, but it rapidly took on a grassroots life of its own that was mostly uncoupled from the elite groups who helped launch it. The Tea Party's elite facilitators rapidly withdrew from the field, providing virtually no additional support to the thousands of local groups that had formed by 2010. While the national groups did maintain a web infrastructure for local Tea Party groups, they provided little else in terms of guidance or leadership, and competed with one another in their claims to represent the "authentic" Tea Party (Skocpol and Williamson 2011). Yet, the Tea Party's evolution did not end with the grassroots ascendency. As grassroots activism began to fade, largely disappearing by 2014, the elite facilitators returned. Leaders of the main umbrella groups widened their set of claims and eventually came to be strong defenders of the Trump administration despite initial trepidations. Overall, we characterize the Tea Party as exhibiting a top-down, bottom-up, top-down trajectory.

Question 4: What Tactics Did the Tea Party Use?

The Tea Party began as a protest movement, when more than one thousand nationally coordinated rallies took place on Tax Day in 2009. These protests and the demonstrations that followed became a cornerstone of research on the insurgency. There were fewer Tax Day rallies in 2010, with about 680 events that year, but more participants. Beyond the initial Tax Day rallies, surprisingly little research has systematically tracked the subsequent protest activities of the Tea Party, other than a study by Cho and colleagues (2012). No research has tracked the Tea Party's activities over time and place.

The tactical choices made by social movement actors are not static (McAdam 1983). A specific tactic effective in one place or time may have little impact later or elsewhere. Though social movements draw from a culturally and temporally informed repertoire of activities (Tilly 2006), the strategies and tactics embraced by social movements to produce social change generally tell a story of diversity. Much the same was true for the Tea Party. We focus on asking which tactics the insurgency used and when, how they evolved over time, and the impact of these decisions on subsequent patterns of mobilization.

Question 5: What Were the Consequences of the Tea Party's Mobilizing Structures?

Soon after Tea Party activism emerged several national coalitions formed, each authoritatively claiming to represent the insurgent activists. The most important of these groups, as we saw earlier, were the 1776 Tea Party, FreedomWorks, Patriot Action Network, Tea Party Nation, and Tea Party Patriots, all of which have been studied extensively by researchers (Blum 2020; Brown 2015; Burghart and Zeskind 2010, 2015; Skocpol and Williamson 2011). We refer to these groups as the *Tea Party umbrella groups*, as they were the main national social movement organizations that sustained the diverse set of local groups that emerged. The umbrella groups were the most important *mobilizing structure* of the insurgency, a concept referring to the social and organizational infrastructures created by activists to sustain mobilization.

Tea Party umbrella groups, to varying degrees, had ties to elite conservative circles. FreedomWorks, for instance, was a descendant of the Koch empire (Leonard 2020). While the umbrella groups varied in their access to resources, all adopted a hands-off strategy to their engagement with local Tea Party chapters, providing little more than access to their web platforms. The insurgency, in short, did not have a central set of leaders and instead operated in a highly decentralized manner. A significant body of research has examined the implications of mobilizing structures. In particular, federated mobilizing structures, which are more centralized, bureaucratic, and professionalized, increase the growth, local strength, and longer-term survival of many social movement groups (McCarthy 1987, 2005; McCarthy and Wolfson 1996) and civil society organizations (Skocpol and Fiorina 1999; Skocpol, Ganz, and Munson 2000). With only minor exceptions, the national Tea Party groups did not follow this historical template in designing their own organizations or in their interactions between umbrella groups and local chapters groups, leaving open questions about the long-term impacts of the choices they made on the trajectory of Tea Party activism.

Question 6: What Became of the Tea Party?

The extensive evidence we present below indicates that the main arc of Tea Party activism occurred between 2009 and 2014. By 2014, there remained scant signs of grassroots activism that had animated the insurgency at its peak. This is the typical trajectory for social movements, which almost always demobilize in the end. Consider, for instance, the relatively rapid rise and fall of the Students for a Democratic Society (SDS) insurgency (Sale 1973). While relatively short-lived, SDS lasted for approximately 14 years, which was quite a bit longer than the Tea Party. Like the Tea Party, however, SDS disappeared with relatively few remaining traces of organized activism.

Why did the Tea Party disappear so quickly? Social movement researchers have advanced several explanations that we employ to analyze and explain the demobilization of the Tea Party. We emphasize 1) the role of the insurgency's chosen organizational structures; 2) a fear of state repression; and 3) the changing economic and political conditions that had so powerfully motivated early activism. In short, a combination of changes in specific internal and external dynamics made local Tea Party mobilization more difficult to sustain. The lessons from the Tea Party's rise and fall, we believe, are widely applicable to other recent episodes of rapid mobilization such as Occupy Wall Street (Calhoun 2013) and Black Lives Matter (Nummi, Jennings, and Feagin 2019).

Question 7: What Were the Political Consequences of the Tea Party?

The Tea Party activists were almost all Republicans, and as a collective force, the insurgency dramatically influenced the GOP by moving the party toward a particular type of fiscal conservatism. Discussions of the political impacts of the Tea Party have disproportionately focused on the political activities of elected Republicans either embedded in, or adjacent to the insurgency. This is for good reason: the founding of the Tea Party Caucus occurred just over a year after the Tea Party emerged. The rapidity of the insurgency's impact on a major political party was astonishing. The emphasis on politicians working in varying proximity to the Tea Party leaves open a series of questions about the impact of local activist efforts on political processes. During its existence, the Tea Party Caucus maintained tenuous ties with the grassroots activists in the Tea Party, many of whom were sharply critical of the Republican Party and its leadership (Blum 2020).

To address this issue, we focus on the political consequences of the Tea Party in two areas. First, we examine how local concentrations of grassroots Tea Party events and organizations were consequential in the political primaries for the GOP in 2010, and how such efforts continued in subsequent electoral cycles. Primaries provide fertile grounds for social movements to influence institutionalized politics (McAdam and Kloos 2014), and communities that are hotbeds of activism can signal dissatisfaction to incumbent politicians (Gillion and Soule 2018) or indicate openings to aspiring leaders (McAdam and Tarrow 2013). We then turn to the ascendency of Donald Trump as the leader of the GOP, a party-level rebuilding that was in many ways at odds with Tea Party dogma. Tea Party activists and leaders admired certain aspects of Trump's Make America Great Again movement (Westermeyer 2022), but reactions to Trump as a political candidate were mixed and often extremely negative. As a result, it remains quite murky what role, if any, Tea Party activism had in the rise of Trumpism.

PRIORITIZING EVIDENCE-BASED CONCLUSIONS ABOUT THE TEA PARTY

A distinguishing characteristic of our work is the unique, extensive, and systematic data we have compiled on the Tea Party. Digging deeply into both the scholarly and popular literature on the Tea Party as our research unfolded, we were sometimes concerned by the gap between the data and conclusions. This was especially the case for discussions about the Tea Party's consequences. This realization led us to engage in extensive original data collection for nearly a decade to carefully document the Tea Party using a variety of sources. These data are grounded in a combination of quantitative and qualitative information that together provides an unprecedented body of evidence about the granular activities of the Tea Party. Our data collection efforts focused on compiling information about where and when Tea Party events occurred, and how activism was related to local community characteristics. We use new research technologies, including web crawlers and text mining, along with traditional techniques such as surveys and newspaper data on protests. In the end, the comprehensive databases we built for this book span several hundred gigabytes and millions of files that are both wide and deep. The variegated body of evidence we have accumulated allowed us to have greater confidence in our substantive conclusions and provided important insights that became essential to our deeper understanding of the Tea Party.

CHAPTER OUTLINES

The remainder of this book is organized around eight chapters which address our research questions, followed by a conclusion and an appendix describing our research designs. Chapter 2 outlines our *main theoretical claims about the Tea Party*. We begin by drawing on decades of research on efforts by conservative activists and elites to encourage the consensus mobilization of White, conservative Christians. We emphasize 1) the role of the elite-driven tax revolt that emphasized cutting or eliminating most forms of taxation; 2) the legacy of Richard Nixon's Southern Strategy; 3) the amplification of White grievances by conservative media; and 4) repeated elite efforts to build a grassroots conservative movement. Together, these efforts created a large, angry sentiment pool whose members were disproportionately drawn to the Tea Party and ready to act. These factors were not sufficient to explain the timing of the Tea Party. Instead, we argue that the Tea Party emerged during the *perfect interpretive moment*, a product of the expanding economic precarity brought about by the Great Recession and the spillover of status threats linked to the electoral victory of Barack Obama.

Chapters 3 and 4 establish the *origins, activists, and mobilizing structures of the Tea Party*. Chapter 3 develops an explanatory account of the earliest wave of Tea Party protests, the Tax Day rallies on April 15, 2009, and the first set of local chapters that emerged following the rallies. We show that in 2009, the Tea Party was set in motion by powerful, well-resourced conservative groups, who honed the insurgency's message and provided an accessible platform to plan events. The influence of these groups on Tea Party mobilization quickly faded, and very likely surprising all involved, the grassroots roared to life. At least 1,022 rallies occurred on Tax Day, and by the end of 2009, 743 local chapters came into existence, which we refer to as the early riser Tea Party groups. We show that Tea Party activism was rooted in a combination of material threats brought about by the Great Recession, and status threats that animated White, conservative Christians.

Chapter 4 focuses on the core characteristics of the Tea Party supporters and activists, how the two groups differed, and the mobilizing structures developed to support the insurgency. Activists were substantially more conservative than supporters, with smaller differences in demographics and educational attainment. Using several sources of evidence, our best estimate is that the Tea Party included between 140,000 and 310,000 dedicated activists, while roughly 30% of US adults supported the insurgency. We then focus on the major mobilizing structures of the Tea Party, outlining the role of five Tea Party umbrella groups that emerged to sustain grassroots activism. These include the 1776 Tea Party, FreedomWorks, Patriot Action Network, Tea Party Nation, and Tea Party Patriots. The mobilizing structures adopted by the Tea Party greatly facilitated its rapid expansion, with 3,587 groups appearing between 2009 and 2014, but individual groups were almost entirely independent in their daily operations.

Our next major theme is the *maturity, evolution, and decline of the Tea Party* in Chapters 5, 6, and 7. Chapter 5 examines the tactical evolution of the Tea Party between 2009 and 2014 using a unique sample of nearly 20,000 protests, meetings, and other activities. The Tea Party captured national attention as an aggressive protest movement, but protest declined quickly and never returned. By 2012, protests were rare, and instead activists shifted their energy to staging what we term maintenance events, including discussion meetings and listening to invited speakers. We explore several reasons for the disappearance of protests, including the role of activist disillusionment with protest's effectiveness, decreasing media attention, the difficulties in staging coordinated events, and a fear of government repression.

In Chapter 6, we turn our focus to the trajectory of the 3,587 local groups that ever participated in the Tea Party insurgency, emphasizing when and where chapters were formed, when they stopped showing any signs of organized activity, and how long they survived. Between 2011 and 2012 – the peak years of the Tea Party's organized actions – there were more than 2,000 active chapters. Beginning in 2012, chapters began to disappear while the establishment of new groups plummeted. By the end of 2014, only 274 chapters remained minimally active, representing only 9% of all Tea Party groups that had ever been established. We demonstrate that the decline in organizational vitality of the Tea Party's local groups was a product of lessening material threats as the economic chaos caused by the Great Recession receded, while status threats and racial politics continued to play a consistent role in organizational survival. Finally, our evidence shows that local insurgent groups located in communities that had elected politicians affiliated with the Tea Party were equally likely to disband.

Chapter 7 describes the evolution in how the Tea Party articulated its grievances between 2009 and 2018. Upon its emergence, the Tea Party occupied a unique discursive space within the conservative movement, embracing an elite-driven vision of lower taxes and reduced government spending in combination with genuine grassroots enthusiasm and an exclusive vision of patriotism. Using a sample of nearly 92,000 Tea Party blog posts published between 2009 and 2018, we show that the Tea Party's initial framing of spending and taxation faded over time and was replaced by more generic conservative talking points. As a result, the insurgency lost its distinctive place within the conservative movement. We argue that this resulted in the discursive demobilization of the Tea Party, which hastened the insurgency's decline.

We close by turning to the *political consequences of the Tea Party* in Chapters 8 and 9. We begin in Chapter 8 by analyzing how grassroots Tea Party activism intervened and shaped institutionalized politics. The impact of Tea Party activism was felt in the 2010 cycle, but its effects varied in the form of activism. The number of Tea Party protests in a district, which we call *mobilization effects*, predicted the number of challengers who ran in its 2010 primary, but not who won. However, the number of local Tea Party groups in a district, which we term *movement infrastructure effects*, did predict who won, but not how many ran in that district. Together, these findings suggest that widespread protests serve to energize individual candidacies, but their effects do not necessarily spill over into electoral success. More organized Tea Party collective action appears to have affected those electoral outcomes. Second, we demonstrate that the members of the Tea Party Caucus were significantly more conservative than their Republican peers originally, but by 2018, only 23 Caucus members remained sitting in the House. Finally, our analyses indicate that local concentrations of Tea Party activism appear to have increased ideological radicalization in the House of Representatives. Overall, grassroots Tea Party mobilization served as a vigorous congressional watchdog for the GOP and was relatively successful in its attempts to ensure that members of Congress voted in alignment with the insurgency's goals.

Chapter 9 analyzes the relationship between the Tea Party and the eventual rise of Donald Trump as the leader of the GOP. Casual observation suggested to many that there was continuity between the Tea Party and Trumpism in that the insurgency and Trump's Make America Great Again movement were both grounded in a surge of grassroots enthusiasm and fierce rhetoric. Upon closer inspection, clear gaps between the Tea Party and Trumpism are evident. Starting in 2009, Tea Party activists enthusiastically endorsed Trump's racist birther[2] attacks on Barack Obama, but most were sharply critical of Trump as a political candidate. A much smaller group of activists expressed measured support. As a result of this ambivalence, grassroots Tea Party mobilization was not associated with support for Trump in the 2016 primaries nor in the general election. Once Trump was elected, however, there was a sea change within the small remnant of the Tea Party, whose members quickly embraced Trumpism at the cost of abandoning their earlier emphasis on fiscal restraint.

Chapter 10, the conclusion, draws on the comprehensive evidence we presented to make several synthetic points about the emergence and demobilization of the Tea Party. While some of the original Tea Party umbrella groups remain, they exist largely as political action committees with few remnants of the grassroots enthusiasm that had defined the insurgency. After its grassroots heyday, we argue that the Tea Party has now returned to its elite origins, evolving between a top-down to bottom-up structure, before finally returning to the top-down dynamic where it began. We close by emphasizing the legacy of the Tea Party, which we believe will persist into the foreseeable future, and the larger theoretical lessons scholars can draw from our work and findings.

The appendix describes the details of the major research designs that we used to assemble the extensive original data collection we completed for this book. Our model of data collection is a template that other scholars can refine, improve, or extend for studying insurgencies like the Tea Party, and social movements and contentious political activity more generally.

---

[2] The birther conspiracy theory rests on the false claim that Barack Obama was not a natural born US citizen, making him ineligible to serve as president.

2

Toward a Theoretical Account of the Tea Party's Rise and Fall

When mass grassroots insurgencies burst into the headlines they are often interpreted as spontaneous, unpredictable, and surprising. One journalist writing for Politico described the Tea Party as "emerging out of nowhere over the summer" (Vogel 2009). Similar observations are typical for a wide variety of uprisings, including the Arab Spring protests of 2010 and 2011. Dupont and Passy (2011:1) remarked that "the events of the Arab Spring caught most experts and analysts by surprise, including social movements scholars. They seemed to be unpredictable protest events." Rarely, however, do such initial judgments stand the test of subsequent analyses. The Arab Spring protests were, in fact, put in motion by decades of activism and organizing (Benkirane 2012). And so it was for the Tea Party. Rather than emerging from obscurity, the Tea Party had deep roots in major conservative advocacy groups like Americans for Prosperity and FreedomWorks, which in turn were linked directly to the Koch brothers, billionaire financiers of a variety of conservative causes (Leonard 2020). Yet, the Tea Party's elite origins only partially explain the substance of the insurgency.

With the benefit of hindsight, social scientists typically develop adequate explanations of the important factors leading up to an unexpected insurgency. Despite this, compelling accounts of the timing of insurgencies often remain underdeveloped and the mythos of surprise remains largely intact. After the Tea Party's emergence, most analysts came to similar conclusions about who the protesters were, and what motivated them to action. Parker and Barreto (2014:3) captured that widespread agreement when they said:

Our argument is very simple. We believe that people are driven to support the Tea Party from the anxiety they feel as they perceive the America they know, the country they love, slipping away, threatened by the rapidly changing face of what they believe is the "real" America: a heterosexual, Christian, middle class (mostly), male, white country.

The explanation outlined by Parker and Barreto (2014) and others (Hochschild 2016) is largely correct, but in important ways incomplete. The reservoir of White anxiety they describe had been available for some time before it became manifest in the wave of Tea Party activism. The election of Barack Obama, the first Black president, was a potent symbol of the broad demographic changes and shifts in political power taking place in America that surely played some role in motivating Tea Party activists. It is less clear how such sentiments were leveraged into an anti-tax, anti-spending insurgency that found its footing in more than 1,000 nationally coordinated protest events on April 15, 2009.

Retrospective accounts of unanticipated insurgencies typically look both to longer-term political and structural changes and to more immediate facilitating conditions. We organize our discussion here in a similar way, emphasizing what we view as the most theoretically central social and political factors that ultimately gave rise to the Tea Party insurgency. These include *longer-run factors* that collectively shaped the political views and mobilization potential of conservatives, and especially White, conservative Christians. These factors are 1) the elite-driven tax revolt; 2) the effective conservative consensus mobilization efforts to characterize poorer African Americans as the "undeserving poor"; 3) the emergence and growth of conservative cable news and radio talk; and 4) continuing efforts by elite-funded conservative organizations to generate grassroots support and citizen mobilization around their policy prescriptions. Much previous debate about the elite facilitation of the Tea Party has revolved around the efforts to directly generate something like the Tea Party (e.g., Fallin, Grana, and Glantz 2014). The longer-run factors we emphasize here differ because they reflect broader efforts to mobilize conservatives. Broader *elite facilitation* of social change had seeded the social and political landscape, making conditions ideal for an insurgency like the Tea Party to emerge.

The longer-run factors cannot explain the Tea Party's timing. Widely held political views among citizens are by themselves insufficient to motivate participation in any social movement mobilization (Olson 1965). To explain why the Tea Party emerged when it did, we focus on two *suddenly imposed grievances that facilitated the Tea Party*. Together, these gave rise to what we call the *perfect interpretative moment* as the central catalysts accounting for the Tea Party's timing. The first is the economic devastation that was unfolding as the Tea Party emerged, which came to be known as the Great Recession. Little prior research on the emergence and trajectory of the Tea Party has taken seriously the notion that the extensive, widespread material threats caused by the Great Recession were important, let alone central. The typical silence about how economic deprivation influenced the origin story of the Tea Party can be seen in the rare acknowledgment by social scientists of the centrality of such causes in what the Tea Party activists and organizers actually said about what they were doing. The rise of the Tea Party cannot be understood without direct consideration of the Great Recession, and the slow, uneven economic recovery that followed. The second catalyst was how the spilling over of status threats was given form and substance with the election of Barack Obama and his subsequent handling of the economic crisis. The work by Parker and Barreto (2014) shows how Tea Party supporters, who were primarily White, Christian conservatives, felt acutely threatened by the Obama presidency as it was understood to be an attack on their superordinate social, economic, and political power. These status threats were powerful motivators for Tea Party activism. White racial resentment, therefore, is a crucial component of the Tea Party's origin story.

Our scope is not limited to explaining only the rapid emergence and content of the Tea Party insurgency. We also analyze its maturation and decline as our evidence shows that most visible signs of grassroots Tea Party activism had largely ceased to exist by 2014. We link the Tea Party's demobilization, first, to its internal dynamics. From its earliest stages, the Tea Party was built around a decentralized organizational structure that provided little centralized leadership beyond the common messaging developed for the 2009 Tax Day rallies. Many local chapters had ties to one or more of the national umbrella groups, each of which claimed to represent the authentic Tea Party movement. Though many chapters used the umbrella groups to publicize their activities, their daily operations were completely independent. This loose organizational network made it difficult, if not impossible, for the Tea Party to coordinate its messaging and activities, which we claim contributed to its demobilization. Second, we argue that the Tea Party's decline was hastened by the economic recovery from the Great Recession. As unemployment slowly decreased, the stock market rebounded, and the overall sense of economic precarity lessened, the Tea Party lost the intense sense of material threat so important to its early activism, as its earlier concerns with the Obama administration's fiscal policies became moot. Finally, we describe the complicated relationship between the Tea Party and the Republican Party (or "Grand Old Party" [GOP]). Our main claim is that while the Tea Party dramatically altered the trajectory of the GOP, the reverse was not the case. Activists stood ready to attack Republican politicians and candidates who broke with Tea Party orthodoxy. Consequently, political integration was not fundamentally related to the larger demobilization of the Tea Party insurgency.

To summarize our major theoretical claims more concisely, we believe that the Tea Party emerged during a perfect interpretive moment, our shorthand for the coalescence of longer-run patterns of conservative mobilization and suddenly imposed facilitating conditions. Together, these factors help explain the timing and substance of the Tea Party. Its emergence was dramatic, but the fall of the Tea Party also came quickly. We link this precipitous decline to its weak internal organizational structure, the declining salience of the material threats that motivated the Tea Party in the first place, and the Tea Party's combative relationship with the GOP. The rest of this chapter lays out these arguments in more detail and concludes with a summary of the major empirical expectations that we evaluate throughout the remainder of the book.

THE CONSENSUS MOBILIZATION OF WHITE CONSERVATIVE CHRISTIANS

The Tea Party emphasized, right from the beginning, taxes and government spending. These two central issues became the animating logic for Tea Party activists. The emphases were inexorably linked to Barack Obama's overwhelming electoral victory in November 2008 during the Great Recession. The anti-tax, anti-spending rhetoric, however, had much deeper roots. Tea Party activists embraced and drew upon a deep reservoir of anti-tax sentiment and concern among large segments of the conservative, White, and largely Christian electorate that had been carefully cultivated for decades by elites and right-wing advocacy groups like Americans for Tax Reform (ATR) and Americans for Prosperity. The success of the Tea Party was in no small part dependent upon that reservoir, and the insurgency itself was put in motion by these same groups before it quickly took on a life of its own.

What do we know about the origins of that reservoir of anti-tax and anti-government spending sentiment? Our answer to this question is framed by the process that Klandermans (1997:7) calls consensus mobilization, or "a struggle for the minds of the people." Activists who hope to mobilize supporters depend upon widespread favorable sentiments held by potential supporters. If such sentiments are not widely held, then consensus mobilization is often a necessary precursor to action mobilization, or the utilization of money, time, skills, and expertise of supporters for collective action, such as protest and advocacy and electioneering. The process of consensus mobilization has been examined in the history of a variety of popular grassroots social movements, and the concept applies generally across the political spectrum. For our purposes, the concept of consensus mobilization is particularly applicable to scenarios where elite actors aim to shape popular attitudes and beliefs to their own ends.

The Tea Party's anti-tax, anti-spending rhetoric can be traced directly to a sequence of consensus mobilization campaigns aimed at White, conservative Christians, a group that turned out to be disproportionately represented in the ranks of the insurgency (see Chapter 4). There are two areas where these consensus mobilization campaigns were most fruitful: first, the elite-driven tax revolt, which aimed at lowering or, in some cases, entirely eliminating federal taxes. These anti-tax attitudes were the product of a series of organized campaigns backed by economic elites who stood to disproportionately benefit themselves from lower taxation. Second, we focus on the longstanding consensus mobilization campaign which succeeded in establishing the linkage of government expenditures to explicitly racist caricatures of which Americans benefited from government spending. These campaigns were amplified by the rapid growth of conservative media and housed in the justifications of repeated elite-driven attempts to foment grassroots activism.

The Elite-Driven Tax Revolt

From its inception, the Tea Party mobilized around the idea of lowering or eliminating taxes and curbing what its activists viewed as excessive government expenditures. These policy positions were rooted in a much longer arc of conservative mobilization. Beginning soon after the passage of the Sixteenth Amendment to the US Constitution in 1913, which secured a nationwide income tax, campaigns to mobilize popular support in opposition to the newly imposed taxation regime became common. These campaigns may be conceptualized as what Martin (2013) calls "rich people's movements," as they aimed to replace the progressive taxation system with one that benefited richer Americans. Crucial to the Tea Party, however, was that such elite-driven policies were readily adopted by the insurgency's grassroots activists even though the policies would have been of little benefit to most participants, given their own socioeconomic status.

Rich people's movements have waxed and waned since 1913, as Martin (2013) exhaustively described. Generally, rich people's movements were led by skilled entrepreneurial organizers embodied in social movement organizations. Major periods of mobilization identified by Martin (2013:6) included 1) the campaign for the Mellon Plan aimed at abolishing the estate tax and limiting top individual tax rates (1924–1929); 2) the campaign for a constitutional tax limitation, again aimed at limiting top individual rates and estate taxes (1936–1957); 3) the campaign to repeal federal income taxes (1951–1964); 4) the campaign for a tax limitation/balanced budget amendment (1978–1989); and 5) the campaign to repeal the estate tax (1933–2001). Generally, these movements were restricted to the activities of highly professionalized social movement organizations, and only rarely engaged in any public protest. Martin's list is not exhaustive of all rich people's movements. Other examples include efforts to cap property taxes in California in Proposition 13, which was passed by a constitutional amendment in 1978 (Henke 1986), or attempts to privatize public education in order to marginalize the power of teachers' unions (Cunningham 2021).

While the success of rich people's movements has been mixed, they succeeded in creating an elite-driven anti-tax narrative as the orthodoxy in the Republican Party. Early in the twenty-first century, as the Tea Party emerged, the efforts of several well-organized rich people's movements cemented an anti-tax platform within the Republican congressional delegation. These efforts are exemplified in the work of Grover Norquist, an influential conservative lobbyist, who formed ATR in 1985. ATR succeeded in convincing the vast majority of Republicans to sign its Taxpayer Protection Pledge. In 2004, 90% of the

Republican delegation in the House had signed the pledge, along with 82% of GOP members in the Senate (Gale and Kelly 2004). By the 212th Congress, elected in 2010, this grew to 97% of Republicans in the House (235 of 242 Members) and 87% of the Senate (41 of 47 Senators) who signed the pledge. They committed to

ONE, oppose any and all efforts to increase the marginal income tax rates for individuals and/or businesses; and TWO, oppose any net reduction or elimination of deductions and credits, unless matched dollar for dollar by further reducing tax rates.

The nearly universal adoption of an anti-tax stance by a major political party provided the groundwork for what would become a signature issue for the Tea Party.

Given the elite origins and policy scope of rich people's movements, it is important to establish that anti-tax ideas also trickled down to non-elite conservatives as well. Figure 2.1 displays the successful efforts of normalizing the anti-tax rhetoric pushed by ATR and anti-tax movements more broadly between 1976 and 2018 (a similar dynamic was noted by Martin (2013)). To achieve this, we used the General Social Survey (GSS), a biennial random sample of the US population. Each round of data collection, or wave, of the GSS retains a common core of questions, allowing us to track and compare trends in opinions about taxation by political orientation. We used a question asking respondents whether they believed current federal income taxes to be too high. To capture political views, we recoded a seven-category scale of political ideology into three categories: conservative, moderate, or liberal. Moderates were excluded from the analysis, as our focal comparison is between the political right and left.

The pattern seen in Figure 2.1 reveals that between the late 1970s and early 1990s, liberals and conservatives held largely comparable views about rates of income taxation. During that period, between 50% and 70% of respondents reported that federal tax rates were too high. Starting in the mid-1990s, a visible shift in views about taxation emerged and persisted through 2018. Conservatives remained consistent in their views that taxes were too high, while liberals became more likely to voice their disagreement. For liberals, less than 50% believed their taxes were too high from 2006 onward. On average, the post-1994 period saw a 12% gap in views about taxation between conservatives and liberals, revealing a major divide between the two political worldviews.

We highlight the post-1994 partisan shift in views about federal taxes because it took place during a key Republican takeover of Congress, similar to the 2010 takeover during the Tea Party wave of activism. Led by Newt Gingrich, the 1994 midterm elections secured majorities in the House and Senate, ending decades of Democratic control in the House. Dubbed the "Republican Revolution," Republican majorities cemented the anti-tax, anti-spending policy described above, and did so in a manner that mobilized and energized the conservative base (Balz and Brownstein 1996). In short, the tax

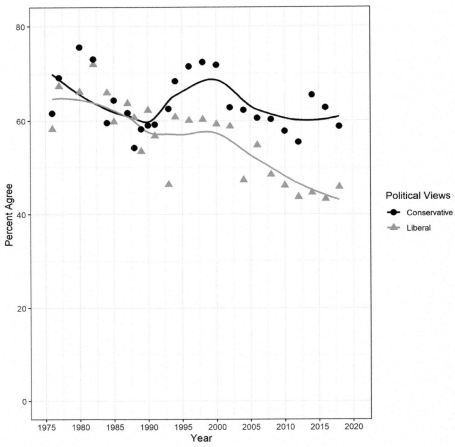

FIGURE 2.1 Percentage of respondents agreeing that federal income taxes are too high, 1976–2018.
Note: Values are based on 25 waves of the GSS and 20,921 respondents. The trend line is a local regression smooth.

policies of the elite-driven, rich people's movements diffused to conservative citizens broadly, creating a sentiment pool that became inextricably linked to the Tea Party in the years that would follow.

Government Spending and the "Undeserving" Black Poor

The elite-driven anti-tax takeover of the GOP and its conservative base is essential to understanding the Tea Party's origins, but leaves open the insurgency's spirited objections to government spending. A second component of our argument posits that the Tea Party's resistance to government spending was the result of years of conservative efforts to characterize spending as analogous to helping the "undeserving," particularly poorer segment of the Black population and other racialized minority groups. The linkages between race and government spending created a false, but nonetheless widely held, view that the *recipients* of government spending were disproportionately racial minorities abusing and exploiting a social safety net funded by White middle-class tax payers.

Starting with Richard Nixon's Southern Strategy in the 1970s, which attempted to secure White southern votes by appealing to anti-Black attitudes (Maxwell and Shields 2019), there was a concerted conservative effort to racialize government spending. The Southern Strategy was successful and resulted in uninterrupted decades of the framing of recipients of public assistance as welfare queens, an explicitly racist, classist, and gendered characterization aimed at stoking White animosity. By the 1990s, a series of studies emphasized the strong connection between attitudes toward race and those toward public welfare among Whites (Gilens 1995, 1996, 1999). By 1995, a significant majority of Whites believed that the root cause of poverty in the US was a lack of effort by the poor. Work by MacLeod and colleagues (1999) aggregated multiple surveys to track attitudes about welfare and welfare recipients. Between 1938 and 1995, the authors found that support for welfare programs remained roughly stable, but the same was not true for how individuals understood the causes of poverty. Over the period between 1982 and 1995, there was a 27% increase in respondents who attributed poverty to a lack of effort, which by then represented 60% of their respondents. Such views came at the expense of attributing poverty to one's circumstances, or a combination of individual effort and circumstantial factors. By the end of the twentieth century, White racial attitudes were tightly coupled with attitudes toward welfare in general. Gilens (1996) argues that racial attitudes are the most important factor for understanding Whites' views on welfare, and in other work notes that such attitudes are informed by the prejudicial stereotypes about welfare recipients (Gilens 1995).

The racialization of poverty, government spending, and welfare expenditures was fostered by Republican politicians, and used effectively to appeal to large segments of the White electorate (Edsall and Edsall 1992). This was yet another instance of a successful elite-driven mobilization campaign that created another sentiment pool essential for understanding the emergence of the Tea Party. The resistance to government spending that the Tea Party came to champion should be viewed not only as a rejection of the expenditures themselves, but also as a rejection of the recipients of those expenditures. The Tea Party's anti-spending platform, therefore, was on its face race neutral but widely understood in racial terms by participants.

Stoking the Fire: Conservative Media Echo Chambers

Perhaps nothing was as important as conservative media in diffusing the elite-driven anti-tax, anti-spending narrative. The growth and widespread influence of conservative media outlets including Fox News (Brock, Rabin-Havt, and Media Matters for America 2012), talk radio (Mort 2012), and eventually social media platforms (Schradie 2019) was instrumental in further popularizing these messages. These outlets provided essential fuel to the nascent Tea Party by popularizing and legitimizing claims about spending and taxation in a way that tapped into existing conservative anger. Scholars have dubbed the conservative media ecosystem an echo chamber, as its constituent outlets distort news in similar ways, while giving airtime to few dissenting voices (Jamieson and Cappella 2008). Widespread agreement exists among researchers that Fox News, in particular played an outsized role in the emergence of the Tea Party (e.g., Skocpol and Williamson 2011), a point we confirm in Chapter 3. This is the result of the outsized role that Fox News has in shaping broad patterns of media attention throughout the right-wing media ecosystem (Benkler, Faris, and Roberts 2018).

The strength of conservative media in its ability to amplify and diffuse issues to its viewers and listeners grew in the 15 years prior to the Tea Party's emergence. Founded in 1996, Fox News had become a major force by the 2000 presidential election (Brock et al. 2012). Reporting by the Associated Press in 2002 indicated that viewership of Fox News had for the first time surpassed rival CNN, and more than doubled MSNBC's (Bauder 2002). Fox's growth continued at a rapid pace. Pew surveys illustrate this point well: in 2000 18% of Republicans reported having watched Fox News regularly, which increased to 34% of Republicans in 2004 (Pew Research Center 2004). The consequences of consuming conservative media are well documented in the research literature. Fox News viewership, for instance, is associated with less political knowledge (Cassino, Woolley, and Jenkins 2012), less societal knowledge (Licari 2020), and a higher propensity to believe misleading or false information (Meirick 2013).

To summarize, by 2009 the conservative mass media was a major force in American politics generally, and among conservatives particularly. We suggest that conservative media played two important roles in the Tea Party's emergence: first, it diffused and legitimized claims about spending and taxation that had been championed by elite conservative movements for decades; second, since conservative media served as an echo chamber, the views articulated by the media elite were rarely questioned or challenged, allowing increasingly fantastical claims to be promulgated unchecked. Consequently, it should have come as no surprise that its viewers and listeners would enthusiastically embrace a grassroots insurgency that directly targeted tax increases, spending, and the newly elected Black president, Barack Obama.

If at First You Don't Succeed: Elite Efforts at Grassroots Facilitation

One of our central claims throughout this book is that the Tea Party is the product of a hybrid between top-down and bottom-up forms of mobilization.

It is top-down because the roots of the Tea Party can be traced directly to elite facilitation by conservative advocacy groups, especially those funded by the Koch brothers. It is simultaneously bottom-up because elite control was fleeting, as the Tea Party quickly transitioned into a principally grassroots wave of contention. Despite this dual formation, we believe that the Tea Party could not have emerged without a broader set of conservative activists and organizations that set the wheels in motion. The Tea Party was shaped, nurtured, and channeled by several conservative advocacy groups who had been largely unable to build a broad, grassroots coalition despite repeated attempts to do so. One group central to these efforts, Americans for Prosperity, and its spin-off FreedomWorks, are examples of organizations that were very much in the mold of previous rich people's movement organizations described by Martin (2013). They were funded by the Koch political machine with the aim of popularizing an anti-tax, anti-regulation, and anti-spending platform (Leonard 2020; Mayer 2016). We see the grassroots Tea Party emerging in 2009 as one iteration of a much longer set of attempts by conservative groups to establish a grassroots movement. The Tea Party insurgency of 2009, however, was by far the most successful – despite sharing tactics and rhetoric, prior anti-tax, anti-spending mobilization fizzled out almost immediately, while the Tea Party dramatically took off.

Attempts either to build a genuine grassroots movement, or at least to produce the plausible appearance of one is embedded in the development of a grassroots lobbying industry detailed meticulously by Walker (2014). Successful efforts by elite groups to generate collective action by citizens in support of their policies are widely called Astroturf campaigns, implying that little organic citizen enthusiasm existed around their issue prior to successful mobilization by professional organizers. Walker's (2014) work convincingly demonstrates that the use of professional grassroots lobbying firms is widespread among corporations attempting to burnish their own images or neutralize their critics. These firms are similarly used by progressive groups to help in mobilizing grassroots support for their causes. For the Tea Party, there is a clear line connecting Citizens for a Sound Economy, its successor, Americans for Prosperity, and FreedomWorks to attempts to mount grassroots action around issues of taxation and spending before the emergence of the Tea Party.

Several decades before the Tea Party insurgency, Citizens for a Sound Economy began experimenting with staging Astroturf citizen rallies. We draw here on the detailed descriptions of these events provided by Mayer (2016:196–199). In 1991 Citizens for a Sound Economy organized a reenactment of the Boston Tea Party of 1773 in Raleigh, North Carolina. Attendance was poor, with those from the media outnumbering the number of participants. There was another attempt by Citizens for a Sound Economy to stage a tea party rally in 1992, this time opposing tax on cigarettes, an important business interest to the Koch brothers. That protest was ultimately canceled after funding by tobacco companies was uncovered by journalists. A final attempt, this time planned by Americans for Prosperity, took place in Texas in 2007. The event garnered little attention or interest despite the deteriorating economic conditions at the time.

Though the grassroots campaigns were unremarkable, the organizational infrastructures created by Americans for Prosperity and related groups were dense and impactful. By 2004, Americans for Prosperity had become the hub of the Koch brother's political operation and the center of its grassroots mobilization efforts. It was well established at the time of the Tea Party insurgency, and involved in planning rallies, knocking on doors, making phone calls, and otherwise engaging in public outreach aimed at expanding the conservative movement (Hertel-Fernandez 2019). According to Leonard (2020), by 2009, the annual budget for Americans for Prosperity was over $10 million, which grew to $17.5 million in 2010. When the Tea Party insurgency began, a wide network of grassroots professional organizers was ready and willing to jump into the fray and aid the fledgling activists. We will show in Chapter 3 that such support was not only vital to successfully capitalize on conservative grassroots rage in 2009, but was also important in shaping the message of the Tea Party.

THE PERFECT INTERPRETIVE MOMENT

The preceding discussion emphasizes long-run trends in politics and conservative mobilization that created symbolic linkages between government spending and race, and an elite-driven anti-tax platform that diffused to conservatives through well-funded advocacy groups and media outlets. None of this explains the timing of the Tea Party. Why did the surge of conservative grassroots activism appear in 2009?

Our theoretical account the Tea Party's timing draws from what social movement scholars call suddenly imposed grievances (Koopmans and Duyvendak 1995; Walsh 1981). When grievances are widespread but chronic, they are not usually helpful in explaining the timing of waves of collective action. In contrast, suddenly imposed grievances have been linked to the timing of bursts of collective action in a variety of contexts (Almeida 2019). Dramatic events, like the nuclear disasters at Three Mile Island and Chernobyl, made clear that when a highly impactful event quickly and appreciably alters the intensity level of grievances among members of a concentrated population, collective action is more likely to occur. This reality motivated searches for other theoretical mechanisms helping to account for timing. Snow and colleagues (1998) point to "disruptions of the quotidian," or radical jolts to elements of the taken-for-granted routines of everyday life. Such disruptions are now familiar to most in light of the recent experiences with the COVID-19 pandemic. Scholars have also emphasized that threats of loss are far more motivating to collective action than are anticipations of potential gains (Kahneman and Tversky 1979).

Our account emphasizes two suddenly imposed grievances that together created the *perfect interpretive moment* for motivating the original Tea Party insurgents. The perfect interpretive moment is a shorthand we use to capture the alignment of an ideal set of social, political, and economic conditions that spurred the Tea Party to emerge and thrive, at least for a time. The first facilitating condition was the Great Recession, which, as we have noted, has largely been minimized in most prior work on the Tea Party (an exception is Rojecki 2016). We find this tendency puzzling, as the economic devastation and widespread anger caused by the Great Recession coincide directly with the emergence of the Tea Party. Our empirical chapters establish that more extensive Tea Party activism emerged in the communities hit hardest by the Great Recession, and mobilization lasted longest there as well. The second key facilitating condition is embodied in the spilling over of status threats resulting from the election of Barack Obama in 2008. Obama's election and his administration's immediate pivot toward creating a massive economic stimulus package designed to reverse the recession, provided a singular target for White anger that had been festering for decades. We now turn to a more detailed discussion of each facilitating condition.

The Great Recession and the Specter of Expanding Economic Precarity

It is essential to begin by recalling the economic circumstances that prevailed in the US when President Barack Obama took office in January of 2009. Those conditions were the elephant in the room when the Tea Party insurgency emerged. The Great Recession had begun in 2007, at the tail-end of the George W. Bush administration, but its effects lasted for years to come. Most researchers agree that a fundamental cause of the Great Recession was the near collapse of the mortgage and housing market, where the thriving industry of subprime mortgage loans brought about millions of foreclosures and defaults. The consequences of the lending crisis were felt in every segment of the economy and across society. Work by Hall and his colleagues (2015:218), for instance, found that nearly one in six households was directly affected by housing foreclosures. The Great Recession had major economic impacts on American households. Between 2005 and 2011, median household wealth had fallen by 35% in the United States (Vornovitsky, Gottschalck, and Smith 2011). Unemployment surged during the Great Recession, growing from approximately 4% before its onset, to a high of 10% (Bureau of Labor Statistics 2012). Another hallmark of the economic crisis was the stock market crash, as several of the major indices dropped sharply in September of 2008 (Grusky, Wimmer, and Western 2011).

A segment of the population then occupying a uniquely precarious position during the recession included retirees and older workers close to retirement. The declining value of their retirement portfolios likely contributed to delays in retirement decisions (Helppie McFall 2011). Workers in the later stages of their careers were also disproportionately impacted by the widespread job losses (Munnell and Rutledge 2013), while other research has indicated that the Great Recession also had disproportionate impacts on the mental and physical health of older workers, who left prescriptions unfiled to make ends meet (Hyclak, Meyerhoefer, and Taylor 2015). The impact of the Great Recession on older Americans appears to have created spillover effects, where depressive symptoms increased in areas with concentrated housing foreclosures even after accounting for an individual's personal financial loss (Settels 2021). The consequences of the Great Recession for older Americans is specifically important, as this group was a core constituency of the Tea Party, a claim we support in Chapter 4.

While the reverberations of the Great Recession expanded, the public was laser focused on the economy. Several surveys that were collected contemporaneously during the Great Recession showed significant growth in the percentage of respondents believing that economic issues were the most important current problem. We show this spike in Figure 2.2, which is based on the "Most Important Problem" dataset collected by Heffington and colleagues (2019). This database harmonizes and combines several hundred random samples of the US population that ask respondents about what they consider to be the most important problem currently facing the nation. We show the temporal trend for all surveys between 1980 and 2015 where respondents indicated that the economy was the most pressing problem.

The evidence in Figure 2.2 indicates a substantial surge of concern about the economy during the Great Recession, visible in the shaded area of the plot. While the general ebb and flow of concern about the economy aligns with larger cycles of economic contraction and growth, reaction to the Great Recession is markedly different. In one survey, administered on October 12, 2008, more than 70% of respondents listed the economy as the most important problem, the highest value over the 35 years of surveys summarized in the figure. The trend declines from that record high but remains elevated for the remaining months of the Great Recession. Across the entire database, a mean of 15% of respondents reported that the economy was the most important problem, a value that more than doubled to an average of 35% during the Great Recession. Overall, concern about the economy was atypically high and widespread during the Great Recession. The deteriorating economic conditions were particularly salient, with suddenly imposed grievances becoming important contributors to the timing of the Tea Party's emergence.

White Rage Spilling Over: Status Threats and the Election of Barack Obama

Perceived declines in social power can be a powerful catalyst for collective action. For instance, McVeigh's (1999, 2001) theory of power devaluation links the mobilization of the Ku Klux Klan to a perceived decline in White

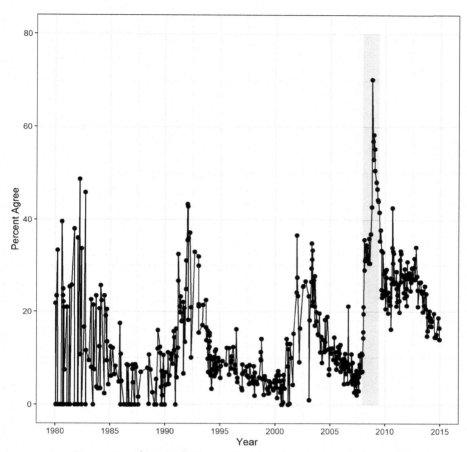

FIGURE 2.2 Percentage of respondents agreeing that the economy is the most important current problem, 1980–2015.
Note: Values are from the Most Important Problem dataset (Heffington et al. 2019) and are based on 514 surveys with 647,530 respondents. The shaded area captures the dates of the Great Recession.

hegemony. A similar phenomenon took place after the 2008 election. By the time that Barack Obama was running for the presidency, social scientists had begun to call increasing attention to the racialization of electoral politics. Exploiting and creating racial division for political gain was a well-established tactic among politicians, of course, but its acceleration with Obama's candidacy and election was particularly stark. Key to this conceptualization is racial resentment. Enders and Scott (2019:276) define racial resentment as "a general orientation toward Blacks characterized by a feeling that Blacks do not try hard enough and receive too many favors." Using 24 years of data drawn from the American National Election Survey (ANES), Enders and Scott concluded that racial issues became especially salient for Whites, and had informed their interpretations of political candidates and government spending since the 1980s. These conclusions have been corroborated in other research. Wetts and Willer (2018) provide compelling evidence that not only had racial resentment among Whites grown, but that it was linked directly to attitudes toward welfare, government spending, and fears of a demographic decline in the White population.

While these arguments point to a general policy disposition disproportionately present in the White electorate, racial resentment found a singular, resonant target in Barack Obama's candidacy and eventual presidency. An extensive literature in political science has concluded that racism was an essential factor in shaping the 2008 election cycle. Scholars found that White acceptance of Black stereotypes lowered support for Obama (Piston 2010), that racism directly influenced how voters evaluated the political candidates (Dwyer et al. 2009), and that the effects of racial resentment were more concentrated on the race for the presidency than emerged in electoral contests more generally (Airstrup 2011). A particularly important contribution by Parker and colleagues (2009) emphasized the coupling of racism and patriotism in the 2008 election. In brief, they argued that Obama was framed as someone other than a "real" American, did not represent "real" American values, and was insufficiently patriotic. We stress this point specifically, as challenges to Obama's legitimacy as a natural born citizen and claims that he did not represent "true" Americans would become major organizing ideas of the Tea Party (see Chapters 7 and 9).

Consistent with what both the Edsalls (1992) and Gilens (1995, 1996, 1999) had so presciently argued before, White racial attitudes became even more tightly coupled with views on spending for governmental services and health care, and this was especially the case with regard to how Whites viewed welfare spending. This coupling was a key part of the logic motivating the widespread opposition to tax increases and enthusiasm for lowering existing taxes among White conservatives, the demographic group most likely to join the ranks of the Tea Party. The campaign and election of Barack Obama exacerbated the racialized resentment held by many Whites, many of whom viewed the election of a Black man, of questionable patriotism, as heading the country toward disaster.

Seizing the Perfect Interpretive Moment: The "Undeserving" Poor and the Santelli Rant

The timing and content of the Tea Party depended on the occurrence of the *perfect interpretive moment*, or the confluence of a large pool of racially resentful, White, conservative Republicans who were acutely concerned with high taxes, government spending, and looming economic precarity. These individuals were suddenly confronted with a serious economic recession and massive government spending bills proposed by a newly elected Black president, who had, himself, previously worked with the "undeserving" poor as a community organizer. What remains is to demonstrate how such narratives became the bedrock of the Tea Party. To do so, we start with the now infamous comments by Rick Santelli, an anchor at CNBC, who played a somewhat surprising but nonetheless essential role in the emergence of the Tea Party.

Rick Santelli's rant has been widely credited as having originated the idea of staging tea parties to showcase the widespread disapproval of the economic stimulus package under consideration by the Obama administration. Santelli's rant is worth examining at length because it clearly outlines the logic of outrage and the allocation of blame that resonated among those who would ultimately join the Tea Party. Here it is:

The government is promoting bad behavior! How is this, president and new adminis-tration, why didn't you put up a website to have people vote on the Internet as a referendum to see if we really want to subsidize the losers' mortgages; or, would we like to at least buy cars and buy houses in foreclosure and give 'em to people that might have a chance to actually prosper down the road and reward people that could carry the water instead of drink the water. This is America! How many of you people want to pay for your neighbor's mortgage that has an extra bathroom and can't pay their bills? Raise their hand. (boos) President Obama, are you listening? . . . Cuba used to have mansions and a relatively decent economy. They moved from the individual to the collective. Now they're driving '54 Chevys, maybe the last great car to come out of Detroit. We're thinking of having a Chicago Tea Party in July. All you capitalists that want to show up at Lake Michigan, I'm going to start organizing. . . . There's only about 5% of the floor population here right now, and I talk loud enough they could all hear me. So if you want to ask them anything, let me know. These guys are pretty straightforward and, my guess is, a pretty good statistical cross section of America, the silent majority. They're pretty much of the notion that you can't buy your way into prosperity, and if the multiplier that all of these Washington economists are selling us is over one, that we never have to worry about the economy again, the government should spend a trillion dollars an hour because we'll get $1.5 trillion back. I'll tell you what, if you read our Founding Fathers, people like Benjamin Franklin and Jefferson, what we're doing in this country now, is making them roll over in their graves. (Conservapedia 2019)

Encoded in Santelli's rant was the widespread understanding among Americans that the housing bubble had been the fault of "losers" and "irresponsible borrowers" whose behavior had been subsidized by the silent majority. This sentiment quickly became more explicitly racist, as conservative media outlets linked the "irresponsible borrowers" to community activist groups like the Association of Community Organizations for Reform Now (ACORN), who primarily served minority and disadvantaged communities. This linkage was particularly salient given Barack Obama's years of work as a community organizer. For example, a blog post of Bader's (2009) posted by the Competitive Enterprise Institute made the following claim: "ACORN lobbyists drafted 'affordable-housing' mandates to pressure the mortgage giants to buy up more risky loans and mortgages from low-income communities." Similar comments were made in an editorial by Pinto (2009) appearing in the *Wall Street Journal* that linked ACORN directly to the housing foreclosure crisis.

These race-neutral complaints about mortgage lending must be understood in the context of decades of linking the "undeserving" poor to racial minority groups, and especially to the Black community. The Santelli rant resonated so widely within White, conservative circles because it confirmed their fears at a time when many believed they faced a real threat of economic devastation. Santelli's rant also provided a tactic for individuals who were angry and wanting to publicly declare their discontent: stage a tea party rally.

The concerns embodied in Santelli's rant had already been accelerating during the final year of the Bush administration, with the passage of what became known as the "bank bailout" in October 2008.[1] After Obama assumed the presidency, the American Recovery and Reinvestment Act passed in February 2009. The Congressional Budget Office (2012) estimated that the legislation would cost more than $830 billion. The reaction to these massive spending packages was sharply partisan. Polling by Gallup indicated that just 34% of Republicans supported the American Recovery and Reinvestment Act in January 2009, which dropped further to only 28% when it became law (Newport 2009). Campbell's (2013) research also emphasized how the Obama campaign's plan to raise taxes on higher earners may have translated into a fear of economic redistribution via major tax-and-spend programs such as this Act. These spending programs enacted during and following the Great Recession, without question represented a significant threat to the sensibilities of fiscal conservatives.

And the proposals translated directly later that year into increasing concern about high taxes among conservative Republicans. Campbell's (2013) analysis of radically different views of taxes by racial liberals versus racial conservatives identified a 27 point gap between the two groups in response to a question about whether taxes were too high. Conservative's deeply held concerns about fiscal responsibility and their general hope for reductions, rather than increases, in taxes were directly threatened by the cataclysmic turn of events embodied in the Great Recession and the resulting policy proposals of the Obama administration. When combined with Santelli's encouragement that concerned citizens stage tea parties, the seeds of the Tea Party insurgency had been firmly planted.

A FRAGILE INSURGENCY

The explanatory scope of this book does not end at the timing and emergence of the Tea Party insurgency, however. Rather, our analyses in Chapters 5, 6, and 7

---

[1] The bank bailout, officially named the Emergency Economic Stabilization Act of 2008, provided a capital injection to the financial sector of more than $700 billion. Such funds were intended to reduce the spiraling subprime mortgage crisis that was partially responsible for the looming economic catastrophe (Shah 2009).

show that by 2014, the Tea Party had largely demobilized as a grassroots insurgency. The demobilization of the Tea Party is perhaps one of the more contentious claims that we make. While there remained small pockets of Tea Party activism across the country through the election of Donald Trump in 2016 (Berry 2017), protests were rare, most local Tea Party chapters had ceased visible signs of activity, and the resonant grievances motivating activism had largely evaporated. The legacy and impacts of the Tea Party continued long after its demobilization, yet it is important that our theoretical account also provide a logic for the precipitous decline of mobilization.

On the one hand, the decline of Tea Party activism is unremarkable. Demobilization is by far the most likely outcome of social movement mobilization. It can result from a variety of sources ranging from repression (Davenport 2015) to cooptation (Gamson 1975). On the other hand, the rapidity of the Tea Party's rise and fall is quite stunning, especially when we consider its widespread impact on American political institutions and society. Our evidence indicates that the effective lifespan of the grassroots Tea Party was roughly six years. How can we account for the decline of the Tea Party? Here we consider three theoretical mechanisms we believe most important for the decline of its activism. First is the weak internal organizational infrastructure adopted by the Tea Party. Second, we emphasize the declining salience of the Tea Party's core set of grievances that had emerged in response to the Great Recession along with the Obama administration's fiscal policies. Finally, we consider the impact of the Tea Party's relationship with, and integration in, the Republican Party.

Organization Building with Weak Infrastructure

In Chapter 3, we will show that the Tea Party insurgency emerged in earnest as a grassroots movement by April 15, 2009, when over 1,000 coordinated protests took place. Soon after, Tea Party groups began to emerge across the country. These local organizations were mostly unattached to any of the several umbrella groups. The umbrella groups, however, soon provided web platforms for hundreds, and sometimes thousands, of the local Tea Party chapters, allowing activists to publicize their events, recruit members, and publish blogs or op-eds. Otherwise, the umbrella groups provided little in the way of resources to the local chapters. There was little cooperation between the umbrella groups, who competed to grow their membership bases while insisting that they represented the authentic Tea Party movement (Skocpol and Williamson 2011). As a result, the Tea Party never adopted a thick organizational infrastructure, but grew into a movement that was at best a loose coalition of mostly disconnected chapters and activists. This internal dynamic of the Tea Party, we argue, played an essential role in its trajectory of both rapid growth and decline.

Scholarship has consistently highlighted the essential role of bureaucracy and professionalization in shaping the trajectory and impact of social movements (McCarthy and Zald 1977). When a social movement adopts an organizational building strategy which emphasizes dedicated leaders, paid staff, and coordination, it tends to survive longer and may be more successful in achieving some social change (Edwards and McCarthy 2004; McCarthy and Walker 2004). The professionalization of a social movement may come at the cost of employing fewer disruptive tactics that are sometimes most effective in producing social change (Piven and Cloward 1977). Protest was a tactic widely embraced by Tea Party activists, but one that is very difficult to maintain in a national grassroots mass movement without at least some minimal level of coordination. The loose organizational infrastructure that came to be adopted by the Tea Party ultimately became a central mechanism behind its demobilization.

Declining Issue Salience

If the timing of the Tea Party was linked to economic conditions stemming from the Great Recession, so too was the timing of its demobilization. As already mentioned, the Obama administration's American Recovery and Reinvestment Act included and estimated $830 billion in spending (Congressional Budget Office 2012), atypically expensive for its time. While debates about the micro- and macro-economic impacts of the legislation are beyond our scope, over time the economy began its recovery from the Great Recession, albeit unevenly and slowly. As conditions improved, the sometimes alarmist claims about the deteriorating state of the economy simply lost relevance and at least in part undermined one of the Tea Party's major grievances.

A similar logic applies to the Tea Party's ability to frame Barack Obama as an existential threat to the nation. Perceptions of the gap between the insurgency's rhetoric and the Obama administration's record of governance, especially concerning taxation and spending, were shaped by partisan preferences (Campbell 2013). Survey data capturing evaluations of Obama's job as president indicated that between 40% and 60% of respondents reported approval, while between 40% and 60% disapproved (Gallup 2018). Obama's performance as president, therefore, fell short of the Tea Party's characterization of it as socialist or radical. These claims lost further salience after 2010, when the Republican Party recaptured the House of Representatives, providing a check on Democratic control of the legislative and executive branches. The newly empowered Republican majority governed aggressively, evident for example in the shutdown of the federal government for 16 days during October 2013.[2]

Scholars have attributed significant importance to the salience of how social movements frame their grievances and articulate solutions (Benford and Snow

---

[2] Notably, Tea Party activists attacked the GOP for working with the Democrats to end the shutdown, an example of the insurgency's willingness to be equally aggressive with Republican leaders (see also Blum 2020).

2000; Snow et al. 1986). Effective frames resonate widely with their intended audiences and can serve as a catalyst for collective action. However, frames evolve in tandem with social, economic, and political processes. What is at one moment an effective frame, serving as an important motive to action, may quickly lose its resonance as conditions change. This line of argument is essential to understanding the decline of the Tea Party. As economic conditions improved, the once effective attacks on spending and potential tax increases were less motivating and effective. The Republican recapture of the House of Representatives partially blunted the status threats posed by the Obama presidency. Such changes left the Tea Party in a difficult position, as the rhetoric which the insurgency had used to capture power needed to evolve. The Tea Party was never successful in articulating an effective subsequent set of grievances.

The Relationship between the Tea Party and Republican Party

Readers will have noticed that we have yet to discuss the role of the institutionalized Tea Party, by which we mean the politicians who affiliated themselves with the insurgency, nor discussed its relationship to the GOP. While the two mechanisms we use to explain the insurgency's decline are relatively straightforward, the final factor – *political integration* – is more complex. We ground our theory of the Tea Party–GOP relationship in work by Tarrow (2021), who provides a detailed analysis emphasizing how the modern hollowing out of political parties makes room for complex movement–party hybrids to emerge. Of these, Tarrow's concept of *blended hybrid formations* best captures the relationship between the Tea Party and Republican Party. Here, Tarrow emphasizes both mutual cooperation between movements and parties (e.g., activists and politicians opposing Obama's Affordable Care Act), while politicians and elites also coopted the Tea Party's rhetoric and grassroots legitimacy to advance their own policy goals and interests.

The blended hybrid concept helps expand our understanding of the effects of political integration on social movement mobilization. This process occurs when a movement's alignment with a political party leads to demobilization as gains in movement demands are achieved in the institutionalized political arena (Gamson 1975; Giugni 1998). A forceful example of political integration is seen in Heaney and Rojas' (Heaney and Rojas 2011, 2015) excellent work on the movement against the war in Iraq, which they argue was tightly linked with the Democratic Party. The eventual demobilization of the movement, they suggest, was the consequence of activists coming to power through the Democratic Party and shifting focus to the institutionalized political arena. The existence of movement ties to political elites need not result in the desired social or policy change (Amenta et al. 2010), but access to institutional political channels is an expedient and efficient way for social movements to influence the political process (Pettinicchio 2017).

Political integration, we argue, does not adequately capture the Tea Party's trajectory. The insurgency achieved rapid political success through the election of politicians aligned with the Tea Party (Gervais and Morris 2018). During the main wave of activism, a rightward-drifting GOP recaptured the House of Representatives in 2010 and the Senate in 2014, and controlled both the legislative and executive branches by 2016. Given the Tea Party's remarkable success in institutional politics, a tactical shift from street-level activism to policymaking would not be entirely surprising.

The Tea Party's hostile takeover of the GOP ran deep. Prior research, especially the excellent work by Skocpol and Williamson (2011) and Blum (2020), thoroughly documents how the Tea Party overtook the GOP. We agree with these authors, but alternatively conclude that the GOP did not entirely absorb the grassroots Tea Party. Instead, the Tea Party's main factions – its elite facilitators, grassroots activists, and the institutionalized Tea Party – all mobilized under the Tea Party banner, with each faction mostly inattentive to what the others were doing at any particular time. Rather, we view the relationship as overwhelmingly asymmetric in that the Tea Party influenced the GOP, but the insurgents remained suspicious and distrustful of Republican leadership. The porousness of movement–party relations, identified by Tarrow (2021), created a scenario where the Tea Party's different factions could work in parallel, and the demobilization of one faction need not have spillover effects on the others. Consequently, we would expect that even the election of politicians who had aligned themselves with the Tea Party should have had little impact on grassroots activism. Instead, like Skocpol and Williamson (2011), we suggest that the Tea Party adopted a watchdog role, and worked to ensure that elected politicians continued to vote in a manner consistent with the insurgency's goals.

CONCLUSION

The swift emergence of what rapidly became a national wave of protests in 2009 surprised many observers. We have asserted that the social, political, and economic stars were perfectly aligned in ways that made the emergence of a movement resembling the Tea Party quite likely as Barack Obama took office. Following the greatest recession since the Great Depression, in the wake of major increases in government spending and widely anticipated increases in stimulus spending by the new administration, conservative Republicans were primed to find the causes of these distressing developments in the irresponsible behavior of the "undeserving" poor, whose behavior had been enabled by activists like Barack Obama.

We have generated several theoretical propositions about the timing, emergence, and trajectory of the Tea Party insurgency that we test in the chapters that follow. These include, first, the importance of the economic chaos caused by the Great Recession in understanding the rise, duration, and decline of the

Tea Party. We employ several indicators, such as unemployment and housing foreclosures, to assess the impact of the Great Recession on the Tea Party's trajectory across multiple chapters. Our expectations here are straightforward: communities hit harder by the Great Recession will have seen more Tea Party activism, and activism should have emerged in those areas more quickly. Second, an unambiguous understanding of what it meant to be a White American animated Tea Party activism. The election of Barack Obama threatened this understanding, and his immediate actions in response to potential economic catastrophe created another set of suddenly imposed grievances. While the Tea Party generally (but not always) adopted race-neutral rhetoric in its economic and policy claims, there was a tacit understanding of who had been receiving "undeserved" benefits causing the economic downturn, and, therefore, who was responsible. Racial politics, in short, were central to the Tea Party's story, but their role must be contextualized within the decades of concerted consensus mobilization. Third, the anti-tax, anti-spending rhetoric of the Tea Party was not mere window dressing. Such views were a product of decades of elite-driven strategizing to create consensus among conservatives and represented the truly and firmly held beliefs of many who participated in the insurgency. Finally, we have argued that as the perfect interpretive moment faded into the past, the salience of the Tea Party was expected to decline in tandem. While there are other important internal dynamics to consider when examining the local longevity of the Tea Party, including cooptation by the Republican Party, we hypothesize that the slow, uneven economic recovery from the Great Recession played an essential role in the decline of the insurgency, particularly as any semblance of national coordination of the many disparate groups failed to take hold.

3

The Birth of the Insurgency

The 2009 Tea Party Protests and the Groups That Staged Them

The Tea Party's first major coordinated show of force occurred on April 15, 2009, when 1,022 Tax Day rallies took place across the United States. A small number of protests had already been staged by Tea Party groups in late February, but the 2009 Tax Day rallies were the first set of widespread protests that put the insurgency on the national stage. The Tax Day rallies were transformative for the Tea Party. Tax Day protests occurred in every state, with hundreds of thousands of individuals attending the events. The protests generated a surge in congratulatory attention across conservative media, as activists promised to stage similar events each year on Tax Day. Soon after the Tax Day rallies, Tea Party chapters began to emerge and expand across the country, with 746 groups appearing by the end of 2009. In short, the Tea Party insurgency roared ferociously to life.

This chapter will develop an explanatory account of the earliest wave of Tea Party protests and the local groups that were created to sustain the nascent insurgency. We focus on the *2009 Tax Day Tea Party rallies* and what we call the insurgency's *early risers*, or the local Tea Party organizations which were founded in 2009. Both are noteworthy because they were a joint product of elite facilitation and more organic, grassroots mobilization, even though the latter came to be the primary mode behind the Tea Party's later expansion. We begin by linking the emergence of the Tea Party to the dramatic opportunity for mobilization created by the Great Recession. Then, we outline the facilitation and testing of the Tea Party template created by conservative advocacy groups, its amplification by conservative media, and the strategic use of online mobilizing infrastructures to connect the Tea Party with grassroots conservative activists. After establishing the origin story of the Tea Party, we analyze the local communities where the 2009 Tax Day rallies took place and where the early riser groups were formed. We conclude by describing the tactics used by the Tea Party during the Tax Day rallies, the insurgency's claims making in the

2009 protests, the organizational sponsors of the events, and the size of the early riser groups.

Our main argument is in two parts. First, the effects of the Great Recession were powerful motivators of early Tea Party activism. Communities where unemployment grew, income declined, and foreclosures were concentrated experienced more Tax Day rallies and also saw the emergence of more early riser Tea Party groups. Status threats, like those posed by racial segregation, large concentrations of welfare recipients, areas with more evangelical Christians, and decreases in the White population, were also associated with Tea Party activity. Second, the Tea Party represented a simultaneous top-down and bottom-up dynamic. Powerful, well-resourced conservative groups, including some with deep ties to the political machine of the Koch brothers (billionaire financiers of a variety of conservative causes), such as FreedomWorks and Americans for Prosperity, were instrumental in creating the Tea Party's message and evaluating its effectiveness. Those groups went on to create an online infrastructure allowing any interested potential activist to independently stage a Tax Day rally or form a functionally independent Tea Party group. The enormous grassroots expansion of the Tea Party, perhaps astonishing even its facilitators, took off and ultimately became the public face of the insurgency by the end of 2009.

SEIZING THE PERFECT INTERPRETIVE MOMENT

Soon after the Tea Party's emergence, a steady stream of journalistic (for example, Zernike 2010) and scholarly (e.g., Williamson, Skocpol, and Coggin 2011) accounts of its origins appeared. That proliferating literature has touched on a variety of issues, including whether the Tea Party represented an authentic surge of grassroots activism (Fallin et al. 2014; Fetner and King 2014), the central role of status-related grievances, particularly those related to a perceived decline in the power of Whites (Parker and Barreto 2014), and the insurgency's impact on electoral processes (Madestam et al. 2013). Others have stressed the reciprocal interaction between Tea Party activism and conservative media attention (Banerjee 2013).

Less work has focused on how economic and material threats might have motivated Tea Party activists; nor has it placed such factors within their existing explanatory accounts emphasizing status threats. Our theoretical account of the Tea Party's rise in Chapter 2 highlights the importance of these considerations. An exclusive emphasis on the cultural and demographic threats linked to Tea Party activism is, and was, limited in explanatory power. It cannot explain why the Tea Party emerged when it did, or account for the elite-driven anti-tax narrative that was the nearly exclusive platform adopted by the insurgency. Our analysis below uncovers a complex interplay between longstanding, well-resourced conservative groups who created the Tea Party's main message, conservative media that amplified those efforts, and the perhaps unexpected surge of grassroots enthusiasm in communities hit hard by the Great Recession.

Our account of the Tea Party's origins differs from prior work in two significant respects. First, our theoretical approach emphasizes the role of suddenly imposed material threats as essential motivators of Tea Party activism. We suggest, for instance, that a growth in unemployment or an elevated housing foreclosure rate – both hallmarks of the economic turmoil caused by the Great Recession – created a fertile community context for Tea Party activism. Second, our emphasis on material threats does not exclude an emphasis on cultural and demographic motivators behind Tea Party activism. For example, we suggest that communities experiencing a decline in the proportion of White citizens along with higher concentrations of what conservatives considered to be the "undeserving" poor were also important hotbeds of Tea Party activism. Similarly, communities thick with evangelical Christian congregations provided a large sentiment pool of potential activists. Consideration of both material threats and status threats are essential to fully capture the rise and fall of the Tea Party. Including both provides a more comprehensive enumeration of the factors motivating the early Tea Party activism.

FACILITATORS OF NASCENT TEA PARTY ACTIVISM

The Tax Day rallies of 2009 were the product of a concerted effort by conservative advocacy groups and conservative media. These early efforts were crucial in testing the main branding of the Tea Party idea, diffusing it widely to a sympathetic audience, and then providing an online infrastructure that facilitated grassroots mobilization. We outline the strategizing that ultimately gave rise to the Tea Party in three aspects: 1) the initial testing of the Tea Party idea by conservative advocacy groups; 2) the amplification of the Tax Day rallies on conservative media generally and Fox News particularly; and 3) the creation of websites designed to facilitate the formation of a largely independent set of local early riser Tea Party groups.

Test-Marketed Astroturf Groups and the First Coordinated Events

Soon after CNBC anchor Rick Santelli's rant in February 2009 (see Chapter 2), a few organizations representing the earliest formulation of the Tea Party idea emerged. The most comprehensive account of these early groups is offered by Lo (2012), who traces the history of what he calls the "test-marketed" Tea Party groups. These groups were formed by established conservative advocacy groups, who collectively settled on the Tea Party concept. Lo convincingly argues that these elite facilitators were examples of "Astroturf" Tea Party activity, in that established conservative groups provided the primary framing, infrastructure, and resources in the earliest stages of organizational formation.

Lo focuses specifically on the outsized role of the Nationwide Tea Party Coalition, which included key conservative groups such as the Dontgo movement, American Liberty Alliance, Smart Girl Politics, American Solutions, FreedomWorks, and the Koch network. Several conservative leaders were deeply involved as well, including Eric Odom and Jenny Beth Martin, who would become leading figures in the insurgency. The goal of these groups was to test the Tea Party concept. Lo identified 18 local Tea party groups that participated in the early test-marketing phase, adopting names such as the Florida Tea Party, Sons and Daughters of Liberty, and the Peach State Tea Party.

Together, these groups staged a coordinated set of protests on February 27, 2009. The events were facilitated and carefully planned by the fledgling Tea Party network, aiming to criticize the Obama administration's American Recovery and Reinvestment Act of 2009. We identified 21 rallies occurring on February 27 using the Tea Party frame in the LexisNexis archive of 785 US newspapers.[1] We coded the details of the early protest events using these media records, which provide important insights about the Tea Party's first activities. We found 18 newspaper articles that collectively referenced the 21 events.

The February protests were representative of the much larger wave of Tax Day rallies that would follow. They were geographically diverse, occurring in 17 states, ranging from southern states such as Georgia and Florida to northern states like Pennsylvania and Michigan, and reaching the west coast in California and Washington. Activists also gathered in Washington, DC. The events were relatively small, most mobilizing fewer than 200 participants. The single exception was a large rally which took place in St. Louis, MO, where media reports indicated that at least 700 participants attended. The protests themselves involved activists giving speeches, waving signs, and chanting, and were thus quite unremarkable in their tactical choices and aesthetics. None of the events had reports of arrests, violence, or other contentious behavior. Newspaper coverage of these events rarely mentioned the groups organizing the rallies. Sponsoring organizations were noted in only three cases: FreedomWorks was listed as a sponsor for an event in Jacksonville, FL; the Atlanta Tea Party sponsored the protest in Atlanta, GA; and the Cumberland County Republican Party organized the event in Fayetteville, NC.

The test-marketed Tea Party groups and the events that they staged were prophetic of the surge of activism that followed. The first push of the insurgency was timely, resonant, and, despite the top-down coordination of the protests, exhibited a plausible level of grassroots authenticity. The small number of groups and events were but a shadow of the explosion of Tea Party activism that soon followed. How did the small scale of the test-marketed

---

[1] The LexisNexis archive is one of the sources we use to build a database of Tea Party events, described in this book's Appendix.

groups become the Tea Party insurgency? We discuss two related factors that are crucial for understanding the rapid growth of the Tea Party: the amplification of the Tea Party frame on conservative media (particularly Fox News) and the online mobilizing infrastructures that were created by the elite groups responsible for the first push toward activism.

Amplifying the Tea Party

The mass mobilization that came to define early Tea Party activism would not have been possible without its amplification in conservative media, social media, and talk radio. Immediately following the protest events of February 27, sympathetic coverage began to appear on Fox News. During Greta Van Susteren's nightly primetime show that evening, she said that "Tea Party protests are erupting across the country. Angry taxpayers, or at least some of them, are taking to the streets in the spirit of the Boston Tea Party. People are protesting President Obama's massive $787 billion stimulus bill, and his $3.55 trillion budget, and a federal government that has been ballooning by the day since the president took office" (see Brock et al. 2012:107–108). Similar sympathetic coverage appeared across the conservative media ecosystem (Fallin et al. 2014; Street and DiMaggio 2015).

Researchers largely agree that Fox News had the most outsized influence on amplifying the Tea Party, in no small part the result of the sheer size of its audience. Skocpol and Williamson (2011:132) document how Fox News' coverage of the Tea Party was substantially greater than attention on CNN leading up to the Tax Day rallies in 2009. To further demonstrate the steady stream of Tea Party amplification on Fox News, we extend Skocpol and Williamson's analysis and compare references to the Tea Party on Fox News, CNN, and MSNBC, and 785 local, state, and national newspapers. We used the full-text transcripts of all content airing on the cable news networks and the full text of the newspaper articles to generate our counts, with the strings "tea party" or "tea parties" to identify references to the insurgency. The newspaper sample exhausts all US-based newspapers in the LexisNexis database (see the appendix). We focus on the period between February 19 and April 14, 2009, which begins with the Santelli rant and ends the day before the Tax Day rallies.

Figure 3.1 illustrates that the Fox News amplification of the Tea Party was substantially more pronounced than that of any other cable news network, or the sample of newspapers. For all sources, the first protests on February 27 received a flash of coverage that quickly dissipated. Fox News began emphasizing the upcoming Tax Day rallies in late March, and this grew in intensity as the Tax Day approached. Starting March 30, it referenced the Tea Party multiple times each day, excluding April 4 and 11, when the insurgency was not mentioned. In the immediate period before Tax Day, Fox News noticeably ramped up its attention, referencing the Tea Party 110 times on

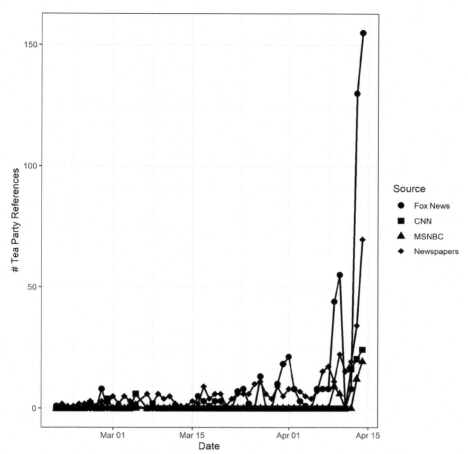

FIGURE 3.1 Media attention to the Tea Party, February 19–April 14, 2009.
Note: Values are based on 537, 74, 48, and 401 references to the Tea Party on Fox News, CNN, MSNBC, and newspapers respectively.

April 13 and 155 times on April 14. The coverage was highly supportive, encouraging viewers to join the rallies and repeatedly mentioning how Fox News hosts Neil Cavuto and Sean Hannity would be broadcasting live from the Tax Day rallies in Sacramento, CA, and Atlanta, GA, respectively. Primetime Fox News star Glenn Beck stated again and again that the protests would not simply be an objection to existing tax policy, but to government spending more broadly.

The comparison between Fox News and other media outlets in Figure 3.1 underscores how extensively Fox News amplified the Tea Party. For instance, CNN did not reference the Tea Party at all in 87% of coverage days between February 19 and April 14, while MSNBC similarly did not mention the Tea

Party in 89% of those coverage days. Newspaper attention to the Tea Party, overall, produced a total of 401 references. The volume of coverage in newspapers was a slow and steady trickle rather than the surge of attention devoted to the insurgency on Fox News. That amplification is especially pronounced since we combined 785 newspapers encompassing a variety of political orientations to create the estimates of newspaper coverage. The resulting comparison starkly illustrates Fox's outsized attention to the Tea Party.

Overall, as did Skocpol and Williamson (2011), we conclude that Fox News played a central initial role in stimulating the Tea Party's initial mass mobilization. Conservative media, and particularly Fox News, were instrumental in amplifying the first large-scale coordinated Tax Day protests. Fox News promoted the rallies and encouraged viewers to attend, and several high-profile hosts like Sean Hannity and Glenn Beck endorsed the Tea Party. However, the amplification by Fox was by itself insufficient to generate protest events across the country. The Tea Party's elite facilitators also built online infrastructures that made it easier for activists to stage a local Tea Party, an act that was crucial to the success of the rallies.

Building Mobilizing Infrastructures Online

The final element in the top-down facilitation of early Tea Party activism was the development of online platforms that allowed virtually any interested individual or group to stage a Tax Day rally, and eventually to form a local Tea Party chapter. The 2009 Tax Day rallies are best characterized as what McCarthy and McPhail (2006) refer to as impromptu protests, in that they were facilitated, organized, and staged on short notice. Impromptu protests differ substantially from many large-scale protests that are the result of elaborate, long-term planning, for instance the famous "March on Washington" in August 1963 when 50,000 people gathered in front of the Lincoln Memorial in Washington, DC. Impromptu protests tend to be smaller and are staged in diverse locations, which substantially increases the complexity of organizing a nationally coordinated set of events. This was particularly salient for the Tea Party, as the insurgency initially lacked any independent organizational infrastructure or local chapter network beyond the test-marketed Astroturf groups identified by Lo (2012).

The creation of online mobilizing infrastructures used to facilitate the Tax Day rallies emerged rapidly, though the platforms necessary to create the loosely structured organizational form that came to define the Tea Party's local chapters took some time. We begin by describing the facilitation of the Tax Day Tea Party rallies, which set the stage for the local organizational building that followed the success of the April 15 events. Mayer (2016:176) notes that within a few hours of the Santelli rant, a website using the domain taxdayteaparty.com was created. The domain became a centralized hub that was used to organize the Tax Day rallies. It was built by Eric Odom, a long-term associate of the

Koch network.[2] Odom also built the Nationwide Tea Party Coalition in collaboration with other leading conservative activists and organizations, including Dick Armey, FreedomWorks, Smart Girl Politics, Top Conservatives on Twitter, and Americans for Prosperity, who appeared as sponsors on the website.

The Tax Day rally website provided an accessible and easy to implement do-it-yourself template for staging a protest on April 15. We exhaustively indexed the Tax Day Tea Party website several times in mid-April to capture the instructions and resources made available to activists, and to track where and when the events took place. The website was meticulous in providing all the information necessary for local organizers who had never participated in planning a protest. It included detailed instructions for working with the media, securing permits, and downloadable templates for signs. The website also summarized the main messaging of the Tea Party, that had been test-marketed by the earlier Astroturf protests. The graphics throughout the website advertised that participants would be the "silent majority no more" and emphasized goals such as abolishing estate tax and taxation on capital gains, as well as reducing the business tax rate (see Chapter 7 for a more extensive discussion of these claims and their evolution). Finally, the website directed interested media outlets to contact several prominent conservative activists, including Eric Odom of the DontGo Movement, Michael Leahy, founder of Top Conservatives on Twitter, and Stacy Mott, co-founder of Smart Girl Politics.

The Tax Day rally website did little to encourage activism after April 15, however. Following the success of the Tax Day rallies, several groups claiming to represent the Tea Party insurgency appeared in mid-to-late 2009, including the 1776 Tea Party, Tea Party Patriots, and Tea Party Nation. These umbrella groups provided web platforms for individual activists to join or form an existing Tea Party group, to network with other Tea Partiers, and continue mobilizing for change. Similar to the sponsors of the Tax Day rally website, the umbrella groups were founded by conservative activists like Judson Phillips (Tea Party Nation), Jenny Beth Martin (Tea Party Patriots), and Matt Kibbe (FreedomWorks). Each of these groups claimed to be the authentic, authoritative source of Tea Party activism, and provided an online platform encouraging activists to form new local Tea Party chapters.

Much like the Tax Day rally website, the umbrella groups exerted little direct control over the formation of local Tea Party chapters. There were few barriers to creating a local Tea Party chapter, which required activists to simply register for an account on an umbrella group's website and select a name. The group was then publicly posted online, allowing other sympathizers to join the group. Once a chapter was formed, it was largely left to its own devices by the

[2] A second website at taxpayerteaparty.com was also built by Americans for Prosperity; however, the bulk of rally planning and organizing appeared to take place on taxdayteaparty.com based on our contemporaneous observations of the rallies.

umbrella groups, whose involvement consisted mostly of providing a platform for mobilization. The websites maintained by the umbrella groups rarely actively encouraged any specific coordinated actions or facilitated coalition building across local chapters beyond the Tax Day rallies.

Summary: The Cultivation of Loosely Facilitated Grassroots Activism

The Tea Party emerged from a carefully planned set of events put in motion by established conservative groups and activists. Following Lo's (2012) work, we suggest that the branding of the Tea Party was the result of test-marketed activism that was resonant and successful. Once the Tea Party idea was widely amplified on conservative media, pushing the anti-tax and lower spending message to conservatives across the country, the advocacy groups built online tools for the Tax Day protests, laying the groundwork for the early riser groups that followed. Together, this loosely linked coterie of top-down facilitators was responsible, we argue, for setting the Tea Party in motion.

We have argued that the rallies and early riser groups were also each a product of grassroots activism. A distinguishing feature of the Tax Day rally website, and the Tea Party umbrella groups that would follow, was their openness. The websites were designed to allow any interested activist to stage an event and/or found a Tea Party chapter. For the Tax Day rallies, the resources made available to potential organizers suggested an expectation that most rallies would be staged by inexperienced participants rather than seasoned activists. The messaging and framing of the Tea Party idea was readily provided, but the national coordinators retained little direct control over how local groups staged events, engaged with the media, or otherwise followed the intended script for the rallies. In other words, it is crucial to emphasize that the Tax Day rallies and early riser groups represent the first examples of the Tea Party's weak coordination, in that the idea was the product of top-down facilitation, but its manifestation was also an example of self-motivated grassroots activism.

FERTILE COMMUNITY CONTEXTS FOR EARLY TEA PARTY ACTIVISM

While the preceding discussion traces the emergence of the Tea Party as a combination of top-down and bottom-up activism, our account has thus far not attended to where the Tea Party took root. We begin building our explanatory account of the Tea Party's origins by analyzing the geographic distribution of early Tea Party activism, using county-level counts to identify where the 2009 Tax Day rallies took place and where the early riser Tea Party groups were founded. This sets the stage for our systematic analysis of the local conditions that led to differences in the extent of Tea Party activity in counties across the country.

Sampling Tax Day Rallies and Early Riser Groups

We used a two-part research strategy to enumerate local Tax Day rallies. First, we collected 806 events listed on taxdayteaparty.com. Organizers listed the time and place of each rally on the Tax Day rally website, which we used to geographically locate each event in its local community. Second, we triangulated the web data with newspaper coverage of the rallies. We used Access World News and LexisNexis, which are full-text searchable archives of local, state, and national newspapers, to collect local newspaper coverage of events. We used a broad search string and drew on 452 daily newspapers from Access World News and, as already noted, 785 from LexisNexis, archiving all articles mentioning the Tea Party movement between April 8, 2009, and April 29, 2009. We then read and content-coded the articles, yielding an additional 216 Tea Party protests not included on the Tax Day rally website. Between the two sources, our sampling strategy generated a total of 1,022 protests in 2009.

Sampling the early riser Tea Party groups involved collecting internet listings of all chapters founded in 2009. Since we are primarily interested in the local community contexts where Tea Party activism took place, we excluded state-level and national Tea Party groups from our analysis. We built a database of early risers using web crawlers that we ran daily on four Tea Party umbrella groups, including the 1776 Tea Party, Patriot Action Network, Tea Party Nation, and Tea Party Patriots.[3] The listings were updated daily and then manually reviewed to capture the group's location and to identify and remove duplicates, spam accounts, and the organizations appearing in the listings of multiple umbrella groups. During data collection, we also retained information about the membership size of each group (when reported), which allowed us to produce a rough estimate of the total number of Tea Party activists who joined an organization through 2009. We found 746 early riser groups using this research design.

Our strategy to identify Tax Day rallies and early riser groups results in a more extensive and comprehensive sample compared to those used in prior research on the Tea Party. For instance, Parkin and his colleagues (2015) used a combination of media sources and websites to sample the Tax Day rallies, and found evidence of 627 protests. Similarly, Banerjee (2013) studied protest counts using data collected by the Institute for Research and Education on Human Rights (IREHR), a group highly critical of the Tea Party and what it stood for, and found only 467 events occurring during 2009 and 2010. Other studies have focused on organizational counts, but most of those use data collected in 2010, when the Tea Party's grassroots chapters were growing exponentially. McVeigh et al. (2014), also using data from IREHR, identified

---

[3] Despite its role in facilitating the Tea Party's emergence, FreedomWorks is excluded from our analysis of early riser groups, as it only provided listings of state-level Tea Party chapters though 2010.

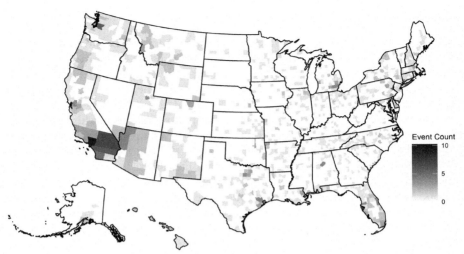

FIGURE 3.2 Spatial distribution of the 2009 Tax Day Tea Party rallies by county.
Note: Estimates are based on 1,022 rallies and 3,143 counties.

2,806 local Tea Party organizations in May 1–5, 2010, approximately one year after the 2009 Tax Day rallies. Overall, we suggest that our unique and more exhaustive triangulated data collection procedures more comprehensively capture this important moment in American protest history.

The Spatial Distribution of Early Tea Party Mobilization

After building the databases of Tax Day rallies and early riser groups, we geocoded each case to the county level, summing them to provide estimates of Tea Party activism across the country. We follow prior work on the Tea Party in our focus on counties (e.g., McVeigh et al. 2014), which provides a reasonable way to approximate local communities and balance considerations of breadth and depth. Maps of the counts of Tax Day rallies and early riser groups are shown in Figures 3.2 and 3.3 respectively.

The 2009 Tax Day mobilization was an outstanding success for the Tea Party. Protests took place in more than 25% of counties across the United States, with at least one event occurring in every state and the District of Columbia. Approximately 21% of counties had one Tax Day rally, and another 5% had between 2 and 10 events. The most extensive Tea Party mobilization took place in Los Angeles County, where 10 demonstrations occurred.[4] States varied substantially in the extent of Tea Party activism by

---

[4] Los Angeles County was the largest in the United States in 2009, with more than 9.8 million residents.

FIGURE 3.3 Spatial distribution of Tea Party organizational formation in 2009 by county.
Note: Estimates are based on 743 organizations and 3,143 counties.

county. In less densely populated states such as Nebraska, North Dakota, and South Dakota, Tax Day Tea Party protests took place in fewer than 10% of counties. It is evident in Figure 3.2 that large pockets of Tea Party mobilization emerged in states such as California, where 65% of counties had at least one event. Washington State was also a hub of Tea Party mobilization, with at least one demonstration taking place in nearly 60% of its counties. There is a moderate level of Tea Party activity in traditionally Republican states such as Texas, where protests took place in 25% of counties, while battleground states such as Florida (63% of counties) and Pennsylvania (40%) had higher levels of mobilization.

Figure 3.3 shows the location of the 743 early riser Tea Party groups. Similar to the wide geographic dispersion of the Tax Day rallies, Tea Party groups emerged in 49 states and the District of Columbia. Rhode Island was the only state that did not have at least one early riser group by the end of 2009. At least one early riser Tea Party group was present in 17% of counties, further underscoring the rapid diffusion of the insurgency. San Diego County, CA had the highest number of Tea Party groups, with a total of 12, followed by Los Angeles County, CA, with 11 chapters. There were also notably high levels of organizational formation in Clark County, NV, with eight chapters, and in Dallas and Harris counties in Texas, which both had seven chapters. There are also clusters of Tea Party groups present across the counties in Tennessee, Florida, and Pennsylvania.

Variables and Measurement

To better understand how local socioeconomic, demographic, and political conditions contributed to the emergence of Tea Party activism, we completed a statistical analysis of where Tax Day rallies took place and where early riser groups were founded. Our dependent variables are the count of 2009 Tax Day rallies and the count of organizations at the county level. Given the structure of our data and units of analysis, we use multilevel negative binomial models with counties nested in states.

We use several groupings of independent variables that are grounded in our theoretical discussion from Chapter 2. These clusters of variables emphasize the joint role of material threats and status threats to account for Tea Party activism, and also control for political context and other demographic factors. We refer to these variable grouping as our *focal independent variables* throughout the book, and in later chapters we use these measures to account for the organizational survival of Tea Party groups and to assess the insurgency's impact on electoral politics. We describe the operationalization of these variables at length here and make reference back to this discussion when we use our focal independent variables in later chapters.

To measure the *material threats* brought about by the Great Recession, we use five predictor variables. The first is the change in the percentage unemployed between 2008 and 2009 based on the values reported in the Bureau of Labor Statistic's Local Area Unemployment series. Second, we use data drawn from the Department of Housing and Urban Development's Neighborhood Stabilization Program to measure the housing foreclosure concentration taking place in each county. To operationalize the variable, we calculated the Gini coefficient of mortgage foreclosures in each county based on census tract-level estimates of foreclosures between 2007 and 2009. We focus on the distribution of foreclosures rather than the rate since we expected that spatial concentrations of foreclosures are more likely to be noticed by individuals living in areas with many foreclosures, relative to communities with a comparable number of foreclosures that are more evenly distributed. The three other variables included in this group come from the five-year estimates of the American Community Survey (ACS) for 2009. We use the Gini coefficient of income for each county to measure income inequality, the change in median income (in thousands) between 2008 and 2009, and, finally, the percentage of residents in a county who receive retirement income. We suggest that counties where the effects of the Great Recession were more pronounced – such as through higher rates of unemployment, declines in median income, or greater existing income inequality – saw heightened Tea Party activism.

We use four variables to capture the effects of *status threats* as predictors of Tea Party activism. The first is the change in the percentage of non-Hispanic Whites between the 2000 Census and the 2009 ACS. We calculate this value by subtracting the 2000 estimate of the percentage of non-Hispanic Whites from the 2009 estimates. As a result, positive values indicated a growth in the relative size of the white population and negative values show a decline in the relative size. Second, we use the dissimilarity index of racial segregation which distinguishes between the non-Hispanic White and all other racialized groups.[5] Third, we include a variable for the percentage of respondents in each county receiving money from the Supplemental Nutrition Assistance Program (SNAP) program, which is widely understood to be a welfare program. As we argued in Chapter 2, welfare recipients are viewed as synonymous with the "undeserving" poor in conservative circles where the Tea Party emerged, and tacitly understood to reference the Black underclass. Last, we used data from the 2000 wave of the Religious Congregations and Membership Study to create a variable for the number of evangelical Christian congregations present in a county.[6] The 2000 wave is the most recent available for our analysis. In line with the status threat explanation, we expected more Tea Party activism in counties with more status threats. For instance, we predicted that counties with an increase in the White population to have less Tea Party activism, while areas with more families receiving SNAP benefits or higher levels of racial segregation may increase the prevalence of Tax Day rallies and the establishment of early riser Tea Party groups. Counties with a strong evangelical presence are likely to provide a larger sentiment pool of potential activists who believe that the social dominance of their faith is in decline, which in turn might motivate activism.

The third cluster of variables accounts for the *political context* in each county. Since the Tea Party is a conservative movement, we include a variable for the percentage of Republican votes in the 2008 election. Second, we developed a state-level variable based on the number of years that Americans for Prosperity (AFP) reported an active chapter. When the Tea Party emerged in 2009, AFP had created many statewide chapters that recruited and trained conservative activists (Hertel-Fernandez 2019; Skocpol and Hertel-Fernandez 2016). As a result, we expect counties in states with an AFP chapter to have had a preexisting network of conservative activists amenable to the Tea Party's goals. To collect information on AFP chapter activity, we reviewed its annual IRS Form 990 filing, a public tax document required for organizations classified as non-profits, between 2004 and 2008. We suggest that more Republican counties and those with more active Americans for Prosperity chapter activity will have more Tea Party activism.

Finally, we employed three variables to account for the *demographics* in our analysis. These were all drawn from the 2009 ACS. We used measures for the percentage of residents over 25 who held a college degree, the median income

[5] While there are several ways to measure segregation (Massey and Denton 2003), we use the dissimilarity index since the main mechanism underpinning status threats emphasizes the changing demographics from majority White to majority non-White.
[6] The Religious Congregations and Membership Study is a national sample of religious groups collected by the Association of Statisticians of American Religious Bodies. Details about the sample are available at the Association of Religious Data Archives (2018).

for families, and the total population size. The latter is necessary to account for the large variation in county size, which by itself could produce different levels of Tea Party activity. We used the natural logarithm of population in our statistical models to reduce skewness.

Local Conditions Associated with Tea Party Activism

The results of our statistical analyses are summarized in Table 3.1, containing estimates for both the number of Tax Day rallies and the number of early riser Tea Party groups. The overall pattern of results for both models strongly supports our central arguments. Tea Party activism was more extensive in areas hit hardest by the Great Recession, as well as where residents where at heightened risk for negative financial consequences resulting from the economic collapse. Counties where unemployment had increased saw more Tax Day rallies and Tea Party organizations, as did communities with high concentrations of housing foreclosures. Higher levels of income inequality were also linked to more Tax Day rallies and Tea Party groups. Counties with a higher percentage of residents receiving retirement income also had greater Tea Party activism. These areas, we suggest, had larger segments of their populations directly impacted by the consequences of the Great Recession's stock market crash. As we have noted, individuals receiving retirement income were disproportionately affected by the Great Recession and the massive declines in the stock market. For instance, those depending upon employer-sponsored, defined-contribution, or personal pension (savings) accounts for retirement, such as 401(K) accounts or other investment vehicles saw sharp declines in their nest eggs. Finally, our analysis shows that counties where income increased between 2008 and 2009 saw fewer Tea Party organizations form, although this measure did not predict the number of Tax Day rallies. Overall, our evidence strongly demonstrates that the economic upheaval created by the Great Recession was a powerful, if often underemphasized correlate of local Tea Party activism.

Additionally, the results in Table 3.1 suggest that status threats, the more common explanation for the Tea Party insurgency, are also important in understanding the prevalence of Tax Day rallies and organizational formation. Counties with higher levels of racial segregation saw more rallies and had more early riser Tea Party groups. We interpret this finding to mean that in more segregated communities, there is less contact, especially, between Whites and other races. As a result, those communities are facilitating contexts for racialized resentment held by White conservatives to grow. The coupling of government spending with White racist attitudes has created amenable community conditions for Tea Party activism to proliferate. Two other measures of status threats are associated with a specific type of Tea Party activity. One is that counties where the percentage of White residents grew over time saw fewer Tax Day rallies, while more early riser groups were formed in areas with a higher percentage of residents receiving SNAP benefits. The second measure is that

TABLE 3.1 *Multilevel negative binomial regression of the factors influencing county-level Tax Day rallies and organizational formation in 2009 (n=3,143).*

	Tea Party Events	*Tea Party Organizations*
Material Threats		
Change in % Unemployed	0.189***	0.317***
	(0.053)	(0.058)
Foreclosure Concentration	1.685***	1.447***
	(0.294)	(0.388)
Income Inequality	3.854**	3.373*
	(1.281)	(1.698)
% Receiving Retirement Income	0.041***	0.025*
	(0.008)	(0.011)
Change in Income	−0.018	−0.040**
	(0.011)	(0.014)
Status Threats		
Racial Segregation	1.540***	1.360***
	(0.282)	(0.368)
% Change in White	−0.037*	−0.023
	(0.015)	(0.018)
% Receiving SNAP Benefits	−0.003	0.032*
	(0.011)	(0.014)
Evangelical Congregations	0.199***	0.151**
	(0.036)	(0.051)
Political Context		
% Republican Votes	0.165***	0.221**
	(0.035)	(0.052)
Americans for Prosperity Chapters	-0.037	−0.015
	(0.031)	(0.041)
Demographic Controls		
% College Graduate	0.029***	0.023*
	(0.007)	(0.009)
Median Income	0.877*	1.723***
	(0.347)	(0.461)
Population Size	−0.228***	−0.162**
	(0.040)	(0.060)
Intercept	−6.716***	−8.298***
	(0.904)	(1.218)
State-Level Variance	0.138	0.241
Dispersion Parameter	1.923	5.180

Note: Counties are nested in states. *p<0.05, **p<0.01, ***p<0.001 (two-tailed tests). Standard errors in parentheses.

counties with more evangelical Christian congregations had higher levels of both Tax Day rallies and early riser groups form. This is consistent with our claim that conservative Christians are a sentiment pool that is highly likely to be amenable to Tea Party messages. Accordingly, higher concentrations of these citizens made Tea Party activism more likely. When considered synthetically, our analyses demonstrate that status threats, indicative of White Christian racial resentment, are associated with the emergence of Tea Party activism.

Tax Day rallies and Tea Party chapters were more prevalent in counties with a higher percentage of votes for the Republican Party in the 2008 presidential election, a finding unsurprising given the lack of political alternatives for conservative voters. We see little evidence that state-level chapters of Americans for Prosperity were associated with the proliferation of Tea Party protests or organizations. This may be a result of the crudeness of the state-level scope of the variable relative to our other measures, which are all better captured at the county-level. We suggest that a more plausible explanation is that Americans for Prosperity, as well as the other advocacy groups that facilitated the Tea Party, had at best played a marginal role in establishing individual early riser chapters or in staging no more than a few specific rallies beyond the test-marketing phase. Instead, these groups, as we pointed out earlier, focused on building online infrastructures allowing any interested citizen or group to plan a Tax Day rally or found a Tea Party group.

Finally, we briefly discuss the demographic controls included in our model. The results show that counties with more college graduates and higher median incomes had more Tea Party activity. As well, the more populous counties had fewer Tax Day rallies, but this variable was not statistically significant for the early riser groups.

Overall, the results from our statistical analyses are consistent with our theoretical arguments about the rise of the Tea Party. Both material and status threats appear to have motivated the first wave of activism, even after controlling for the political conservatism and demographic characteristics of counties. It is especially important to underscore the strong impact of material threats, since they have so rarely been a focal point of attention in previous work on the Tea Party. It is clear from our results, however, that the rapid economic decline spawned by the Great Recession played a key role in generating a sense of precarity among conservatives, a large many of whom went on either to stage or to attend Tea Party protests on Tax Day, while more committed activists took the initiative to create an early riser chapter.

THE CHARACTER OF EARLY TEA PARTY ACTIVISM

The Tax Day rallies drew wide attention as the insurgency continued to grow. Yet few observers have described either the protests themselves in much detail, or how they set the stage for the early riser Tea Party groups that emerged soon thereafter. The work of Ehrhardt (2020) is an exception, as he spent seven years doing fieldwork on Tea Party activists and their efforts in Western North Carolina. He says:

There's something missing from our picture of the Tea Party Movement. Researchers use survey data to describe members' demographics and beliefs, and investigate the elites and advocacy group portrayed as Tea Party leaders. But what about the actual "practice of protests": . . .the rallies, the meetings and the other events? National elites and social forces don't organize themselves; nor do they occur spontaneously because of public opinion. (Ehrhardt 2020:373)

We agree with Ehrhardt and aim to fill the gap he identifies by outlining the surge of genuine, grassroots enthusiasm that quickly came to dominate early Tea Party activism.

The final part of this chapter offers detailed descriptions of the Tax Day rallies, which help to inform our understanding of the early riser groups. Our approach to capturing the main characteristics of the 2009 Tax Day rallies employs what social scientists call protest event analysis (Hutter 2014; Koopmans and Rucht 2002). This methodology uses newspaper reports of events to describe the variable features of protest activity. A major difficulty of using newspapers, or indeed any media reports of protests events, is that many gatherings are not reported (Earl et al. 2004). Researchers have systematically established several factors that help explain localized patterns of media attention to social movement mobilization (e.g., Rafail, McCarthy, and Sullivan 2019).

As already mentioned, our triangulated research design employed to identify Tax Day rallies identified 1,022 events. Newspaper coverage of the Tax Day rallies was extensive, with more than 74% of events receiving some level of media attention. We coded the details of each event using a standardized set of variables, allowing us to identify patterns within the Tax Day rallies. We focus particularly on the tactics used during the rallies, the claims made by partici-pants, and the organizational dynamics that emerged during and after the rallies.

The Tactical Repertoires of the Tax Day Rallies

Scholars use the concept of protest repertoires to bound the tactical decisions made by contentious political actors. The concept of protest repertoires was introduced by Tilly (1986, 2006) and consists of temporally and historically rooted templates employed by citizens while staging protests. Variation in tactical repertoires is widely used by researchers to compare the decisions organizers make before, during, and sometimes after, protest events (Tarrow 2011). Our evidence indicates that the Tea Party closely followed common existing repertoires of protest during the Tax Day rallies. The events were boisterous and quite festive in tone. Participants donned colonial garb, carried tea bags, and in certain cases attempted to recreate the Boston Tea Party of 1773. The Tax Day protests almost entirely took the form of rallies, with a few also including a short march either before or after the rally.

More than 85% of the Tax Day rallies took place in traditional public spaces, such as parks, courthouses, or town squares, consistent with most contemporary protest activity. These spaces have the highest level of Constitutional protections for assembly (McCarthy and McPhail 2006), and the site selection is consistent with the recommendations appearing on the taxdayteaparty.com website used to coordinate the events. The turnout at the Tax Day rallies varied, but most were fairly small with a median estimate of 400 protestors and a mean of approximately 1,000 participants. Our data show that 81% of Tax Day rallies had at least 100 participants and 25% had more than 1,000 people attend. The largest rally took place in Atlanta, GA, with at least 15,000 participants attending, including Fox News anchor Sean Hannity.

The Tax Day rallies were strikingly consistent in their avoidance of contentious or illegal tactics. There was not a single arrest, incident of property damage or vandalism, violence against persons, an act of civil disobedience, or other conduct that may have produced a clash with law enforcement. Counter-protestors who came to challenge the Tea Party were also quite rare, appearing at just 4% of protests. There was a notable police presence at only 7% of all the Tax Day rallies, and the officers present were primarily described to be directing traffic. The tactical uniformity, overall, is remarkable given the loose coordination of the events and the fact that they were staged by hundreds of largely disconnected activists.

Articulating the Tea Party's Message

During the planning stages of the Tax Day rallies, the conservative advocacy groups who organized the initial Tea Party wave settled on a message emphasizing fiscal responsibility and the reduction of government spending. The facilitators of the rallies provided a detailed list of grievances and talking points that rally organizers were encouraged to adopt. Our evidence suggests that these efforts were highly successful. Speeches articulating these claims were almost universal at the Tax Day rallies, and evoked supportive crowd responses. Many events gave opportunities for participants to sign petitions demanding a reduction in taxation and government spending. Rally planners linked their agenda to hyperpatriotism, encouraging attendees to sign patriotic documents such as the US Constitution and to sing patriotic songs, including the Star-Spangled Banner and America the Beautiful. Activists used a series of props to give color to their claims, including phony million-dollar bills or muskets resembling those used during the colonial era.

As we will explain in detail in Chapter 4, participants in this first wave of Tax Day protests were staunch conservatives who held political preferences in common far beyond fiscal policy alone. However, our data suggest that messaging during the Tax Day rallies was laser-focused on core economic issues, with claims about other major conservative policy positions largely invisible across the protests. For example, we coded whether the reports of each event referred to abortion or immigration, two longstanding issue arenas of conservative consensus mobilization. Across those rallies that received newspaper coverage, only 2% mentioned abortion and just 3% mentioned immigration. The Tax Day rallies remained largely on message with an anti-tax, anti-spending populist focus.

A final question about the messaging at the Tax Day rallies concerns who made the speeches. Despite the facilitation by conservative advocacy groups and media outlets, our evidence indicates that the speakers articulating the message of fiscal restraint were ordinary activists in the substantial majority of protests. We coded whether a celebrity such as Sean Hannity participated in an event, as well as politicians who were either elected or running for office. In more than 74% of Tax Day rallies, there were no such individuals reported to be present. The speakers and organizers were described as community residents and conservatives who claimed to have been motivated by concerns about the direction of the country. This finding is particularly important because it provides early evidence about the grassroots base of activists who embodied the Tea Party.

Organizational Sponsors of the Tax Day Rallies

The newspaper coverage of the Tax Day rallies also provides valuable clues about the preexisting structural ties of the founding set of Tea Party groups and their initial organizational building. We coded the newspaper reports to capture any sponsoring organization linked to each of the Tax Day rallies.[7] The results show two clear patterns. First, the organizations mentioned as sponsors of the rallies mimic the facilitating groups that worked together to launch the Tea Party. Second, there was no mention of any local or national sponsor for a majority of protests. We describe each pattern in turn.

The most common sponsoring organizations in the newspaper coverage of the rallies are listed in Figure 3.4. Fox News was mentioned for nearly 35% of the events covered by the media. This is not unexpected given the network's amplification of the Tea Party. At one rally, attendees were described as watching Fox coverage of the protests on a large TV screen. Fox News had already amplified the Tax Day rallies, rather than taking any active role in actually organizing them. Consequently, while the outsized role of Fox News in encouraging participation should not be minimized, it was conservative activists and advocacy groups who accomplished the day-to-day work in test-marketing the Tea Party concept and building the online infrastructures that were so crucial to the success of the protests.

---

[7] A potential concern about this approach is that the extent, and therefore comprehensiveness, of the coverage may have been insufficient to accurately describe sponsoring groups. To assess this concern, we coded the relative length of each article. Only about 2% of the stories were coded as "Short," or spanning two sentences or less or a photo caption. Almost 94% of the stories were coded as "Long," meaning they consisted of at least three paragraphs.

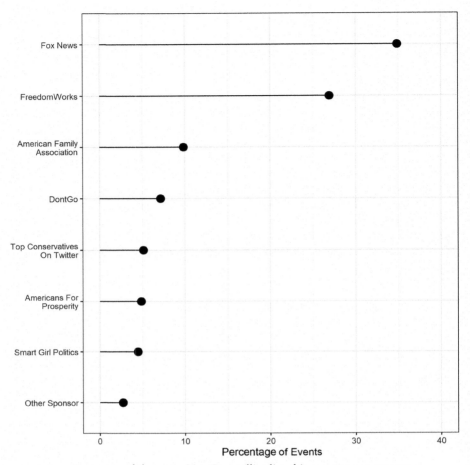

FIGURE 3.4 Sponsors of the 2009 Tax Day rallies listed in newspaper reports.
Note: Percentages are based on the 743 Tax Day rallies covered by the media. Sponsors are not mutually exclusive.

The media coverage listed several conservative advocacy groups as sponsoring the events. FreedomWorks featured most prominently and was listed as sponsoring organization in 27% of protests. Other conservative groups such as the American Family Association, DontGo, Top Conservatives on Twitter, Americans for Prosperity, and Smart Girl Politics were all mentioned as sponsoring between 5% and 10% of events. Glenn Beck's 9/12 project was reported to have sponsored only four events, suggesting it had little impact on launching the Tea Party. A small number of other sponsoring organizations were noted at 3% of rallies. These were generally local or state conservative groups. For example, the Taxpayer League of Minnesota sponsored 13 events.

Last, we see little evidence of coordinated involvement of local, state, or county, Republican groups in sponsoring the Tax Day rallies, as 97% of events did not list one in any sponsoring role. About 52% of the media coverage of the Tax Day rallies did not list any sponsor. Instead, participants interviewed at many of the rallies described themselves as regular citizens rather than activists.

This evidence about the organizational sponsors of the Tax Day rallies in 2009 reemphasizes the top-down/bottom-up dynamic of the Tea Party that quickly settled into place. More than half of the events did not have a reported sponsor, and for those that did, the ties between the national conservative advocacy groups like FreedomWorks or Americans for Prosperity were not dominant. Many of these groups provided both the test-marketing of the idea of the Tax Day rallies and the technological infrastructure that helped activists to plan and to stage a rally. But beyond that, we saw little evidence of direct cooperation, resource sharing, or other support.

From Protest to Organization Building: The Early Riser Tea Party Groups

After the tremendous success of the first national wave of Tax Day rallies, many of the activists who staged the events kept the insurgency's momentum moving forward by creating local Tea Party organizations. We analyze the Tea Party's organizational structure more extensively in Chapter 4, and the trajectory of local Tea Party groups in Chapter 6. Here, we characterize the membership size of the early riser chapters. The concept of an early riser is typically used to describe insurgent groups that emerge on the scene early in what eventually turns out to be a much larger wave of interlinked protest mobilization (Tarrow 2011). There are good theoretical and empirical reasons to believe that these early riser groups may differ from those founded later in an insurgency, and, for the Tea Party, they had the closest ties to the elite conservative advocacy groups that initially facilitated the Tea Party. The early risers also emerged at a time when the insurgency focused strictly on economic policy, government spending, and taxation rather than the broader array of conservative issues that characterized the focus of many later forming groups.

Our estimate of 743 early riser groups being active in 2009 tallies with two other attempts to document the first surge of Tea Party organizational formation, although both also include chapter growth beyond 2009 alone. First, Skocpol and Williamson (2011:90) employed a multifaceted strategy to identify local Tea Party groups in 2011, ultimately concluding that there were approximately 968 chapters who had been active at one point since 2009. Of these, 804 remained engaged. Second, a survey by the *Washington Post* estimated that more than 1,400 groups existed in September of 2010, of which 647 could be verified and contacted directly (Gardner 2010). Our estimate of the number of Tea Party groups active in 2009, then, is consistent with the best efforts by previous researchers.

TABLE 3.2 *Reported membership counts of early riser Tea Party groups.*

Percentile	# of Members
1	1
5	1
10	2
20	4
30	5
40	7
50	8
60	9
70	11
80	24
90	39
95	65
99	108

Note: Estimates are based on online lists of membership for 743 groups on December 31, 2009.

Most of the early riser groups were small. Together, the chapters reported a total membership of 11,244 individuals.[8] The percentiles of chapter membership size are summarized in Table 3.2. Our evidence shows that 5% of early riser groups had only a single member. The median group size was 8 members with a mean size of just 10. There were a small number of larger groups, though even here the total membership counts were relatively small. For instance, the 99th percentile was 108 members, and the maximum number of members reported by a single group was 129. These estimates are comparable to the other serious attempts to sample Tea Party groups. Skocpol and Williamson (2011) identify only a handful of Tea Party groups with online membership exceeding 500 individuals. The *Washington Post* provides more details about the size of the 647 groups they identified. The results indicate that 51% of the groups reported having 50 members or fewer and only 6% claimed to have more than 1,000 members. These estimates are comparable to our own estimates especially since Skocpol and Williamson and the *Washington Post* survey sampled Tea Party organizations during 2010, a period when the Tea Party was experiencing exponential growth.

CONCLUSION

We developed an explanatory account of the emergence of the Tea Party in this chapter. Drawing on prior scholarship and a variety of data sources, we

---

[8] These membership counts are based on the online listings for each organization. We discuss the complexity of estimating group size more comprehensively in Chapter 4.

showed that the Tea Party had strong roots in elite-driven conservative activism and media outlets, yet the insurgency quickly became more grassroots in character. Activists made use of online tools created by the aforementioned groups in order to stage Tax Day rallies, and eventually to found early riser groups that shaped the tone and tenor of the early Tea Party. Our evidence suggests that communities that were hit particularly hard by the Great Recession, those that had higher levels of status threats, and conservative communities were most likely to have seen extensive Tea Party activism. Tea Party activists used well-established protest tactics and remained quite loyal to the anti-tax, anti-Obama, anti-spending framing first tested by conservative advocacy groups. The Tax Day rallies were loosely organized, and most appeared to be entirely grassroots efforts put together by local activists that lacked any formal organizational sponsors. Over that first year, Tea Partiers went on to found early riser groups, again replicating the loosely coordinated structure of the Tax Day rallies. The early riser groups were small in size and number, but as we show in subsequent chapters, were highly consequential.

The Tax Day protests in 2009 were singularly important events, and were intended to become the signature tactic as the Tea Party insurgency spread across the US. The protest surge on Tax Day pales in contrast to several more recent American protest waves, notably the women's marches of 2016 (Beyerlein et al. 2018) and the Black Lives Matter protests of 2020 (Pressman et al. 2022). When contextualized contemporaneously, however, the size, total attendance, and geographical extensity of the Tea Party protests were nothing short of transformative. Despite plans to carry the Tax Day rallies into the future, the 2009 protests represented the peak number of events compared to the years that followed, a claim we substantiate in Chapter 5.

Despite the remarkable success represented by the Tea Party's rapid emergence and diffusion, the seeds of its decline were also embedded in the insurgency's earliest period of mobilization. Leaders with deep roots in the conservative movement were able to build what came to be largely unprecedented grassroots enthusiasm for traditional elite-backed policy positions on taxation and spending. The localized consequences of the Great Recession were a salient motivator for activists to stage Tea Party protests on Tax Day and to subsequently form local chapters to carry on their activities. Nevertheless, the economy went on to recover, albeit unevenly, making it more difficult to sustain the rage and frustration many early Tea Partiers had felt. The highly decentralized organizational form adopted by the Tea Party was mimicked in many ways by major progressive movements that followed after it, such as Occupy Wall Street (Gillham et al. 2019; Gould-Wartofsky 2015). This organizational form can be highly effective in generating rapid growth but also complicate coordinated action, messaging, and sustained mobilization. We describe these processes extensively in the chapters that follow, since they are linked directly to the decline of Tea Party activism, which seemingly occurred just as quickly as had its rise.

4

Tea Party Supporters, Activists, and Mobilizing Structures

Social movements are embodied in the efforts of the activists who mobilize supporters to implement their visions of social change. Movements are also embedded in the mobilizing structures that activists build and sometimes appropriate from preexisting communities, such as churches or community organizations. Scholars conceive of these as the social infrastructures of mobilization (McCarthy 1987; Tarrow 2011; Tilly 1978). These theoretical tools emphasize the centrality of agency in explaining insurgencies and collective action more generally, and how the organizational choices made by activists and leaders shape the tactics, longevity, and success of their campaigns.

Activists are the primary actors in contentious political activity. Popular insurgencies and social movements typically find widespread societal support beyond the activists who lead them. This contrasts with insurgencies that are unpopular, stillborn, or lacking any semblance of support beyond the few activists who led them.[1] It is rare that activists and leaders of even the most popular insurgencies succeed in mobilizing more than a very small proportion of their adherents through their individual and organizational efforts. We find it useful, therefore, to make a conceptual distinction between supporters and activists, since the former are typically much more numerous than the latter and the social characteristics of the two groups may differ in important ways.

In this chapter we make a serious effort to identify the individuals who together formed the Tea Party, and then to analyze the mobilizing structures they chose to build the insurgency. We begin by comparing the characteristics of supporters and activists, deploying a previously unexamined survey of Tea

---

[1] Examples of unpopular insurgencies include the Republic of New Africa (Davenport 2015), the Aryan Nations, the Branch Davidians, and the Freemen (McCarthy and McPhail 1998).

Party participation. We then generate estimates of the peak number of Tea Party activists ever involved in the insurgency.

Next, we describe the main mobilizing structures of the Tea Party from its beginning through 2014; these were essential in shaping the insurgency's decline. We start by examining the role of the major Tea Party umbrella groups – the 1776 Tea Party, FreedomWorks, the Patriot Action Network, Tea Party Nation, and Tea Party Patriots. These umbrella groups housed the majority of the local chapters that composed the insurgency.[2] Of these, the Tea Party Patriots and FreedomWorks were most central. We draw on earlier theoretical work describing the functions of the most widely used templates for social movement mobilizing structures in order to differentiate those used by Tea Party activists: the *federated* and the *spin* forms. The Tea Party insurgency employed a hybrid mobilizing structure, combining elements of these two forms. We then examine the dynamics of Tea Party local chapters, including their size, Internal Revenue Service (IRS) contact experience, and financial resources. The body of evidence we assemble in the chapter provides us the basis for several grounded claims about the role of the Tea Party insurgency's particular mobilizing structural profile on both its precipitous rise and rapid decline.

TEA PARTY SUPPORTERS AND ACTIVISTS

Researchers who study contentious political activity make a distinction between adherents and activists (McCarthy and Zald 1977). Adherents, more typically called supporters, are those who support the aims of a movement or insurgency from afar without getting actively involved. Activists, on the other hand, are those adherents who contribute resources, including time and money, to the cause. It is rare in any insurgency for activists to consist of more than just a small proportion of those who support the goals of the movement. For instance, most African Americans did not take an active part in the Civil Rights movement despite widespread support for its goals, while thousands of activists took part in the movement following both their local leaders and well-known national leaders (Morris 1986).

Much of what we know of the demographic, political, and social characteristics of Tea Party supporters is drawn from surveys using national random samples. A significant limitation for most of these surveys is that they are restricted to capturing *supporters* of the Tea Party, and are typically unable to produce a sufficiently large pool of *activists* for analysis. National random samples are generally not ideal for capturing rare populations unless deliberate

---

[2] These groups were the main national mobilizing structures for the insurgency. Unless an exception is noted, our references to the umbrella groups are based on these five groups. We distinguish these groups from the Tea Party Express, which was not a membership group and did not host local chapters. We exclude the Tea Party Express from our analysis.

ameliorative strategies are used, such as screening methods (Kalton and Anderson 1986). As a result of their rarity in the general population, developing representative samples of activists normally poses a serious problem for researchers.

A fortuitous exception to this problem in the case of the Tea Party is a set of surveys conducted by cable news channel CNN in partnership with the Opinion Research Corporation (ORC), which, to our knowledge, has not been previously analyzed. These surveys employed a consistent question gauging different types of engagement with the Tea Party across 36 separate surveys administered between 2010 and 2014. The question, first appearing in a survey administered in August of 2010 (CNN and Opinion Research Corporation 2010), asked respondents whether they best described themselves as 1) an active member of the Tea Party movement; 2) a supporter of the movement but not an active member; 3) having no view about the Tea Party one way or another; 4) an opposer of the Tea Party movement; or 5) don't know, undecided, or refused. Across the iterations of the survey, CNN/ORC polled more than 35,005 total respondents who answered the Tea Party question. While none of the individual surveys yielded a feasibly sized sample of self-reported Tea Party activists, the cumulative number of respondents allowed us to produce, by harmonizing responses for each iteration of the survey, a defensible sample of self-reported activists. The time-series of total self-reported Tea Party membership and supporters is shown in Figure 4.1.[3]

Overall, 1% of 35,005 respondents indicated that they were members of the Tea Party, 28% described themselves as supporters, 39% had no opinion, and 32% were opposed to the Tea Party. The temporal trends seen in Figure 4.1 are useful in establishing the stability of Tea Party support. First, a very small proportion of survey respondents ever reported membership in the Tea Party, and this rate of participation was constant between 2010 and 2014. The range of this value varied between a minimum value of 0.5% and a maximum of 2% across the surveys, pointing to relative consistency in membership reports. Second, a healthy segment of the population supported the Tea Party, although wide support declined over time. By early 2011, the proportion of Tea Party supporters was eclipsed by the proportion who opposed the Tea Party, a trend that continued through 2014. Last, across all 36 surveys, the most common response was "no opinion" about the Tea Party and that group increased in size after early 2011. The increasing ambivalence about the Tea Party seen in these data is quite striking given the insurgency's continuing impact on American political processes during this period. It is consistent, as well, with our prevailing emphasis on the fragility of the insurgency, as it quickly began to vanish from the public's attention.

---

[3] Since we are harmonizing multiple surveys, all our analyses adjust the estimates using accompanying survey weights.

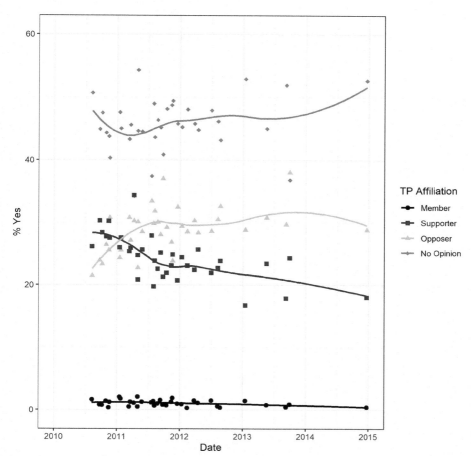

FIGURE 4.1 Trends in membership and support for the Tea Party, 2010–2014.
Note: Data are drawn from 36 surveys conducted by CNN and the Opinion Research Corporation. Lines are based on the LOESS regression smooth. The pooled *n* is 35,005.

How do Tea Party activists compare with supporters on key demographic, social, and political characteristics? Using the pooled survey data on both groups, we are able to assess key similarities and differences. Figure 4.2 shows the contrasting estimates on key demographic variables for Tea Party members (i.e., activists) and supporters, alongside the average percentages for all respondents, which provides a baseline for comparisons. All the comparisons in Figure 4.2 are statistically significant at the 95% level of confidence.

The pattern of results in Figure 4.2 supports our contention that Tea Party activists and supporters differ not only from one another, but from the general population. More than 83% of Tea Party activists identified as White as did 90% of supporters. Across all these surveys, 82% of respondents identified as

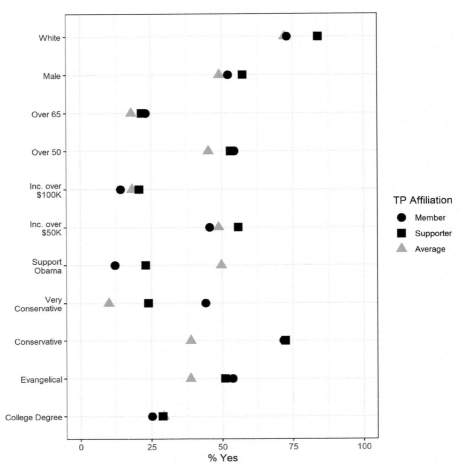

FIGURE 4.2 Demographic and political characteristics of Tea Party members and supporters, 2010–2014.
Note: Data are drawn from 36 surveys conducted by CNN and the Opinion Research Corporation. The pooled *n* is 35,005.

White. Although upon initial inspection these values may appear roughly comparable, our calculations using the 2010 Census of Population indicates that 64% of the US population identified as non-Hispanic White.[4] Consequently, we can conclude that Tea Party activists were substantially

[4] Of course, this finding raises concerns that samples themselves were not representative of the US population. To address this, we compared the other demographic variables to the Census estimates and found that they were generally consistent with the survey values. This indicates that, overall, the harmonized survey data is representative of the general population, although non-Whites are underrepresented.

Whiter than the general population, as were supporters too. Activists and supporters were also slightly more likely to be male relative to all survey respondents, likely due to the importance of status threat arguments that we and others have emphasized (e.g., Parker and Barreto 2014) as important motivators for the Tea Party.

The patterns in Figure 4.2 also indicate that Tea Party activists and supporters were older than the typical survey respondent. Tea Party activists were less likely to earn both over $100,000 and over $50,000 than the general population. Tea Party supporters, in contrast, were financially better-off, including atypically high percentages earning more than $50,000 or $100,000. These findings are particularly important considering the Great Recession's disproportionate impact on those of retirement age and those close to retirement. The pervasive sense that economic precarity was looming likely influenced the decision to take part in the Tea Party. As the stock market crash deepened, the retirement portfolios of retirees and of those on the cusp of retirement plunged in tandem. As we noted in Chapter 2, research has established that many older Americans delayed their decision to retire as a result of the Great Recession (Helppie McFall 2011). That Tea Party activists were older with fewer economic resources, then, is unsurprising considering the disproportionate risk that they faced. Tea Party activism likely served as an outlet for older Americans and seniors to express their frustration at being exposed to major economic risk.

The political views of Tea Party activists and supporters point to another important contrast. Tea Party activists were substantially more conservative than supporters, who in turn were substantially more conservative than the general population of adults. We see this clearly by comparing the groups across the percentage of respondents who identified as "very conservative." Approximately 44% of Tea Party activists answered they were "very conservative" compared to 24% of supporters and 10% of all respondents, while approximately 72% of activists and supporters identified as either "very conservative" or "conservative." There existed a major gap, then, between supporters and activists in extreme conservative views; the insurgency's activist corps was substantially more conservative. A similar gap is replicated in support for Barack Obama's performance as president. Just 12% of Tea Party activists approved of Obama's performance, well below the 24% for Tea Party supporters, and 50% of all respondents. In sum, Tea Party activists were highly conservative and were distinguished by their disproportionate disapproval of Obama. This pattern of findings is consistent, too, with our theoretical discussion in Chapter 2 that emphasized the impact of perceptions of Obama on Tea Party activism.

The demographics at the bottom of Figure 4.2 are also consistent with some of our central claims about Tea Party activism and support. First, while at least 50% of Tea Party supporters and activists identified as evangelical Christian, the activists showed slightly higher adherence levels. Both activists and supporters are more highly represented among the ranks of evangelicals compared with 39% of all respondents who so identified. Last, the data show the Tea Party supporters had comparable levels of education attainment to the general public, while Tea Party activists were slightly less likely to be college educated.

Taken together, this pattern of findings indicates that Tea Party activists were distinguishable from both supporters of the insurgency and from the general population. They were Whiter, older, extremely conservative, slightly more likely to be male, disproportionately evangelical, and on the cusp of joining the middle class in terms of education and income. Activists were the most critical of Barack Obama. These demographic and political differences are consistent with our contention that the economic precarity created by the Great Recession and the status threats embodied in the person and policies of the Obama presidency very likely provided strong bases for the suddenly imposed grievances that generated the burst of collective action that was the Tea Party insurgency.

Activist Distrust of the Republican Party

These survey results underscore how distinctive Tea Party activists were in their extremely conservative political views. But the pattern requires elaboration, particularly about how activists viewed the Republican Party. Several scholars, particularly Blum (2020), have emphasized the animosity that many Tea Party activists expressed toward the Republican Party, particularly the party leaders who were derided as self-interested and corrupt. Consistently, Skocpol and Williamson (2011) emphasized how the Tea Party activists viewed themselves as congressional watchdogs, with a goal of pressuring the Republican Party to adopt the Tea Party's preferred policies, and candidates, over any others.

We now contextualize the unique political, social, and demographic position occupied by Tea Party activists using two qualitative sources of evidence which reveal how Tea Party activists viewed the Republican Party. The first consists of 37 interviews conducted between March and August of 2013. The interviews, directed by Michael Heaney and Fabio Rojas, engaged leaders and organizational representatives of local Tea Party groups across the US who had participated in a larger study of ties between social movements and political parties (see Heaney and Rojas (2015) for a more detailed discussion).[5] We identify the main substantive themes in those interviews based on summative content analysis of the interview transcripts (Hsieh and Shannon 2005). Second, we draw on responses to a web survey of surviving local Tea Party organizations that we, with colleagues, administered during the summer and fall of 2015. We sent the survey to the leaders of any Tea Party group for which we could generate an email address based on exhaustive web searches. The searches gathered contact information from online directories of Tea Party umbrella groups. These results were combined with our online monitoring of Tea Party

---

[5] Michael Heaney generously made these transcripts available to us.

organizations starting in 2009. In total, our survey elicited some form of response from 211 groups, and 87 of the respondents returned fully completed surveys. Respondents were provided a series of open-ended questions, which we coded assessing consistent substantive themes. These qualitative sources are consistent in their main themes and also contextualize the quantitatively based claims we have made thus far.

Many of the Tea Party activists expressed distrust that the Republican Party would itself increase spending and taxation if not monitored and pressed to hold the line. Activists framed the tenuous relationship between the Tea Party and Republican Party as transactional and conflictual. Several explicitly framed the alliance between the Tea Party and the Republican Party as a means to an end. Mary, an activist from Utah noted:

I thought about it and I realized right now we are a two-party system and just because I don't like either party right now particularly, the Republican Party is closer to what I want to see and if I want change within that then I need to work within that framework that's there to make that change. (Interview #302; Utah)

Respondents also insisted that the Tea Party maintain an identity distinct from the Republican Party:

I've been campaigning but as a Tea Party [sic] not as a Republican. (Interview #327; Pennsylvania)

Everyone thinks that we're just Republicans doing Republican stuff and it's like well, no... (Interview #326; California)

The day we start believing we are a party like the Republican Party or the Democratic Party that's the day we start losing. (Interview #316; Iowa)

Respondents routinely reported that the conservative Tea Party was a thorn in the side of Republicans because of their attempts to pull the party to the right. One activist bluntly stated: "The Republicans in our county are like 'oh no here they come'" (Interview #323; Michigan), while another noted that his group was "trying to steer the Republicans back on course" (Interview #318; Nebraska). A common sentiment was that the Republican Party directly interfered with the Tea Party to block movement-affiliated candidates from taking power. One activist, referring to primary campaigns for federal office stated that "we tried and we got a few Tea Party people in and they were squashed by the Republican Party. By the lobbyists I should say" (Interview #307; Michigan).

The disillusionment with the Republican Party had important consequences on the trajectory of the Tea Party. This view is summarized most clearly by Lawrence, who had founded a Tea Party chapter that had seen a decline in activity since 2009. Reflecting on the decline, he noted:

[It was a product of the] midterm election and member frustration with the Republican Party after seeing how party leaders acted after the 2010 election, and in 2012 and subsequently. In short, there were few candidates of interest in 2014 as the party leaders continued to try to reject grassroots pressure for change. Their priority was the preservation of their own political power as incumbents, rather than to listen and respond to grassroots concerns by voters. This prompted a shift in tactics for 2016 and less activism in the 2014 cycle as a group. Individuals were still active in support of the campaigns or issues of their choice, but the group became less active. (Web Survey #99)

Here we see that frustration with Republican leaders resulted in a reshuffling of tactics within elements of the Tea Party, where individual activists became engaged with campaigns or issues which extended beyond their initial activities. This was not a unique experience. Though some Tea Party activists reported prior involvement in institutionalized politics (e.g., working on campaigns), the majority did not, and for these novices, participation in the Tea Party was a profoundly politicizing experience.

The political motivations of Tea Party activists, by and large, were quite complex. Few activists were fully committed to securing electoral victories for the Republican Party as the primary goal of their efforts. Instead, for many of the activists, the alliance between the Republican Party and the Tea Party might better be described as a Faustian bargain. As the Tea Party evolved from top-down to grassroots mobilization, the extent of disenchantment with the Republican Party grew, as the career Republican politicians came to be viewed as self-interested and misaligned with the insurgency's goals. For many, if not all, of the Tea Party activists, then, movement identity transcended party identity.

ESTIMATING THE NUMBER OF TEA PARTY ACTIVISTS

Despite the rapid growth and impact of the Tea Party, the size of its activist core remains difficult to pin down. Developing plausible estimates of the number of Tea Party activists speaks directly to the depth of the Tea Party's grassroots base across the country. Evidence of an activist pool numbering more than 100,000 people, for instance, is difficult to reconcile with claims that the Tea Party remained an "Astroturf," or elite-driven, insurgency without an activist core as some have claimed (DiMaggio 2011). But how many of them were there?

We summarize two attempts to estimate the number of Tea Party activists, each using a different conceptualization of what it means to be an activist, and each based on a different data source. The first uses relatively straightforward extrapolations from survey data conditional on the size of the American adult population to estimate the number of activists.[6] While such estimates are instructive, they are based on a very weak view of membership and activism

---

[6] We estimate total attendance at the annual Tax Day rallies in Chapter 5. However, our goal here is to estimate the size of the Tea Party's activist core rather than its maximum turnout. Protest participation is an incomplete reflection of the number of committed activists, and the Tax Day rallies represent a partial set of the insurgency's larger set of activities.

that conflates active participation in a local Tea Party chapter with attending a single protest. It is substantially more difficult to produce evidence-based estimates of the number of the most committed activists – those who regularly organized and attended chapter meetings, worked to secure the permits for events, and otherwise maintained the ongoing insurgency. The second effort relies on estimating numbers of activists using membership counts of the Tea Party groups listed online by the several umbrella groups.

Estimating Activists Using Survey Data

Earlier research on the Tea Party produced sharply different estimates of the overall size of the insurgency's activist base using questionnaires and surveys to develop the figures. Skocpol and Williamson (2011:144) made an effort to estimate how many supporters claimed to be activists in 2010 in several ways. Similar to our approach, they aggregated multiple surveys – a total of 45 in their case – to gauge activism. They found that an average of 13% of respondents considered themselves part of the Tea Party, while a mean of 8% reported active participation, such as donating money or attending Tea Party events. Data from the 2010 Census of Population suggests that the adult population of the US was 234,564,071 people. Even the lower estimate of 8% participation would yield 18,765,126 activists, a number that Skocpol and Williamson (2011:145) acknowledge is implausibly high. Ultimately, they conclude there were approximately 200,000 activists who took part in the Tea Party insurgency though 2011. We contend that this estimate is either too low if we define activists as individuals who ever participated in any Tea Party activity, or too high if we constrain activism to mean those who joined Tea Party chapters.

The survey data we have already analyzed point to a much lower number of activists in the Tea Party than was estimated by Skocpol and Williamson, and we suggest that the average of 8% participation is likely far too high. In the 36 surveys collected by CNN/ORC, just 1% of respondents described themselves as activists, and disaggregating by individual survey never yielded an estimate above 2% of respondents identifying as activists. Extrapolating again from the adult population of the 2010 Census using the CNN/ORC values suggests that there were about 2,345,641 Tea Party activists. We find this estimate to be plausible. In our analysis of Tea Party events presented in Chapter 5, we estimate that approximately 2.7 million activists took part in the Tax Day rallies between 2009 and 2014 (see Figure 5.2 and the accompanying discussion). The estimates aggregate annual turnout and, as a result, are inflated upward since many individual activists likely attended more than one annual rally. But even a lower bound of two million participants is supported by trends in turnout at Tea Party events. Overall, if we use a very weak definition of activist to mean anyone who ever participated in Tea Party activities in any capacity, an estimate of approximately 1% of the adult population seems plausible, given patterns of attendance at the Tea Party's flagship events.

Estimating Activists Using Website Listings

To date, one of the most exhaustive attempts to estimate the size of the Tea Party's committed activists comes from Burghart and Zeskind's (2015) report published by the Institute for Research and Education on Human Rights (IREHR). IREHR aggregated reports of the number of participants who appeared on the websites for the Tea Party umbrella groups between 2010 and 2015, including 1776 Tea Party, FreedomWorks, Patriot Action Network, Tea Party Patriots, and Tea Party Nation.[7] Burghart and Zeskind (2015) estimated that, in 2010, there were approximately 184,000 activists, which grew to 541,000 activists by 2015.

Our approach to estimating the number of activists, like Burghart and Zeskind's (2015), uses web listings of local Tea Party chapters. We built web scrapers that ran once every 24 hours between 2009 and 2014 for each umbrella group, harvesting local chapter listings. This allowed us to collect exhaustive lists of the membership for each group, which we aggregated every three months to estimate membership size. Our approach to estimating the number of activists deviates from Burghart and Zeskind (2015) in two important ways. First, Burghart and Zeskind (2015) appear to use all of the Tea Party groups that were listed to generate their estimates. In contrast, we used a curated list that contained only the groups that were plausibly members of the Tea Party insurgency. Many groups appearing on the websites for FreedomWorks and Patriot Action Network, for instance, were better described as conservative, but not necessarily aligned with the Tea Party. For example, a group named "Rand Paul for President 2012" was at best only tangentially related to the Tea Party, so we concluded that its members should not have been included in counts of Tea Party activists. Second, our interpretation of the estimates differs as well. Whereas Burghart and Zeskind conclude that there was a monotonic increase of Tea Party members, our daily tracking of local chapters indicated that these estimates contained many groups that had entirely demobilized but nonetheless remained listed as active online (see Chapter 6). We interpret our estimates as number of activists who had ever participated in the Tea Party, rather than assuming a group's cumulative size reflected its actual current membership roster.

Using our granular data on membership we estimate that between 144,851 and 308,667 activists ever participated in the Tea Party. The lower bound of this range, which we expect skews too low, is based on the curated list of 3,587 local Tea Party groups that we identified from our daily tracking. We believe this estimate undercounts the size of the Tea Party by excluding the activists who did not join their local chapter online listing. To produce the upper band

---

[7] Burghart and Zeskind (2015) also include the Tea Party Express, though they use the number of donations for that group. Since the Tea Party Express is not a membership organization, we omit it from our calculations.

of our estimate, we included all the local, state, and national chapters of the Tea Party as they appeared online. This estimate, we believe, is likely to be too high as many of the members of local and national chapters did not meet, stage events, or otherwise engage in any on-ground activity beyond joining a group online. Since our goal here is to estimate the activists who participated in day-to-day mobilization, we caution that online group membership alone may not reflect the extent of activism. Our total estimate of activists, then, is lower than Burghart and Zeskind's (2015), but still points to a surprisingly large number of activists who ever took part in the Tea Party's organizational work during its peak phase of mobilization.

What Is the Relative Size of the Tea Party?

How did the size of the activist corps of the Tea Party compare with other conservative social movements? One anchoring point useful in assessing the relative size of the Tea Party is the number of Pro-Life activists. Scholars have claimed that the Pro-Life movement has been among the most impactful and durable instances of social mobilization which emerged from the political right (Munson 2010). Consequently, it makes an appropriate comparison with the Tea Party. Many of the complications that come with estimating the size of Tea Party are also pertinent to making similar estimates for the Pro-Life movement: there exists no definitive list of activists.

Fortunately, an analysis by Swank (2020) used the 2010–2012 wave of the American National Election Survey (ANES) to provide a credible estimate of the number of Pro-Life activists. The ANES is a large probability sample, making its use comparable to our efforts to estimate the size of the Tea Party with survey data. The data collection period for the ANES also overlaps with the main period of Tea Party mobilization. According to Swank (2020:369), approximately 2.7% of the ANES respondents reported some level of activity in the Pro-Life movement. Extrapolating from the adult population in 2010 documented in the US Census yields an estimate of 6,333,230 people who reported ever participating in the Pro-Life movement. The activist core of the Tea Party, then, plausibly appears to have been smaller than that of the Pro-Life movement. Both movements, however, are widely present in the general population, if we use a very weak conception of membership that means ever having participated in a movement event. For both the Tea Party and Pro-Life movements, we suspect that the size of the regular activist contingent was probably quite a bit smaller.

THE TEA PARTY'S MOBILIZING STRUCTURES

Our analysis of the early riser Tea Party groups in Chapter 3 largely left open questions about the nature of its organizational structures as it emerged. These mobilizing structures – the choices made by activists about tactics and organizational forms that are used to produce social change – are essential components of any social movement (McCarthy 1996). By the end of 2010, the Tea Party's distinctive mobilizing structures were in place, including a few national umbrella groups that housed largely independent local chapters. This structure remained stable over the course of the Tea Party's lifecycle, and consequently significantly influenced the trajectory that the insurgency would take. We begin by reviewing two well-known organizational forms widely used by social movement activists as their mobilizing structures, and then describe how well each fits the empirical patterns of the Tea Party's mobilizing structures. We then describe the structure of the Tea Party network identifying its most important actors.

Two Major Mobilizing Structures for Social Movements

The term social movement organization (SMO) describes the component organizational entities of insurgencies and social movements (McCarthy 2013). During the Tea Party insurgency, SMOs included local groups such as the Burgoyne County Tea Party or Adams County Tea Party discussed by Westermeyer (2016) along with national groups like the Tea Party Patriots (Meckler and Martin 2012). SMOs proliferated dramatically in the US in the late twentieth and early twenty-first centuries (McCarthy and Zald 1977), displaying great variation in structure, deliberative processes, longevity, and impact.

The *federated form* is one of the most common mobilizing structures used by social movements (McCarthy 2005). Federated mobilizing structures are hierarchical, usually with some combination of national, state, and community-level chapters. Larger-scale strategic planning flows downward from the national group, which typically commands the most resources (e.g., income or professional staff). For example, the Sierra Club, a leading environmental group, exhibits the federated form. The Sierra Club includes a national headquarters, state-level chapters, and local groups. The state-level groups coordinate the efforts of several hundred local groups and serve as a conduit between the local groups and national headquarters (Andrews et al. 2010). McCarthy and Wolfson (1996) described a similar structure for Mothers Against Drunk Driving (MADD). In the mid-1980s during the peak of MADD's mobilization, there were more than 400 local chapters and state offices active in most states along with a well-staffed national headquarters that provided extensive services including financial, managerial, and technical support. Skocpol and colleagues (2000) chronicled this same distinctive form among many prominent examples of such groups active across the US before the 1960s, with examples ranging from the Women's Christian Temperance Movement to the Ku Klux Klan (see also Skocpol 2003). The federated SMO form presents several important advantages to the activists who adopt it. Such structures benefit from their established social legitimacy (DiMaggio and Powell 1983), as well as mapping closely to the American political structure's federal, state, and local centers of power (Skocpol et al. 2000). Social movements and insurgencies that adopt the federated form can be expected to survive longer, even in the face of declining activism.

The federated organizational form, of course, does not exhaust the many options available to activists. One alternative, the *spin form*, is described by Gerlach and Hine (1970) with subsequent revision by Gerlach (2001). The spin form is a "segmented, usually polysepalous, cellular organizational structure composed of units reticulated by various personal, structural, and ideological ties" (Gerlach and Hine 1970:xvii).[8] In general terms, the spin form decenters the role of hierarchy and bureaucracy as tools for creating social change, placing it at odds with the federated form. Examples of causes that ultimately adopted the spin form include the US Pentecostal and Black Power movements (Gerlach 2001; Gerlach and Hine 1970). A more contemporary example is the Occupy Wall Street movement, which was almost completely decentralized in its daily operations (Gould-Wartofsky 2015). There are strong advantages to the spin form, such as its ability to facilitate rapid growth for newly emergent social movements and insurgencies. New groups need not gain permission to affiliate with the insurgency or be subject to any central control by umbrella groups, nor do they need to adhere to any rigid established consensus messaging. These features allow independent groups to emerge in many varied political and social locations, encouraging a wide diversity in the mix of goals and tactics that are adopted, as well as facilitating ideological plurality. The diffuse and decentralized nature of the spin form also makes insurgencies less vulnerable to social control efforts by authorities since they contain no organizational center vulnerable to being targeted.

The Tea Party's Hybrid Organizational Structure

The federated and spin forms provide two well-documented mobilizing structures that social movements have adapted to their own purposes. Neither completely captures the Tea Party's core organizational form. Despite the emergence of five umbrella groups that claimed to represent the Tea Party, it never succeeded in developing any semblance of a stable national organizational structure that reliably mimicked the federated form. Summarizing their observations of the Tea Party, Skocpol and Williamson (2011) reach a similar conclusion, saying that "there is not, therefore, a single Tea Party organization,

---

[8] Gerlach (2001) later changed their terms polysepalous to polycentric and reticulate to networks in a second formulation of the spin model. These revisions, however, did not substantially alter the key insights embodied in his and Hine's original formulation, so we use the initial spin terminology throughout.

not even a well-coordinated network. Instead, [it is] a gaggle of jostling and sometimes competing local and national organizations" (p. 84). This observation was made when the Tea Party was at its peak, but continued to be a valid description of it in subsequent years.

The insurgency did not exactly mimic the spin form either. On the one hand, there is strong evidence that most local Tea Party groups operated independently from the umbrella groups. Blum (2020:46) identifies a total of 270 network clusters of Tea Party groups using linkages between websites to measure ties between groups. Within these clusters, 88% of ties were exclusively between some combination of local and state Tea Party groups, putting these groups at a distance from the national umbrella groups. This is consistent with the spin form's emphasis on minimal vertical hierarchies within a social movement's mobilizing structures. On the other hand, the Tea Party umbrella groups and their precursors did play an outsized role in the insurgency's emergence, as we demonstrated in Chapter 3. The top-down initial mobilization apparent for the 2009 Tax Day rallies is a striking example of nationally focused groups and activists building the core mobilizing structures that grassroots activists would ultimately adopt. Other scholars have arrived at similar conclusions. Fetner and King (2014), stressing the early elite resource flows to Tea Parties, argue that analysts should include those resource providers as another organizational level for modern insurgencies like the Tea Party.

We argue that the Tea Party's mobilizing structure represents a hybrid approach, somewhere between the federated and spin forms for two reasons. First, the local Tea Party groups extensively used the web platforms created by the umbrella groups to further their agendas. In Chapter 5, we will analyze nearly 20,000 Tea Party gatherings, with nearly 90% of these events having been announced on the website of at least one umbrella group. Thus, though ties between the umbrella groups and local chapters did exist, they were quite weak and used strategically by the grassroots activists for their own purposes, a claim similarly made by Ehrhardt (2020) based upon his ethnography of local groups. This is additional evidence of a partially federated form. Second, there is little evidence of top-down leadership, especially after 2010, as would be expected with the federated form but consistent with the spin form. The umbrella groups offered few resources to local chapters beyond web hosting, and we saw little evidence of top-down strategic planning of the Tea Party's activities. As well, the local Tea Party group's affiliations were spread out across the five umbrella groups, further complicating any form of consolidated action, an issue to which we now turn.

Mapping the Tea Party Network

The five umbrella groups differed significantly in their impact on the Tea Party insurgency. Each umbrella group gave local chapters a roughly comparable set of online tools, including a dedicated webpage, a locale to make and publicize events, and hosting services for individual and chapter blog posts. The umbrella groups were nevertheless quite hands-off the local chapters, as the web data for these chapters indicated little direct public interaction with the user accounts held by the national organizations. The total number of local chapters that became attached to each umbrella groups varied quite significantly, with some chapters joining multiple umbrella groups. Which national umbrella groups were most important based on these affiliation patterns?

To answer this question, we draw on our daily web scrapes capturing each local Tea Party group's appearance on the website of the five umbrella organizations, which we treat as a large social network.[9] We also include fully independent Tea Party groups that were active on Meetup, a widely used general social media platform designed to facilitate gatherings, one that was used by many of the independent Tea Party groups. Our full research design is described in this book's appendix. However, in brief, our web crawlers harvested an exhaustive list of groups interacting with each umbrella group each 24-hour cycle. This research design required constant supervision of the performance of every web crawler, allowing atypical error rates to be identified and corrected immediately. The process produced a detailed portrait of groups that had ever affiliated with an umbrella group. Since local groups could appear on a website of multiple umbrella groups – many groups appeared repeatedly – we manually reviewed the list of groups, identifying and correcting errors and overlaps. This process generated a sample of 3,587 local groups distributed across the five umbrella groups and Meetup.

Figure 4.3 portrays the Tea Party's local chapter network, including the connections between individual groups and the umbrella groups.[10] It is apparent from the plot that the Tea Party Patriots and FreedomWorks were the two primary umbrella groups. A total of 2,135 local groups were affiliated with the Tea Party Patriots, with another 1,335 groups linked to the FreedomWorks. These vastly overshadow the 202 groups linked to Tea Party Nation, the 164 groups on Patriot Action Network, 106 groups on Meetup, and 68 groups on the 1776 Tea Party. Approximately 11% of local Tea Party groups were linked to more than one umbrella group. The most common pairing was the 162 groups appearing on the websites for both FreedomWorks and Tea Party Patriots, followed by 93 groups listed on Tea Party Nation and Tea Party Patriots. No group appeared on all five umbrella groups and Meetup. Overall, the pattern of Tea Party network ties tells us that while FreedomWorks and Tea Party Patriots were the most important national

---

[9] In the jargon used by social network analysts, this is a two-mode network as individual chapters could be affiliated with more than one umbrella group.

[10] Blum (2020) also used network tools to visualize the Tea Party's mobilizing structures; however, she used website linkages to assess ties. Our data indicated that most local groups did not have a website beyond ones they built on the platforms provided by the umbrella groups.

FIGURE 4.3 Network structure of the Tea Party insurgency across the umbrella groups. *Note*: The abbreviations are: 1776=1776 Tea Party; FW=FreedomWorks; MU=Meetup; PAN=Patriot Action Network; TPN=Tea Party Nation; and TPP=Tea Party Patriots.

mobilizing structures, those groups did not have a complete monopoly on the grassroots insurgency. No single umbrella group could reasonably claim to be the sole representative of the Tea Party insurgency.

THE CHARACTERISTICS OF LOCAL TEA PARTY GROUPS

We next describe some organizational features of the local groups, their size, resources, and indication of being more institutionalized through filing for tax-exempt status with the IRS. We draw on a combination of data sources, including our web survey of surviving Tea Party groups, online membership lists, and publicly available IRS records. We use the results to establish a comparative understanding of the strength of local groups; we investigate their activities and longevity in subsequent chapters.

The Size of Local Groups

While we have estimated that there were between 144,000 and 310,000 activists who ever participated in the Tea Party, our web scrapes of organizational and membership lists allow us to analyze the distribution of membership by chapter. Focusing on the curated list of 3,587 local Tea Party groups identified above, we use their highest count of membership anytime between 2009 and 2014 in our analyses. The distribution of chapter size is summarized in Figure 4.4.

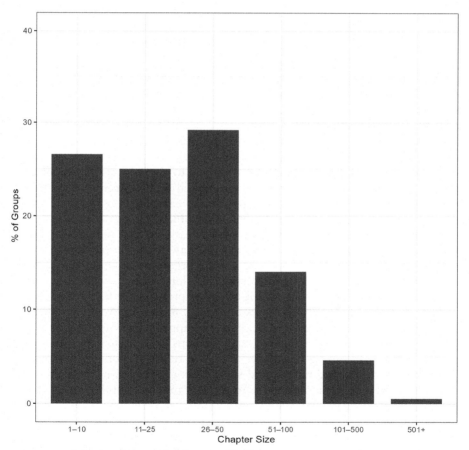

FIGURE 4.4 Membership counts of 3,587 Tea Party groups, 2009–2014.
Note: Estimates are based on the maximum size appearing on each chapter's website listing.

A substantial majority of local groups were quite small. The median size was 25 with a mean of 38 members. Approximately 22% of groups had fewer than 10 members, while 95% of groups had fewer than 100 members, and just 2% of them had more than 200 members. The distribution of group size narrows dramatically between a total membership size of 50 and 100. The pattern again reinforces our claim that most groups had very few members. It is important to emphasize that the size estimates are based on the total count of members who were ever active, rather than reflecting a group's size at any specific point in time. It became clear to us during our data collection that few groups deleted members, regardless of their activity status, since membership size almost never declined. This fact falsely created a trend of monotonic membership growth for groups. In short, most Tea Party groups were quite small, and nearly all of them had fewer than 100 active members.

Trends in Seeking Tax-Exempt Status through IRS Registrations

Another way to assess the distinctive tactics of local Tea Party groups is by determining whether they attempted to register with the US IRS. Many social movement organizations seek out tax-exempt status by applying for IRS registration. Registration is optional, but groups who successfully receive tax-exempt status benefit from important financial advantages. The two most commonly sought statuses conferred by the IRS are 501(c)(3) and 501(c)(4) designations (McCarthy, Britt, and Wolfson 1991). A major advantage of receiving 501(c)(3) status is that contributions to a group are tax deductible for the donor; however, groups are prohibited from directly or indirectly participating in, or intervening in, any political campaign on behalf of (or in opposition to) any candidate for elective public office. The 501(c)(4) status does not confer tax deductibility advantages for donations, although the organization itself remains tax-exempt. These groups may engage in partisan political activity, as long as such activities are not the organization's primary activity. A more detailed discussion of these statuses, along with how they are interpreted and used by movement organizations, is provided by Berry (2003).

Registration with the IRS requires applying for an Employer Identification Number (EIN), completing a form about the applicant group, and paying a filing fee. Once a determination is made, groups are required to file annual returns with the IRS using Form 990, and these returns become public record. Given the effort required to gain and sustain tax-exempt status, only the most stable Tea Party groups were likely to initiate and successfully complete the process. While this was no doubt only a small number of the more highly professionalized groups, IRS filing records remain helpful as they provide a window into the internal characteristics of those chapters.

Some Tea Party groups that had applied for IRS status became involved in what was referred to as "the IRS scandal" by Tea Party activists and the conservative media. In the spring of 2010, the IRS began flagging applications

TABLE 4.1 *Trends in IRS registration for Tea Party groups, 2009–2018.*

	N	%
Total Number of Groups Listed from IRS Search	133	100
Total Number with a Ruling Date	79	59
501(c)(3)	11	14
501(c)(4)	68	86
Total Number of Groups Ever Filing a 990	36	46
Filed More than Once	19	24
Filed After 2013	8	10
Total Number of Statuses Listed as Revoked	16	20

Note: Estimates exclude national Tea Party groups.

for scrutiny containing keywords such as "Tea Party" or "9/12 Project"[11] in their name. Evidence eventually emerged that the IRS monitored groups across the political spectrum, not only conservative groups. Nevertheless, the false narrative of lopsided political targeting widely proliferated across right-wing media outlets. Though the claim that the IRS exclusively targeted conservatives was rooted in disinformation, the perception of enhanced scrutiny almost certainly further reduced the already scant number of applications that had been submitted by Tea Party groups. We postpone a discussion of the effects of the IRS scandal until Chapter 5. We note, however, that the incident did not gain much widespread public attention until 2013. As a result, it likely had a modest impact on the propensity of groups to file through the end of 2012.

To locate Tea Party groups that had begun the filing process with the IRS, we used a combination of three searchable databases that track organizations filing for 501(c) status. These are the Tax-Exempt Organization platform maintained by the IRS, the National Center for Charitable Statistics, and Guidestar. We used the search term "tea party" to identify candidate groups. Searches were conducted in 2014 and repeated in 2020. We reviewed all the results returned by our search terms and retained only those organizations plausibly part of the Tea Party insurgency. This strategy ultimately identified 133 Tea Party organizations that had at some time begun the registration process.

Table 4.1 shows the pattern of IRS registration for Tea Party groups between 2009 and 2018. Of the 133 chapters that began the filing process, based on its issuance of an EIN to the group, just 59% received a final determination. The remaining 41% had either abandoned their application process during the filing

---

[11] The 9/12 Project was a conservative movement founded by conservative commentator Glenn Beck in 2009. It was loosely affiliated with the Tea Party, but did not match the insurgency's size and ferocity.

process or otherwise did not complete all the necessary forms required by the IRS to arrive at a final determination. Most Tea Party groups filed as 501(c)(4) organizations, representing 86% of chapters where the IRS made a final determination, with the rest filing as 501(c)(3) organizations. The more common preference for a 501(c)(4) status stems from the sharply partisan stance of the Tea Party.

Few of the Tea Party groups that completed the registration process appeared to substantially benefit from doing so. Only 46% of groups that had received a determination went on to file a Form 990 with the IRS, and 24% of groups filed more than once. By the time that the IRS scandal became national news in 2013, only 10% of the registered Tea Party groups were still filing their 990s, suggesting that the majority of the registered groups had elected to abandon maintaining their tax-exempt status. About 20% of chapters that received a determination eventually had their status revoked by IRS, as a consequence of not having filed their required 990 for three consecutive years.

Overall, these data clearly show that only a small minority of the several thousand Tea Party groups had begun or succeeded in registering as tax-exempt nonprofits with the IRS. No more than 4% of the 3,587 organizations we identified as active at some point between 2009 and 2014 attempted to seek tax-exempt status. In other words, 96% of Tea Party groups had operated off the IRS radar, and did not secure any of the advantages available to more professionalized social movement organizations. This is a common pattern for small grassroots organizations with few financial resources. Work by Smith (1997) found that most of the smallest local groups do not register with the state. He refers to these groups as comprising the "dark matter" of the nonprofit organizational landscape. Our data indicate that a similar pattern held for the Tea Party: groups that either had begun or completed the filing process with the IRS were rare.

Estimating the Financial Resources of Local Tea Party Groups

Finally, we estimated local groups' financial resources. We relied on two primary sources of evidence: first, we used the completed Form 990s for the Tea Party groups that had registered with the IRS to track their reported income; second, our web survey of Tea Party groups asked about a chapter's operating expenses. Both sources are weighted toward the most professionalized, well-resourced, and firmly established groups, given the barriers to IRS registration and the fact that respondents to our web survey were among the longest-lasting local chapters, having survived through early 2015. The patterns we discuss, therefore, refer to the most highly resourced Tea Party groups.

Table 4.2 provides the income for 93 chapters that filed at least one Form 990 with the IRS, and 66 groups that reported their operating expenses in our

TABLE 4.2 *Percentiles of Tea Party income and expenses.*

Percentile	Income ($)	Expenses ($)
5	0	0
10	217	0
20	1,920	100
30	3,674	250
40	13,323	500
50	17,444	1,000
60	26,764	1,500
70	44,411	2,250
80	86,983	4,000
90	124,872	8,750
95	186,098	11,500

Note: Estimates for income are from 93 complete Form 990s; estimates for expenses are from 66 survey responses.

web survey. We show the reported income and operating costs in percentiles to capture the overall patterns from each source. The primary implication of Table 4.2 is that Tea Party groups were able to accomplish quite a lot with quite meager resources. The median group reported $17,444 in income to the IRS, with significant diversity across the organizations that had secured tax-exempt status. Notably, at the 5th percentile groups did not have any income for that tax year, while even by the 20th percentile groups had less than $2,000 in income. The top 10% of Tea Party groups were quite successful at fundraising, and secured more than $100,000 during a tax year, with the top 5% securing approximately $186,000. These groups were typically large regional coalitions, making it difficult to determine the financial resources that were available to any particular local group within a local network.

As a point of comparison, evidence collected from Mothers Against Drunk Driving (MADD) local chapters in 1985 showed that the median annual revenue of a chapter was $1,500 (McCarthy and Wolfson 1996). Those groups also reported a median of 36 members, and 67% of the groups published a newsletter. MADD exhibited a classic federated mobilizing structure. Our estimates of these wealthiest local Tea Party group's annual income appear quite low, but comparable with the more established chapters of MADD.

The operating expenses reported by the groups answering our web survey are significantly lower than the income figures reported to the IRS. The median group reported that it had cost approximately $1,000 to sustain its activities for a year; however, 40% of groups in the sample reported having been able to do so with less than $500. A small number of groups reported relatively high expenses, as seen in the 90th and 95th percentile values of $8,750 and $11,500 respectively. These groups nearly all answered that they had secured nonprofit status with the IRS and claimed to have several thousand members. Comparing the responses from those groups with the organizations that reported values on the IRS Form 990s indicates that these answers were plausible. Overall, large groups with significant operating expenses were quite rare. Indeed, on our web survey, many groups responded that their expenses were so small that they did not keep records of them, again confirming to us that the values in Table 4.2, modest as they are, may be inflated. Our data on Tea Party chapter income points to a clear pattern: most groups operated with very modest resources, at best, while only a handful of chapters commanded substantial resources.

CONCLUSION

By almost any measure, the Tea Party insurgency was enormously consequential. The major findings in this chapter indicate that the insurgency's success was unlikely, and even surprising given the bird's eye view of the Tea Party that we have provided here. The core number of activists who took part in the Tea Party was much smaller compared with other prominent conservative causes such as the Pro-Life movement. Using a combination of qualitative and quantitative data about Tea Party activists, we have demonstrated that they were a unique subset of American conservatives. Activists faced a more precarious personal financial situation than supporters, and were markedly more conservative in their views. We suggest this made activists less compromising, which was perhaps most clearly manifested in how the activists were so suspicious and critical of Republican leaders.

The mobilizing structures built by Tea Party leaders and activists complicated long-term coordination and planning, making their successes all the more remarkable. The hybrid federated/spin organizational form adopted by the insurgency facilitated its rapid spawning of several thousand local groups, but the chapters were largely isolated from each other. Since the major umbrella groups elected to work in competition with each other rather than cooperate, local groups in a single community were often split in their affiliation between multiple umbrella groups and sometimes disconnected from other nearby chapters. The two most prominent umbrella organizations, FreedomWorks and Tea Party Patriots, displayed little consistent effort in helping local Tea Parties to organize and communicate with one another beyond providing web hosting services. The local chapters, in general, were relatively small and had modest financial resources to enable them to continue their work. Nearly all the groups lacked the tax-exempt status commonly sought by contemporary social movement organizations. Given their scant financial resources, the application process was likely not worth the effort for most groups.

Now that we have established the origin story and sketched some important dimensions of the internal structure of the Tea Party groups, the remainder of the book will focus on their activities and the consequences of their activism. The weak mobilizing structures we have described here are particularly important, since they set the stage for what ultimately became the rapid dissolution of Tea Party activism by late 2014. Despite the evaporation of political mobilization, however, traces of that activism continued to have major consequences for American politics that would last for years to come.

5

The Trajectory of the Tea Party Insurgency

Local Activism and Its Rapid Decline

Despite the initial high-profile burst of activity, Tea Party activism declined quickly and never returned to its original ferocity. The decline in protest was more immediate than local organizational vitality, which declined more slowly. We analyze the two trajectories separately, first discussing the tactical evolution of the Tea Party insurgency, then taking up the demobilization of local Tea Party organizations in Chapter 6. We emphasize two primary trends in the activities and events staged by activists: first, we dissect the decline of the signature Tax Day rallies and, second, we describe the results of our granular accounting of 19,758 Tea Party events staged between 2009 and 2014. After establishing the outline of the insurgency's tactical evolution, we generate a synthetic, theoretical account to explain why the Tea Party so abruptly changed its tactical mix. Our explanation emphasizes the combined impact of declining media attention, the activists' evolving views of protest's effectiveness, and a fear of state repression that developed in response to the Internal Revenue Service (IRS) scandal of 2013 (discussed later in this chapter).

We highlight several important insights about the evolution of Tea Party activism. Most notably, we show that the insurgency's reliance on the most common tactics – rallies and protests – quickly fell by the wayside and never resurfaced. Especially following the Tax Day rallies of 2009 and 2010, there is little evidence of any coherent, large-scale national coordination between Tea Party groups. This lack of coordination is at odds with the top-down model of activism which was so highly emphasized in earlier research (e.g., DiMaggio 2011; Fallin et al. 2014; Langman and Lundskow 2012; Nesbit 2016). As we demonstrated in Chapter 4, the Tea Party's local chapter network largely operated in a manner almost entirely independent from the insurgency's elite facilitators. As a result, the level of coordination possible in federated social movements was absent for the Tea Party. By 2011, the dominant form of Tea Party activity had become monthly or bimonthly chapter meetings, with the consequence of shifting the activities of local groups out of public view and hidden from the eyes of even sympathetic media, whose favorable coverage had initially supercharged activism.

THE DISAPPEARANCE OF TAX DAY RALLIES

We provided a detailed portrait of the 2009 Tax Day rallies in Chapter 3, assessing how a combination of local material threats and status threats were associated with their prevalence. We identified 1,022 events in 2009, but the scope and breadth of Tax Day rallies declined precipitously over the next four years. By 2014, only 22 Tax Day rallies took place. What happened to the flagship tactic of the insurgency?

Tracking Tax Day Rallies over Time

We developed our analysis of the Tax Day rallies through a dynamic, multifaceted research design which tracked Tea Party events over time. In 2009, the rallies were organized using a single website (taxdayteaparty.com; now defunct).[1] We exhaustively indexed those events using a web crawler. To track the rallies between 2010 and 2014, we modified our workflow to match the splintering and expansion of the Tea Party into a series of umbrella groups, combined with capturing independent Tea Party activity. We built web crawlers for each umbrella group to capture pertinent information, modifying the groups each year to match the organizational evolution of the Tea Party itself. Our data is ultimately based on event information compiled from American for Prosperity, FreedomWorks, Meetup, Patriot Action Network, taxdayteaparty.com, 1776 Tea Party, Tea Party Express, Tea Party Nation, Tea Party Patriots, and Tea Party Perspective. For independent groups, we included all Tea Party organizations present on Meetup, a social media platform designed to facilitate gatherings, to look for evidence of Tax Day rallies. In all cases, we supplemented that event data with extractions of organizational information and other event listings starting in early 2010 and continuing through the end of 2014.

We combined the web data with the results from systematic newspaper searches identifying reports of Tea Party activities in the one-week period before and after Tax Day each year between 2009 and 2014. Together, these steps allowed us to build a comprehensive database of Tax Day rallies. Social movement researchers have long used newspaper data to study protest events. Importantly, they have consistently found that newspapers devote more attention to events spatially proximate to their editorial offices (e.g., Earl et al. 2004; Rafail et al. 2019). To minimize the effects of this bias, we used 452 local, state,

---

[1] This website has oscillated as a front for the Tea Party or a source of cybersquatting over the years that we have followed the movement. The website was only actively used to promote the Tax Day rallies in 2009.

and national newspapers from Access World News and an additional 785 news-papers from LexisNexis, both full-text searchable archives of newspapers. We identified candidate articles with full-text searches using the string '"tea party" or "tea parties."' Then , we reviewed all articles returned each year between April 7 and April 22. Articles describing any Tax Day mobilization were coded and added to our main database.

Our analysis of the trajectory and location of the Tax Day rallies is based on the combination of these two data sources. Triangulating multiple sources of information significantly increased the comprehensiveness of our annual enu-meration of Tax Day rallies. This multifaceted approach to data collection proved especially useful in this case, as between 28% and 68% of each year's annual rallies were exclusively posted online. Had we depended only upon newspaper sources, we would have significantly underestimated the annual number of Tax Day rallies each year.

The Trend of Tax Day Rallies, 2009–2014

The number of rallies we identified each year is shown in Figure 5.1. We distinguish between the total number of events and the subset of rallies that were reported by news media. In 2009, the Tea Party's initial wave of mobiliza-tion was highly successful with 1,022 rallies. By 2010 this number fell to 679 events, a decline of 34%. The decline in protest activity continued through 2011 when 395 protests occurred, representing a 41% decline from the previous year. By 2012, only 128 Tax Day rallies took place, which represents another major year-to-year decline of 68%. The final two years of our analysis, 2013 and 2014, had just 27 and 22 events respectively, effectively marking the end of Tea Party activists' use of what had once been their signature tactic.

The decline in the raw count of Tax Day rallies also carried over to patterns of media attention, plotted in Figure 5.1. In 2009, a stunning 73% of Tax Day rallies received some level of media attention – a notable achievement for the fledgling Tea Party. Rallies in 2010 also received considerable media coverage, with 56% of protests appearing in our newspaper data. A marked shift in media attention to the Tax Day rallies became apparent in 2011, when just 26% of events were covered. The lack of media attention largely continued between 2012 and 2014, where between 18% and 41% of events received coverage. The high of 41% coverage took place in 2013, where 11 of 27 events were discussed by the media. This coverage pattern barely registers as a blip in the larger media landscape. The decline in media attention to the rallies no doubt dampened activist's enthusiasm for continuing to stage Tax Day rallies, as their efforts were going largely unnoticed by local or national media sources.

A second consequential implication of the decline in the number of Tax Day rallies was the corresponding decrease in activist turnout. This was true in terms of both the average size of an event and the total number of participants across the nation who attended. The initial wave of Tax Day rallies in 2009 was not just remarkable for its geographic breadth and raw volume, but also for the sheer

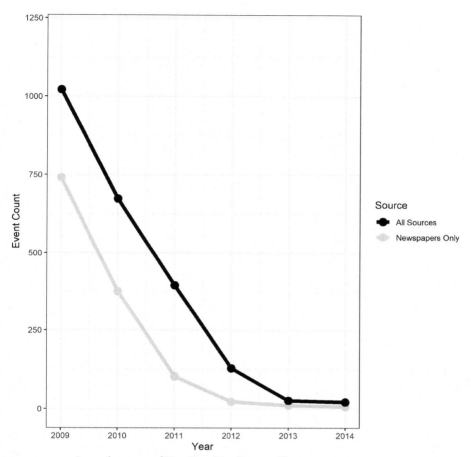

FIGURE 5.1 Annual counts of Tax Day Tea Party rallies, 2009–2014.

number of conservative activists who took part. Previous research on the insurgency found that between 440,000 and 810,000 people participated in the 2009 events (Madestam et al. 2013), though these estimates are based on smaller samples of rallies compared with our more comprehensive enumeration of the events. We plot the average size of Tax Day rallies in Figure 5.2a and the estimated total activist turnout in Figure 5.2b, both for the period 2009 through 2014.[2]

There are two sharply contrasting periods in the trajectory of the Tax Day rallies: the active phase and the decline phase. In the active phase, between

---

[2] These estimates are based on the crowd counts for the events reported in our sample of newspaper coverage. To patch in plausible values for the non-reported events, we used a simulation routine to randomly draw from the crowd sizes for a specific year. We repeated the process 10,000 times to generate the average turnout and total participant estimate in Figure 5.2.

(a)   (b)

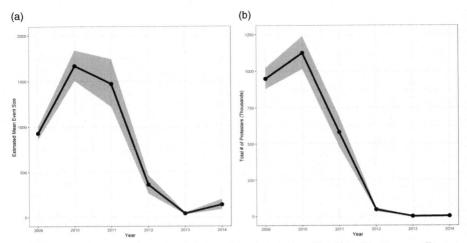

FIGURE 5.2 Estimated (a) size and (b) total participants at Tax Day Tea Party rallies, 2009–2014.
Note: Estimates are based on 10,000 simulations of all rallies using size estimates from media reports each year. We estimate that approximately 2.7 million activists took part in the Tax Day rallies between 2009 and 2014.

2009 and 2011, events were large and national turnout was high. We estimate that in 2009 between 860 and 1,001 activists participated in a typical Tax Day rally, a number which grew to a high of between 1,504 and 1,838 in 2010, and then decreased slightly to a range of 1,218 and 1,743 participants by 2011. The Tax Day rallies of 2012 show a sharp decline, with between 261 and 467 estimated participants. The lowest point was in 2013, where between 31 and 52 protestors gathered for the average Tax Day rally. Finally, by 2014, there was a slight growth in the average event size, which ranged between 87 and 200 participants.

The trend of total activist turnout in Figure 5.2b mirrors the mean participation rates in Figure 5.2a. By our estimates, between 878,752 and 1,023,197 total demonstrators participated in the 2009 rallies, which grew to an estimate of between 1,014,316 and 1,239,121 in 2010. These protests were enormous by historical standards, but not sustainable. There was a more noteworthy decline between 2010 and 2011, where we estimate a turnout of between 481,270 and 688,437; these remain remarkably large overall turnout numbers. The decline phase in 2012, 2013, and 2014 had an estimated national turnout of 45,964, 1,112, and 3,057 respectively, a mere shadow of the number of protestors seen just a few years earlier.

Evidence of Annual Intent

Tea Party activists originally conceived of the Tax Day rallies as annual events, and retained that vision over time, so the precipitous decline in rallies needs to

TABLE 5.1 *References to annual intent in newspaper coverage and website content on the Tax Day rallies, 2009–2014.*

	Newspaper Coverage		Web Content	
	Annual Intent (%)	*Total N*	*Annual Intent (%)*	*Total N*
2009	7.98	3899	25.37	70
2010	6.14	4596	9.04	1084
2011	16.49	2013	14.53	1851
2012	13.37	1129	18.14	3765
2013	13.45	446	10.61	1216
2014	22.52	151	7.79	1283

Note: Sources include 1776 Tea Party, Americans for Prosperity, FreedomWorks, Google, Meetup, Tea Party Express, Tea Party Nation, and Tea Party Patriots, and 1,287 newspapers. Newspaper Ns are based on all Tea Party coverage between April 1 and April 22 of each year.

be interpreted in terms of the stated intentions of the participants. There is ample evidence of annual intent. Table 5.1 contains the results of keyword searches of the Tea Party's web content and newspaper coverage of the rallies. In the 21,503 source documents we used to build the Tax Day rally databases, we searched for references to the strings "yearly" and "annual" to identify plans to stage the rallies each year. Between 6% and 23% of newspaper articles on the Tax Day rallies contained these keywords. The same is true for between 8% and 25% of the web content. This evidence points to a fair amount of variability in the use of these keywords over time. Nevertheless, the pattern provides support for our conclusion that, from the onset, many Tea Party organizers entertained the intention of staging Tax Day rallies annually, and intended to keep staging protests into the foreseeable future.

Summary

We have shown that by several metrics the Tax Day rallies, initially the primary tactic deployed by activists of the Tea Party insurgency, had declined dramatically by 2012 and largely disappeared after 2013. As the raw count of Tax Day rallies declined, so too did the total participant turnout and the average size of the typical event. Taken together, these trends contradict the Tea Party's rhetorical hook that its activists and members continued to reflect the true political sentiments of a silent majority. While in 2009 events were organized rapidly, occurring just two months after the famous rant by Rick Santelli, CNBC anchor (see Chapter 2), the Tax Day rallies in 2010 were the product of more than a year's intensive mobilization, rapid organizational growth, and expressions of support from key leaders in the Republican Party. By any account, it was a tremendous accomplishment to mobilize more than a million people across the country in a loosely coordinated, but primarily decentralized manner. Just as significant was the swiftness of the decline. Transitioning quickly from more than 1,000 events across the country with millions of participants to a mere handful of protests with a combined attendance in the low thousands indicates that the insurgency had rapidly begun to run out of steam. Despite ensuing widespread gains for the Tea Party in the institutionalized political sphere, these trends point to major shifts in the internal dynamics of the insurgency.

THE TRAJECTORY OF LOCAL TEA PARTY EVENTS: PROTESTS TO MEETINGS

Perhaps the most obvious explanation for the decline in the number and size of Tax Day rallies was simply that Tea Party activists had changed their minds about preferred tactics. Activists are adept at reading changes in the political or social systems they confront and modifying their tactics accordingly. McAdam's (1983) work on the civil rights movement makes it clear that activists regularly modified the scale and type of their activities based on the mix of repressive tactics used by their segregationist opponents (also see Tilly 2006). For the Tea Party, the decline of Tax Day rallies was consistent with a larger pattern of demobilization. In particular, the insurgency shifted from street-level activism to more routine organizational maintenance, and eventually, an end to public gatherings. That transition appears to have marked a strategic choice by Tea Party activists, as many local chapters continued to stage meetings, book clubs, and other events out of the public eye. We substantiate these claims with an analysis of nearly 20,000 events, including protests and other kinds of gatherings, arranged by local Tea Party organizations and activists occurring between 2009 and 2014.

Creating Granular Estimates of Tea Party Activity

We used a triangulated approach to identify as many local Tea Party events as possible, similar to the research design we used to track the Tax Day rallies. Using a series of web crawlers, we identified events hosted by local Tea Party groups beginning in late 2009 and 2010 when such listings began to appear online. These listings allowed any affiliated Tea Party group or activist to post events, such as protests, chapter meetings, speaker series, and other gatherings. These listings also typically included a time, date, place, and description of the event. We modified our scrapers as needed when a specific website altered how local groups could post and publicize events.[3] These groups included the 1776 Tea Party, FreedomWorks, Patriot Action Network, Tea Party Nation,

---

[3] A good example of such website shifts was the launch of Freedom Connector platform that was publicly released by FreedomWorks in early 2011. The platform greatly simplified the process of creating events for affiliated groups, which we believe generated the small boost in daily events starting in 2011 visible in Figure 5.3.

and Tea Party Patriots. As before, we used Meetup to capture the activities of Tea Party groups that were unaffiliated with any of the major umbrella organizations.

We also collected 70,834 newspaper articles, editorials, letters to the editor, and other coverage of the Tea Party drawn from 785 local, state, and national newspapers to supplement the web data. This content was drawn from all US-based, English language newspapers available in the LexisNexis database at the time of data collection. As with our approach to identifying Tax Day rallies, we used the search string '"tea party" or "tea parties"' and collected all articles published from February 19, 2009, through December 31, 2014. Many of these articles focused on the Tea Party more generally rather than the specific activities of any group or groups, so we used a combination of keyword restrictions and machine learning to create a subsample of articles that featured any events.[4] This ultimately allowed us to generate 34,929 pieces of media content. Each was manually screened, and when necessary, coded by a team of research assistants.

We combined the web data with the newspaper activities to create a merged activity database, geocoding each event to the county-level, and then retaining all unique events. This required manually reviewing any two (or more) events occurring in the same county on the same day, regardless of the description of a specific event. This step proved necessary, as 15% of the events that we analyzed were reported by multiple sources (e.g., two umbrella groups, or an umbrella group and newspaper article). The final step involved developing a decision tree to code the events into four categories. The first category, *protest events*, included Tax Day rallies, demonstrations, and other comparable events; the second category included all *chapter meetings*; third, we created a category for *awareness events*, including speaker series, bus tours, or other non-protest events used by activists to promote the Tea Party's message; the last category included *political events*, such as Tea Party participation in town halls, "get out the vote" events, phone banking for candidates for public office, and direct engagements with elected representatives or candidates at the local, state, and federal level. We omitted spam events, those held entirely online, or otherwise not appearing to have a clear purpose.[5] Our final analytic sample included 19,758 events that we used to analyze Tea Party activism. The measure has great utility in describing the trajectory of Tea Party activism and unpacking the larger impacts of the Tea Party on political processes.

---

[4] We used the keywords "protest" and "meeting" to make a first rough cut of articles for our research assistants to examine, and then used a support vector machine on the remaining articles. This latter model had a precision of 0.94 and a recall of 0.73, indicating strong performance (see Murphy 2012).

[5] These also included more than 2,000 events that were listed at least twice on the same website, or groups that organized events far into the future. One group organized more than 1,000 events through 2035.

The Ebb and Flow of Tea Party Activism

We begin by analyzing the temporal evolution of Tea Party activity from February 2009 through December 2014. The daily count of Tea Party events is shown in Figure 5.3. There are notable spikes of activity during the 2009, 2010, 2011, and 2012 reflecting Tax Day rallies, consistent with the surge of protests we already described. In 2009, another coordinated event took place on July 4, where 170 protest events occurred in 87 counties. A final coordinated event took place on May 21, 2013, when 166 protests occurred in 76 counties to oppose what the Tea Party believed was biased oversight of its membership and activities by the IRS. We expand on what came to be called the "IRS scandal" further below, as it highlights a relatively anemic response to what many activists considered an existential threat to the Tea

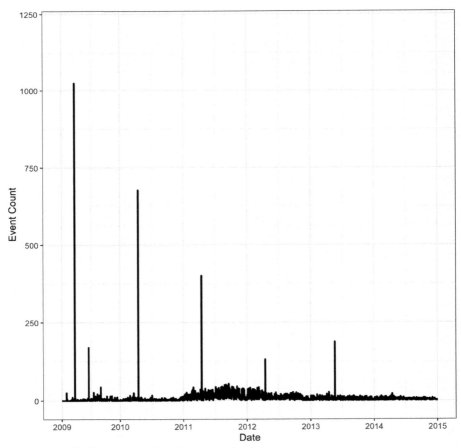

FIGURE 5.3 Daily counts of Tea Party activity, 2009–2014.

Party. Aside from these peaks, there is little evidence of any further broad coordination among local groups for the duration of our analysis. The evidence indicates that, apart from the first few annual Tax Day protest waves, there was never another surge of Tea Party activity. The average daily event count for the Tea Party was merely nine total events across the nation. Only 26% of days between 2009 and 2014 saw a total of 10 or more Tea Party events, and that frequency declines to less than 10% of days when using 20 or more events as the cut-off.

Daily aggregate counts of Tea Party events do not differentiate between the major types of activities chosen by activists, thus masking the profound changes in the character of Tea Party activities over its effective lifespan. There was a rapid and durable shift away from protest as the tactic of choice for the insurgents. Simultaneously, however, the activists came to settle quickly on what we call *maintenance events*, or gatherings that consisted primarily of semiregular meetings among members of local Tea Party groups. These maintenance events were highly localized and were rarely advertised beyond online listings. The events were also unlikely to appreciably contribute to organizational growth, recruitment, or even retention. The annual breakdown of the types of events staged by the groups is shown in Table 5.2.

During 2009, the Tea Party insurgency was marked by loud, boisterous protests. While such events were most apparent in the Tax Day rallies, similar tactics were also used during town halls designed to confront local politicians about Barack Obama's plans for healthcare reform, which was typically derided as a government takeover of healthcare. Protests were the dominant form of Tea Party activism, accounting for nearly 79% of all events staged in 2009. The move away from protests began in 2010, when 55% of all events were protest related. This trend was solidified by 2011. During that year, less than 10% of Tea Party events were protests. Between 2012 and 2014, protests continued to be only a minor part of the broader portfolio of tactics used by activists. A small increase in protests took place in 2013, the result of the coordinated effort to counteract the IRS surveillance of Tea Party groups. By 2014, less than 4% of Tea Party events were protests.

TABLE 5.2 *Annual percentages of Tea Party events by type (n=19,758).*

	2009	2010	2011	2012	2013	2014
Protest	79.45	54.69	9.55	5.81	9.71	3.89
Meeting	7.31	28.81	78.29	80.57	82.18	89.40
Awareness Event	6.02	8.64	7.47	6.56	5.55	4.52
Political Event	7.22	7.86	4.69	7.05	2.57	2.18
Total N	2092	1909	6869	4494	2648	1746

Note: Estimates are based on events listed by Tea Party umbrella groups, Meetup, and 785 newspapers.

As protests declined, there was a corresponding increase in maintenance events. In 2009, just 7% of events were meetings. This ballooned to nearly 80% of all activities by 2011. At the end of our analysis in 2014, almost 90% of all Tea Party gatherings were meetings, a stunning departure from the tactic that had defined the insurgency's early years. What was the content of a typical meeting? Using information from the web description of events allowed us to piece together some patterns. Three kinds of meetings were most typical. First, many were conversational gatherings for attendees to discuss "current political issues" or "defending liberty." Second, meetings with guest speakers were common, especially featuring conservatives from other political organizations, local and state politicians, as well as law enforcement representatives (e.g., county sheriffs). Finally, many meetings were used to motivate current and prospective members and supporters to vote in municipal, county, state, and federal electoral contests. These meetings were staged in hopes of electing Tea Party sympathizers, or in rare cases one of the group's own members.

Table 5.2 provides important evidence of the Tea Party's use of more institutionalized and traditional political tactics. While the Tea Party unquestionably had a major impact on the Republican Party, political events were never a dominant part of the tactical repertoire of most local groups. This is in contrast to the widespread belief that the opposite had been the case – that Tea Party activists devoted extensive effort in helping to nominate and subsequently directly support sympathetic candidates. Blum (2020), for instance, outlines how a main Tea Party goal was a hostile takeover of the Republican Party. We agree that this was true. However, our evidence indicates that pursuing this goal made up only a tiny share of what activists actually did. The data in Table 5.2 show that political activities did become more common during the height of the key election years of 2010 and 2012, making up respectively 8% and 7% of all Tea Party events. Election-related gatherings never exceeded a 10% threshold in any year between 2009 and 2014.

As the Tea Party matured, its organizational structure became increasingly decentralized, consisting primarily of local organizations at best loosely connected to any the national Tea Party groups (Skocpol and Williamson 2011). As a consequence, it is especially important to supplement our aggregate analyses with a more detailed assessment of the spatiotemporal patterns of Tea Party events. This is useful to help evaluate the consistency of the trends in activism across local communities. Is it possible that some communities and regions were hotbeds of Tea Party activism in contrast with the larger aggregate trends we have shown? To that end, we turn to a county-level analysis of the trajectory of local Tea Party activism.

Using the date and place of each Tea Party event, we created a database of monthly patterns of Tea Party activity for each county. Our use of counties helps reflect the dynamic nature of local Tea Party groups as well as the extensive mortality of local groups (see Chapter 6). Using counties as unit of analysis also allows us to capture the activities of multiple Tea Party organizations that were simultaneously active in single location. Our primary analytic tool for investigating this issue is sequence analysis, an approach that facilitates the identification of activity patterns by using the entire sequence of Tea Party activism as the unit of analysis (Abbott 1995; Cornwell 2015).

Basic descriptive statistics underscore that vast range of Tea Party activity across the nation. Between 2009 and 2014, at least one event took place in 1,477 counties, or 46% of all counties. The distribution of Tea Party activism was positively skewed with a mean and median of 6.8 and 3 events, respectively. This pattern suggests that a small number of counties saw a disproportionate share of Tea Party activity. Broward County, FL, and Allegheny County, PA, were the most active counties seen in our data, where events took place in 59 of the 71 months in our analytic period.[6] These were followed closely by Hillsborough County, FL, and Los Angeles County, CA, where events occurred in 56 and 55 months respectively of 71 months. Such cases were relatively rare. The 90th percentile of Tea Party activism was just 16 months where we found evidence of activity, or conversely, in 77% of months the most active counties did not have any activity.

Figure 5.4 shows the county-level event sequences by month for all active counties. Each thin horizontal line in the plot represents the monthly activity that occurred in each county through the end of 2014, using grayscale contrasts for the different type of events that may have taken place (if any). The sequences in the figure provide important context for understanding the trajectory of all Tea Party activity at the local level, and how those patterns inform inferences about national trends in events. There is strong evidence of coordinated actions visible during the Tax Day rallies of 2009, 2010, and 2011 and the IRS protests of 2013, based on the clustering of the horizontal lines marking protest activity in Figure 5.4. Over time, these thick bands fade into the chaotic pattern in the plot between 2013 and 2014, providing strong evidence that the Tea Party did not replace the Tax Day rallies with an alternative predictable dominant tactic at the national, state, or local levels.

Our sequence analysis illustrates several important trends in Tea Party activism. By far the most common sequence of local chapter activity consisted of a Tax Day rally in 2009 followed by inactivity through 2014, which occurred in 10% of active counties. The second most common event sequence was the 4% of active counties where a Tax Day rally took place in 2009 and 2010, with inactivity before, between, and after these events. The third most frequent sequence, present in just 3% of active counties, was a Tax Day rally in 2010 without other activity before or after. Finally, 1% of active counties hosted a Tax Day rally in 2009, 2010, and 2011, without any other events.

---

[6] Neither of these counties is among the top 25 largest in terms of population size. Except for Los Angeles County, communities with the highest concentrations of aggregate Tea Party activity through the life of the insurgency are not the ones that had seen the largest number of 2009 protests.

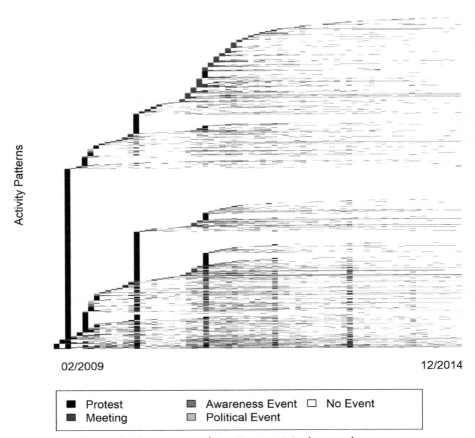

02/2009   12/2014

- ■ Protest   ■ Awareness Event   □ No Event
- ■ Meeting   ▨ Political Event

FIGURE 5.4 County-level sequences of Tea Party activity by month, 2009–2014.
Note: A color version of the plot is available at www.patrickrafail.com/Tea_Party/
Sequence.pdf, which we strongly encourage readers to consult.

None of the other activity sequences exceeded a 1% threshold in frequency. In total, over 17% of counties where Tea Party activity took place *only* experienced Tax Day rallies without any other events. The local picture of Tea Party activism, therefore, could be described as sporadic, with little evidence of national coordination or regularly occurring events beyond the first three Tax Day and the IRS rallies.

Maybe surprisingly, the modal county experienced a Tax Day rally in 2009 after which all activity ceased. The sequence count is based on a strict match of month and activity, making high frequencies of activity patterns unlikely. The visual representation of event sequences in Figure 5.4 reinforces the sporadic, largely independent trajectory of the local chapters over time. There was no clear and coherent timing in the pattern of events, but instead, individual Tea Party groups in local areas forged their own distinct paths, organizing varying mixes of events at different times, likely based on what appealed to their local memberships.

Two final observations about the patterns seen in Figure 5.4 are worth emphasizing. First, there was at best marginal growth and expansion of activism into new counties after 2011, and the areas where activism took root in the early years were also most likely to see sustained sequences of activism, despite some sporadic gaps in activity. Second, particularly after the 2012 Tax Day rallies (and arguably after the 2011 rallies), the sequences of activity underscore our conclusion that there was little coordination of activism among even smaller regional clusters of local groups. This is consistent with our argument that the Tea Party lacked an organizational structure through which national leadership worked closely with local chapters. Instead, these findings are consistent with the larger tactical shift from protests to maintenance events. These maintenance events, especially the meetings, were typically insular and organized primarily around discussing issues of interest to established members of the sponsoring organizations, rather than serving as a vehicle for pressing collective demands or wider membership recruitment.

In summary, we have demonstrated that the trajectory of local Tea Party organizing soon took a rapid turn away from protest events. Across the country, groups appeared to operate largely independently, with little effort to coordinate with other groups, including those in their immediate area. Protests were replaced primarily by meetings, which represented nearly 90% of all events by 2014. Over time, the volume of Tea Party events declined dramatically, too, after peaking in 2011. As we will show in Chapter 6, this was in large part the result of organizational mortality linked to larger structural changes in the local environments where Tea Party groups had been active. Nevertheless, empirically establishing the rapid transformation of the insurgency's tactical repertoire is important, and one that has eluded the efforts of prior researchers. We turn now to a more synthetic account of the Tea Party's declining use of protest, and the eventual steep decline of its activism altogether.

EXPLAINING THE TRANSITION AWAY FROM PROTEST

Protests are the canonical form of mobilization in western democracies (Meyer and Tarrow 1998), but they are only one among the myriad tactical approaches available to social movements, insurgencies, and other contentious political actors. In particular contexts, certain tactics, such as protest, may prove to be significantly more or less effective than other forms of mobilization (Tilly 2006). The choice of a tactical repertoire is related to the target of a social movement (Walker, Martin, and McCarthy 2008), and expectations about how targets will respond to demands, particularly when movement actors anticipate repression (Davenport 2015).

We emphasize three factors to help explain the Tea Party's movement from protest to maintenance events: first, with little centralized leadership, resources, and public interest, local Tea Party activists came to question the efficacy of protest tactics, instead emphasizing other types of activities, particularly meetings. Second, protest events staged by local groups in previously sympathetic media markets began to receive less attention. Instead, press coverage of the Tea Party came to emphasize Republican politicians, many of whom took credit for the Tea Party, despite having at best weak connections to local groups. Last, we discuss the IRS scandal of 2013, which involved allegations that the IRS had systematically undertaken heavy scrutiny of conservative groups in general, and Tea Party groups particularly when they sought non-profit status. Together, we argue, these factors hastened the decline of Tea Party activity.

The Perceived Utility of Protest

Our quantitative analyses thus far have not spoken to how rank-and-file activists in local Tea Party groups understood the impact of their activities, especially their use of protest. Activists' understanding of their own tactical choices, however, were clearly revealed in our qualitative interviews and the open-ended web survey questions discussed in Chapter 4. A consistent pattern was an evolution in participant's views about protest. Most respondents had come to believe that the protest tactic had lost its effectiveness for them as a vehicle for creating social change. Activists emphasized how they had moved on to other tactics, helping to contextualize the replacement of street-level activism with maintenance events.

These sentiments were pervasive in the qualitative interviews. For instance, Samantha, a Tea Party leader in Michigan, suggested "That's [protest] become much less important, because even though those are exciting, they don't change anything" (Interview #314; Michigan). A similar view was echoed by Gary, who said: "I don't think that's [protesting] being effective anymore ... we've moved beyond that" (Interview #308; Nebraska). Some Tea Party activists bristled at the idea of further protests, such as Ronald, who noted: "I think they [protests] are completely ineffective and have become a joke" (Interview #322; Nevada). The common core of these remarks questions the utility of what was initially the flagship tactic of the Tea Party, culminating in statements by a few activist leaders even ridiculing continuing efforts to stage protest events.

Responses to open-ended questions about protest activity drawn from our web survey of Tea Party organizational leaders provide additional supporting evidence for these claims. More than 35% of responding group leaders indicated that either protests were not productive or that their group was busy with more important activities. Albert, co-founder of a Tea Party group still active in 2014 said: "This symbolic gesture [protest] was not deemed useful in generating any change. Our members are more inclined to be productive that [sic] stand around making empty gestures" (Web Survey #103; Pennsylvania). Second, many groups reported a lack of interest among their members as a major factor shaping their decision to discontinue staging protests. When explaining why his Tea Party group did not host a Tax Day rally in 2014, Jim responded simply: "Not enough interest" (Web Survey # 71; Missouri). Several leaders pointed to difficulties in hosting a rally because they, personally, were either too burned out or otherwise occupied to organize an event. Chris explained it as: "I also succumbed to activist burnout and this time no one else was able to organize such an event" (Web Survey #157; New York). Joseph further exemplified this sentiment, noting that his group did not host an event because "I had conflicts and nobody else wanted to organize it (Web Survey #24; California).

When comparing both our qualitative interviews and survey responses we conclude that Tea Party activists had altered their views about the efficacy and usefulness of protest. While participant burnout appears to have shaped the choices of many, we emphasize two factors external to the activists that also may have influenced their views. First, the election of many Tea Party–aligned candidates may have reduced interest in protest activities as elites sympathetic to the insurgency were in the halls of power. We return to a more comprehensive discussion of this claim in Chapter 8. Second, dwindling media attention to the protest activities of the Tea Party, especially on Fox News, may have also helped drive the shift in perceptions among both leaders and rank-and-file activists. Since ongoing protest activity received little coverage on Fox News, the network of choice for most Tea Party members, they were reinforced in their view that protests no longer provided additional value in advancing the goals of the insurgency. We now turn to this issue.

Changes in the Content of Media Attention

Media coverage, patterns of protests, rallies, demonstrations, and other forms of mobilization directly influence the likelihood that similar subsequent activities will receive attention (e.g., Andrews and Biggs 2006; Banerjee 2013; Myers 2000). Research has consistently shown that, all other things being equal, protests that are larger, violent, sensationalistic, or otherwise remarkable are more likely to receive newspaper attention. This regularity is one of the most common and stable patterns of research on media bias in the coverage of protest (Andrews and Caren 2010; Earl et al. 2004; McCarthy et al. 2008, 1996; Myers and Caniglia 2004; Oliver and Maney 2000).

The tactical shift from protests to maintenance events by insurgents may have been, at least in part, a consequence of declining media interest in the grassroots Tea Party's activities after the initial avalanche of coverage in 2009. Figure 5.5 shows the annual percentage of media articles mentioning protest activity and political activity in all coverage of the Tea Party. We employ two

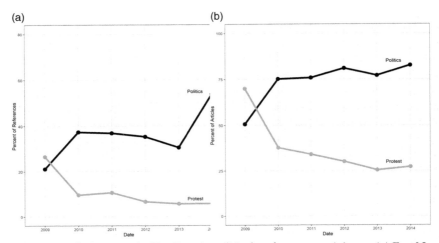

FIGURE 5.5 References to the Tea Party's political and protest activity on (a) Fox News and (b) in newspapers articles, 2009–2014.

sources of information. First, there were 33,188 references to the Tea Party on Fox. Second, we identified 70,834 newspaper articles from 785 local and national newspapers referencing the Tea Party (our sampling protocols are described in the appendix). It is essential to separately compare protest-related coverage with discussions of the institutionalized faction of the Tea Party – that is, the political leaders who adopted, and sometimes coopted, the Tea Party's rhetoric. This distinction allows us to establish when media attention emphasized the institutionalized Tea Party, rather than the grassroots activities of local chapters. To calculate the percentages shown in Figure 5.5, we used keyword searches to identify media content with at least one reference to protest activity or to the insurgency's relationship with the Republican Party.[7] We then divided these counts by the total annual number of articles or references to the Tea Party. These variables are not mutually exclusive, as a single article or reference to the Tea Party could mention both protest activity and the Tea Party's relationship with the Republican Party.

Fox News and newspaper coverage of the Tea Party were each more likely to emphasize protest-related activities in 2009. Mentions of protests were present in 27% of references to the Tea Party on Fox News and in 70% of the newspaper articles. There was a decline in the relative amount of media attention to protest activities starting in 2010, where just 10% and 38% of Tea Party content on Fox News and newspapers respectively mentioned grassroots mobilization. This is a striking finding, as the Tea Party still turned out more than one

---

[7] We used "protest," "rally," "demonstration," and "vigil" as search strings for protests, and "Republican" and "GOP" in searches to capture linkages to institutionalized politics. Syntactic variations of our keywords were used in all cases.

million activists for the 2010 Tax Day rally. The media's attention to the Tea Party's protests never returned. By 2014, just 1 in 20 references to the Tea Party on Fox News focused on protest activity. In contrast, our data in Figure 5.5 show a rapid and permanent surge in the political coupling of the Tea Party and the GOP (the Republican Party or "Grand Old Party"). By 2010, when Tea Party candidates were part of the groundswell of Republican effort to reclaim the House of Representatives, 37% of Fox News references mentioned the GOP which grew to 54% in 2014. A similar trend is seen in Figure 5.5b where, by 2014, 83% of articles about the Tea Party emphasized its institutionalized political activities. In short, media attention to the grassroots constituency of the Tea Party began to fade quickly, and was replaced by an emphasis on the activities of Republican politicians who were loosely connected to the insurgency.

The preceding account of the radical shift in the content of Tea Party coverage in the media adds important context to our claims about the origins, frequency, consistency, and participant turnout at Tea Party protests over time. The corresponding decline in media attention to protest events seems likely to have helped discourage activists from allocating the required time and resources needed to seek permits, advertise, and otherwise engage in the invisible labor necessary to stage a public event. These findings are consistent with the patterns of media attention not only among newspapers, which varied in their support of the Tea Party, but also for Fox News, a network that had dedicated significant airtime to the insurgency, with several hosts among its most vocal supporters. We show that across both sources, the substance of media coverage about the Tea Party quickly turned away from grassroots activities staged by local activists, instead placing primary attention on the Tea Party's role in shaping institutionalized politics. This is likely also a consequence of the movement away from street-level protests, as Tea Party groups increasingly staged maintenance events, more mundane and less newsworthy than the colorful rallies of the past.

Fear of Surveillance and the IRS Scandal of 2013

Tactical choices are shaped by expectations of how authorities will respond to episodes of mobilization (Davenport 2015). For example, arrests are commonly used as proxies for state repression, which have been linked to subsequent demobilization (Earl 2005). Episodes of overt repression were rare during Tea Party gatherings. Across all the events we examined, arrests occurred only 12 times. On the other hand, there is compelling evidence that some Tea Party groups were fearful of government surveillance, a form of state repression that can be effective in undermining efforts to mobilize for social and political change (Boykoff 2007; Marx 1974; Rafail 2014).

We argue that perceptions of repression played a significant role in explaining the tactical evolution of Tea Party activism. The move away from protests was hastened, we claim, by the IRS scandal of the same year, that is, 2013, that may have served as a death knell for the prospects of a return to the Tea Party's aggressive repertoire of protest activity. Though the IRS scandal was, in actuality, a minor event distorted and amplified by conservative media, for many activists it confirmed preexisting fears about intrusive, big government oversight. The Tea Party's inability to mount a sustained campaign against the IRS only served to underscore how organizationally thin and fragmented the insurgency had become by 2013. The IRS scandal has not received much in the way of scholarly attention (but see the law review articles by Hackney 2014; Kahng 2013; Mueller 2014). We, therefore, briefly highlight the main points of the controversy drawing upon a combination of journalistic accounts and reports of the US Treasury Inspector General for Tax Administration (TIGTA) and US Senate Committee on Finance.

The IRS scandal revolved around determinations of 501(c)(3) or 501(c)(4) status by the IRS. As discussed in Chapter 4, those classifications grant an organization tax-exempt status and both are routinely provided to social movement groups. Both types prohibit a certified organization from attempting to influence legislation or engaging with political campaigns. Upon review by the IRS, violations result in the loss of a tax-exempt status. The determination process starts with a group applying to the IRS seeking tax-exempt status. Beginning in February 2012, conservative online media began reporting that Tea Party groups appeared to be receiving disproportionate attention from the IRS through requests for atypically intrusive documentation of a group's activities, and long delays in correspondence (a representative example is Opelka 2012). This additional scrutiny dated back to 2010, although it appeared to have become more common in 2012. The national Tea Party umbrella groups had mostly achieved nonprofit status by then and had encouraged their local affiliates to do so as well. The IRS appeared especially concerned with political activities that occurred during the 2012 election cycle. The issue received a limited amount of national media attention by March, 2012, including the *New York Times* article by Weisman (2012) noting that dozens of Tea Party organizations had received correspondence from the IRS requesting additional information. Representatives Darrell Issa (Republican, California) and Jim Jordan (Republican, Ohio) pressed for an investigation by the TIGTA to determine whether any Tea Party groups, specifically, and conservative groups more generally, were receiving undue scrutiny from the IRS. The issue quickly faded from widespread public attention for nearly another year.

By May 2013, evidence had emerged that the IRS was deliberately targeting groups with "tea party" or "patriot" in their name, a breach of the IRS protocol to impartially review tax-exempt applications for groups. This created an explosion of media attention to the issue and extensive discussion on social media accusing the IRS of repressing conservative voices. The coverage was quite misleading, as the IRS had also been scrutinizing groups on the political left at the same time. Nonetheless, the narrative pushed by conservative media was treated as compelling evidence that a powerful government agency was targeting conservatives and elicited strong reactions from Tea Party groups. In what would ultimately become the final coordinated action for the Tea Party, 166 protest events were hastily organized using the Tea Party Patriot's website and scheduled for May 21, 2013.

The IRS ultimately issued an apology to the targeted Tea Party groups, but went on to deny that its targeting was based on politics, but resulted from prohibited political activities. The IRS noted that none of the 75 groups inappropriately selected for extensive review had lost their tax-exempt status (Ohlemacher 2013). A report by the TIGTA affirmed that inappropriate review criteria were used for an 18-month period which resulted in delays in processing and erroneous inferences about political activity (TIGTA 2017), a finding consistent with an earlier report prepared by the US Senate Committee on Finance (2015). Both reports, however, held that even though conservative groups were highlighted for additional scrutiny, the IRS had similarly launched investigations of liberal groups, a fact that had also been noted by journalists (Weisman 2013). In 2017, the Department of Justice settled two lawsuits resulting from the IRS scandal that had been filed by a coalition of several dozen impacted groups, and issued another apology, this time admitting wrongdoing on behalf of the IRS (Reuters 2017).

While the IRS scandal was a breach of protocol and misuse of government resources, our findings in Chapter 4 showed that registration with the IRS by Tea Party groups was extremely rare. Just 133 of the 3,587 Tea Party groups we identified as existing between 2009 and 2014 started the filing process. While the final count of Tea Party groups that registered with the IRS was certainly above zero, these groups made up a tiny fraction of the total population of local Tea Party groups. Even if few chapters were registered with the IRS, the scandal had profound effects on conservatives, including not only Tea Party activists, but also traditional Republicans. The IRS scandal's motivation of the brief return to protest on May 21, 2013, visible in both Figures 5.3 and 5.4, did not last.

Since the Tea Party did not mount a sustained street-level response to the IRS scandal, to gauge conservative concerns about the issue we turn to social media posts that we collected contemporaneously. We collected 814,812 tweets about the IRS scandal as our primary source. Twitter data about the issue is especially helpful, allowing us to examine activists' reactions to the IRS scandal in real-time. The tweets were collected for the period between May 20, 2013, and June 5, 2013. This timeframe begins when the IRS scandal became a major news story and captures the rhetoric surrounding the issue. We used a wide variety of search terms and the Twitter Search API (see Rafail 2018a) to create as exhaustive a set of tweets about the IRS scandal as was possible. We then conducted a sentiment analysis of the tweets, which is a computational technique that quantifies the emotions and emotional intensity of textual material (Liu 2015). We highlight three core emotional responses that could have arisen in response to the IRS scandal: anger, disgust, and fear. In order to machine code these emotions, we used Mohammad's (2018) NRC Emotion Intensity Lexicon, which assigns an intensity score between 0 and 1 to a set of words associated with each emotion. We cross-referenced the words in each tweet with the lists of emotionally tagged words, which returned a sum of emotional intensity for each tweet. These values were then averaged each day to capture the temporal evolution of the emotions expressed on Twitter concerning the IRS scandal. The resulting statistics have a lower bound of 0, indicating a total lack of a specific type of emotional expression, and could theoretically range to infinity, with higher values pointing to a more intense response.

Figure 5.6 summarizes our sentiment analysis. The dominant emotion in Twitter responses to the IRS scandal was fear. Between May 20 and June 5, the

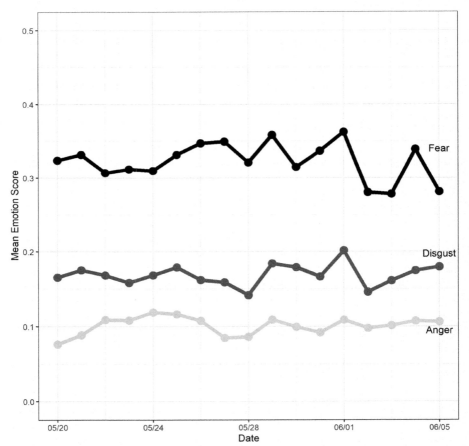

FIGURE 5.6 Mean emotional intensity scores from Twitter posts about the IRS scandal and the Tea Party, May 20–June 5, 2015.
Note: Estimates are based on the content of 814,812 tweets.

daily mean fear score ranged between 0.3 and 0.4, which was triple the score for anger and nearly double the score for disgust. Most of the tweets did not register any expressions of either anger or disgust, which were only evident in 27% and 19% of the tweets respectively. In contrast, at least one word expressing fear was present in 47% of the tweets. It is also noteworthy that the daily mean emotional expression remained relatively consistent over time, suggesting that the views of Tea Party activists, conservatives, and supporters did not change as additional information about the IRS scandal unfolded. There is little evidence that emotions such as anger came to replace the more fearful reactions that were initially dominant on social media.

Sentiment analysis provides only a coarse depiction of emotional content. It is therefore helpful to ground the quantitative analysis in concrete examples from the Twitter database.[8] The consistent pattern in Twitter responses to the IRS scandal was that it represented overreach from big government, and would be likely to spill over to other domains. One user, for instance, suggested that "IRS tyranny against Tea Parties is same IRS tyranny that will lead to ObamaCare death panels. #PJNET #TeaParty"; a reference to the Patient Protection and Affordable Care Act passed by the Obama administration. Another poster shared an op-ed, arguing that "The #IRS scandal show [sic] right-wing fear of government isn't always paranoid." A common suggestion was that the IRS scandal was orchestrated by the Democratic Party, or directed by Barack Obama, with the goal of undermining not only the Tea Party, but also conservatives, Republicans, and others on the right. For example, one widely retweeted comment claimed: "[the] Goal of the IRS Scandal: Scare GOP Donors - #intimidation #suppression #corruptObama" while many agreed with the sentiment that "[the] IRS War On Tea Party Began Day After @BarackObama Met With IRS Union Chief At White House." The notion that the IRS was targeting the Tea Party to undermine the conservative donor base was widespread. Another example is a poster who tweeted "#intimidation #IRS #DOJ Big Donors afraid to give money, fear being tagged. Along w/voter fraud, we're doomed." Finally, many participants on Twitter linked the IRS scandal to a broader set of Soviet-style repression techniques, stemming from what was perceived as the Obama Administration's adoption of socialism, for instance, posting content such as "#IRS using tactics the KGB would find admirable! So who really won the Cold War?"

In conclusion, we suggest that the IRS scandal was another important factor nudging the Tea Party out of the public square. The insurgency moved away from protest activity toward less public forms of activism. Though few Tea Party groups were registered with the IRS, and the scandal itself was in large part a fiction amplified by conservative media, the issue took on significant

---

[8] Since these tweets were overwhelmingly posted by individuals, we anonymize the tweets by removing affiliated accounts or other identifying information.

symbolic importance for the insurgency and its sympathizers. These individuals reacted in fear to the specter of big government overreach and the systematic targeting of conservatives. The Twitter data does not allow us to address the longer-term fear levels of state surveillance and repression that had been articulated in the tweets. Nonetheless it does clearly indicate that the IRS scandal had a substantial impact on morale among local Tea Party activists. Soft repression can be an important cause of demobilization and the temporal pattern of the IRS incident is consistent with the arc of Tea Party activism.

CONCLUSION

This chapter analyzed the trajectory of Tea Party activism, using extensive and diverse evidence collected from multiple sources. We built a comprehensive snapshot of what the Tea Party did, when they did it, where it happened, and what its activists wanted. The consistent pattern was that even though the Tea Party emerged as a powerhouse of disruptive protest, that piece of its repertoire quickly waned. Grassroots groups, lacking any national leadership, instead each forged a path of their own. Activists became either uninterested in protest activity or convinced that it would not influence government policy, a process hastened by declining Fox News coverage of their demonstrations and rallies along with an increasing fear of government surveillance. Groups increasingly mobilized within narrow spaces embedded within local communities, concentrating on hosting meetings to discuss issues important to the larger conservative movement. By 2014, effectively none of the boisterous Tea Party activism of the early years remained.

These findings also underscore several other important observations about the Tea Party. First, its grassroots side quickly became dominant. Local groups, however, were disconnected from one another in their event planning, a fact quite consequential in limiting the insurgency's ability to coordinate national action. Unified displays of the Tea Party's strength became difficult, if not impossible, to display. Second, there was a shift in the Tea Party's tactical repertoire, as local groups came to view protests as ineffective. Instead, they turned their efforts to staging maintenance events, which were primarily discussion or information sessions. Protests can be a major conduit of media attention for social movements, yet for the Tea Party, as protest activity declined, so too did media coverage of the activities of local groups, a finding seen even in highly sympathetic media outlets like Fox News. Finally, while this chapter has focused primarily on the internal dynamics of the Tea Party, between 2009 and 2014 major social structural changes were occurring in the aftermath of the Great Recession. Chapter 6 turns to these important trends, showing how the organizational decline of the Tea Party insurgency was also linked to changing local contextual conditions.

6

Threat, Political Integration, and the Disappearance of Local Tea Party Groups

After 2009, the Tea Party's local chapter network began to grow rapidly. Within two years, thousands of new Tea Party chapters emerged across the country, providing activists with structured opportunities to take part in the insurgency. The preceding chapters have focused on the emergence, prevailing mobilizing structures, and tactical trajectory deployed by those groups, leaving the insurgency's organizational evolution unexamined. An account of the rise and fall of the Tea Party cannot be complete without exploring the evolution of the groups that activists built to sustain and grow the insurgency. Local groups are essential to understanding the vibrancy and dynamism of the Tea Party, and its decline (Westermeyer 2016). This chapter extends our discussion of the organizational structure of Tea Party groups begun in Chapter 4 and develops a theoretical account of their persistence and demise.

Scholarly attention to local Tea Party groups has almost exclusively concentrated on understanding their emergence. As we demonstrated in Chapter 3, early riser Tea Party groups emerged in communities with high material and status threats (see also McVeigh et al. 2014). The origins of local groups are an essential precursor to understanding what became of them, but little previous research has tracked what became of the local groups that staged the rallies, organized speakers, and otherwise sustained the insurgency. The entire lifecycle of the insurgency's local chapters, then, is an important topic that remains unexamined. Using a unique database systematically tracking each local Tea Party group, we show that the trajectory quickly became one of demobilization. By 2014, the roar of the Tea Party rapidly became a whisper, with more than 90% of local chapters ceasing all visible signs of activity.

What happened to the thousands of Tea Party groups that emerged during the insurgency, and how can we explain their disappearance? Aside from work by Berry (2017), no other attempts to systematically explain the trajectory and decline in organization building and maintenance after the first few years of the insurgency exist. Berry shows that, by 2017, 40% of Tea Party chapters in his sample of 95 groups had either dissolved entirely or were on the verge of disbanding. The process, Berry argues, was hastened by low organizational capacity, as local Tea Party chapters were unable to utilize their minimal resources in ways that allowed them to meet their goals. His finding is consistent with many previous accounts of decline among local social movement chapters (Edwards and Marullo 1995; Edwards and McCarthy 2004; McCarthy and Zald 1977). The explanation is convincing, but incomplete in the case of the Tea Party. As we showed in Chapter 4, the lack of centralized leadership was chronic across the Tea Party groups, but their individual lifecycles were quite diverse.

This chapter traces local Tea Party groups through time and across space, emphasizing how local contextual conditions were related to organizational survival. We draw from our theoretical account of the emergence and timing of the insurgency developed in in Chapter 2 to emphasize the role of material and status threats in shaping the longevity and trajectory of individual chapters. We also consider the potential importance of the political integration of the Tea Party into the Republican Party (or "Grand Old Party" [GOP]) as a mechanism to explain the lifecycle of the local groups. Our analysis is grounded in the unique database of 3,587 local Tea Party groups introduced in Chapter 4. We situate each group geographically and temporally, allowing us to link organizations to their evolving local economic, political, and demographic environments. Our findings show that the vast majority of local Tea Party groups died: less than 8% of the chapters in our sample showed any signs of activity by the end of December 2014. We conclude that the Tea Party's organizational decline appears to be associated with a broad reduction in the material threats brought on by the Great Recession, along with lingering status threats linked to the declining power of White conservative Christians. In contrast, political cooptation of the Tea Party by the Republican Party had little impact on the survival of local groups. Overall, this chapter provides important new evidence about the local groups central to the insurgency. Examining these dynamics is essential to understanding the rise and fall of the Tea Party.

EXPLAINING THE LIFECYCLE OF TEA PARTY GROUPS

Social movement organizations (SMOs) are the lifeblood of modern political activism (McCarthy and Zald 1977). A substantial body of work has emphasized how internal characteristics of SMOs can influence both patterns of emergence and survival. These include factors such as deliberative processes (Polletta 2004), resource utilization, and the cultivation of legitimacy (Walker and McCarthy 2010). As well, features of SMO organizational structure have a profound impact on the survival of local groups (Edwards and Marullo 1995). Networks of SMOs pursuing similar goals can take a variety of forms, ranging from strictly hierarchical group structures that are led by professional staff, to almost totally disconnected cells lacking any central coordination.

From its earliest stages, the Tea Party adopted a loose organizational form where individuals or small groups of activists were able to independently create chapters within a framework created and controlled by national Tea Party umbrella groups. In Chapter 4, we showed how the organizational form ultimately adopted by the Tea Party was a hybrid, bridging the more hierarchical federated approach to organizational building and the spin form, which typically exhibits little top-down coordination. While the national groups did maintain a web infrastructure for local groups, they provided little else in terms of guidance or leadership, and competed with each other in their claims to represent the authentic Tea Party (Skocpol and Williamson 2011). To be sure, well-established and well-funded conservative organizations such as FreedomWorks and Americans for Prosperity were instrumental in putting the original wheels in motion for the earliest Tea Party groups (Skocpol and Hertel-Fernandez 2016), such as the test-marketed "Astroturf" groups we identified in Chapter 3 (see also Lo 2012). However, after the initial push, Tea Party activists and organizations were largely left to their own devices (Berry 2017) with a notable absence of centralized leadership (Courser 2012). The lack of a cadre of professional leaders maintaining and expanding the Tea Party, should, by itself, have heightened the risk of movement decline (McCarthy and Zald 1977). However, attention to the organizational dynamics of the insurgency provides an incomplete account of its decline. We suggest that the timing of the Tea Party's decline is not easily reconciled with its internal dynamics, as they solidified soon after the insurgency's emergence.

It is necessary to situate local Tea Party groups in their broader community contexts to understand their lifecycles. A large body of scholarship has investigated how local environments facilitate and impede the emergence and continuity of social movement organizations, but this approach has not yet been used to explain the trajectory of the thousands of local Tea Party groups that emerged, evolved, and mostly disappeared over the course of the insurgency.

Material Threats: The Great Recession and the Uneven, Slow Financial Recovery

The Great Recession began in late 2007 and lasted approximately 18 months, through the middle of 2009. By most accounts, it was among the most profound economic events in nearly a century, and it was routinely compared to the Great Depression of the 1930s. While opinions among researchers vary, most agree that its central features included a sudden decline of nearly half the value in major stock indices, a doubling of the unemployment rate, and a dramatic increase in housing foreclosures, especially concentrated in the subprime mortgage market (see for example Grusky, Wimmer, and Western 2011;

Hetzel 2012). In addition, they generally agree that the Great Recession was a rare, acutely impactful economic event with broad impacts.

The Great Recession was national in scope, but its impact was disproportionately concentrated in specific regions across the US and across different social groups. For example, unemployment was spatially concentrated: especially vulnerable were communities with high concentrations of racial minorities, residents with lower educational attainment, and retirees directly impacted by the stock market crash (Thiede and Monnat 2016). Work by Hall and his colleagues (2015) found that by 2009, 10.7% of Black homeowners had already experienced foreclosure starts, more than double the 4.9% that took place in White households. Recall that we have argued that such racialized concentrations of foreclosures probably contributed to many Tea Partiers' conclusion that governmental attempts to blunt the devastating impact of the Great Recession would inevitably translate into yet more handouts to "undeserving" minority groups, the costs of which they expected would be borne by White taxpayers.

Our argument that the Great Recession motivated Tea Party activism extends readily to the dynamics of local groups. The Great Recession was unevenly distributed in its impact, and the same is true of the economic recovery that followed. The growth in economic inequality and material precarity brought on by the Great Recession was spatially concentrated and disproportionate in its impacts on local communities, with effects lasting for several years beyond the end of the recession in June 2009 (Bennett, Yuen, and Blanco-Silva 2018). Scholars have largely agreed that the recovery from the Great Recession was slow, weak, and uneven (e.g., Cynamon and Fazzari 2016; Taylor 2014). In terms of its effect on Tea Party activism, this recovery was just as consequential as its initial set of economic shocks had been.

We established in Chapter 3 that material threats attributable to the Great Recession were important catalysts for the Tea Party's Tax Day rallies in 2009 and the founding of the early riser Tea Party organizations. The underlying mechanisms translating the impact of the Great Recession into Tea Party activism follows from our conclusion in Chapter 4 that the social and demographic attributes of Tea Party activists put them at heightened risk of economic precarity. We focused on the role of suddenly imposed grievances and the perceived risk of precarity they generated. Even if activists did not directly experience the deleterious impacts of the Great Recession personally, we suspect they did feel heightened precarity where the devastation was most concentrated. The threats, we suggest, provided important motivation for even middle-class activists to continue maintaining their local Tea Party group.

Status Threats: The Declining Social Power of White Christians

Much as the suddenly imposed grievances of the Great Recession motivated Tea Partiers to action, so too did the status threats, forged and honed over decades by linkages created by conservative politicians, activists, and media outlets between non-White groups and increased government spending. Tea Party activists, who were disproportionately White conservative Christians, viewed their core identities as under attack by what they perceived to be continuing rapid demographic and cultural change (Parker and Barreto 2014), feelings further exacerbated by the election of Barack Obama. These status threats, we have shown, were importantly linked to the emergence of the first set of Tax Day rallies as well as the formation of early riser Tea Party groups.

Extensive research has connected such status threats to political action, particularly right-wing mobilization. For instance, a series of studies by McVeigh (1999, 2001, 2009), and other scholars (Cunningham 2004; Cunningham and Phillips 2007; Owens, Cunningham, and Ward 2015) have shown that localized manifestations of status threats, whether perceived or actual, were instrumental in explaining populist collective action. McVeigh (2009) in particular has emphasized the role of *power devaluation* as a catalyst for action. Power devaluation occurs when individuals perceive threats to their social status, motivating them to engage in collective action when provided the opportunity. Such threats emerge directly from an individual's immediate environment. Power devaluation has been fruitful in explaining early Tea Party activism (Parkin et al. 2015). McVeigh and colleagues (2014) also identified perceptions of distributional justice as a significant factor in shaping where Tea Party groups emerged. Similar status threats also appear to have increased support for the Tea Party in the general population (Parker and Barreto 2014).

The theoretical model of the Tea Party's timing and emergence we developed in Chapter 2 emphasized the role of status threats as essential contributors to the insurgency's rapid growth. Similar to our expectations about the slow recovery from the Great Recession, we also expect that status threats were important predictors of the organizational survival of local Tea Party groups. In areas where status threats grew or remained elevated, we expect that Tea Party groups would survive longer. Similarly, in communities where larger sentiment pools of potential activists existed, Tea Party organizations should have a longer period of activity.

The Tea Party, the Republican Party, and Political Integration

A final reason for organizational decline is that a group simply outlived its usefulness as a vehicle of political change. Scholars have consistently emphasized how formal alliances between social movements and political actors can lead to cooptation (Gamson 1975), or hybrid forms of movement–party relationships (Tarrow 2021). A central feature of Tilly's (1978) influential polity model of social movement mobilization emphasized the importance of regular, institutionalized access to policymakers. To the degree that such channels are created and maintained, social movement mobilization and tactics such as protests, boycotts, and pressure campaigns become substantially less useful.

The Tea Party was remarkable in its ability to rapidly embed its central tenets in the Republican Party's platform (Skocpol and Williamson 2011). Dubbed by Blum (2020) a faction-based hostile takeover of the GOP, the wave of anger associated with the Tea Party insurgency is often credited with helping Republicans retake the House of Representatives and diluting Democratic control of the Senate during the 2010 midterm elections (Gervais and Morris 2012, 2018; Madestam et al. 2013). After the 2010 elections, nearly 70 members of the House of Representatives formed the Tea Party Caucus, formalizing the centrality of the insurgency in a successful rebrand of Republican politics. That portrait likely understates the impact of the Tea Party on the Republican Party, as the hollowing out of American political parties created openings for social movements to influence party platforms (Tarrow 2021). As Gervais and Morris (2018) explain, the relationship between the Tea Party and the Republican Party was multidimensional. Membership in the Tea Party Caucus was only one indicator of a politician's support of the Tea Party, and did not necessarily reflect the preferences of activists. The Tea Party's demands of the Republican Party were initially quite inflexible (Skocpol and Williamson 2011), and activists were happily willing to cause significant damage to Republican politicians and the Republican Party more broadly to secure their desired policy changes (Blum 2020). But once a local Tea Party group managed to secure institutionalized political representation, such as with the election of a Tea Party Caucus member, the motivation for continued local activism may have disappeared.

In sum, then, it is plausible that survival of Tea Party groups was shaped by the timing and location of the insurgency's inroads into the Republican Party. Such cooptation could manifest itself in two ways: first, organizations located in areas represented by a Tea Party Caucus member in Congress were less likely to survive because the group had achieved formal representation in Congress. Second, organizations active in congressional districts held by Republican politicians (but who were not Tea Party Caucus members) may similarly have been less likely to survive. We take up these possibilities below.

Summary

We have argued that the survival of local Tea Party organizations was shaped by their social, political, and economic environment. Features of communities surrounding local chapters directly and indirectly inform individual decisions about whether to participate in collective action and for how long. We expect that groups survived longer in areas where the recovery from the Great Recession was slower and where status threats were greater. While the integration of local Tea Party groups into institutionalized politics may also account for demobilization, we believe that both material and status threats provide a more robust account for the continuity of local activism. Rather than focusing solely on the internal dynamics of organizational decline, which decontextualizes chapters from the communities where they mobilize, local issue salience and sentiment pools are also important in accounting for sustained mobilization. If we are correct, then the survival and decline of local groups will be shown to be more powerfully shaped by local contextual forces. This line of reasoning has been particularly fruitful in explaining both the surge of populist mobilization that has flourished globally during the last several decades (McCarthy 2019) and particularly, we argue, the Tea Party's organizational dynamics through its lifespan.

CAPTURING THE DYNAMICS OF LOCAL TEA PARTY GROUPS

We aim to analyze the emergence, survival, and mortality of local Tea Party organizations across the US between 2009 and 2014. We use our database of 3,587 Tea Party chapters, introduced in Chapter 4, which were nested in their local contexts. Our sample of local Tea Party organizations is ideal for this purpose. We used web crawlers to exhaustively capture all Tea Party groups appearing on the websites for the main umbrella groups: 1776 Tea Party, FreedomWorks, Patriot Action Network, Tea Party Patriots, and Tea Party Nation. We supplement these sources by using listings of Tea Party groups from Meetup. We started crawling the umbrella groups as they began to publish organizational listings, ranging between mid-2009 and late 2010, and running software every 24 hours through December 31, 2014. We also collected information from the dedicated webpage(s) for each national organization, supplementing the listings aimed at enumerating all groups.

After compiling a comprehensive list of organizations, we manually reviewed each organization name and webpage to identify and remove groups not related to the Tea Party (e.g., those promoting conservative ideologues or politicians), groups spamming the Tea Party websites, or groups dropped for typographical errors in their names. Since our focus was on local conditions where Tea Party groups operated, we also removed organizations with a state or federal-level scope, and those exclusively emphasizing online activism. Last, since an organization could appear on more than one Tea Party umbrella group or Meetup, we used the name and location of each organization to identify and delete duplicate cases. This proved to be a necessary step since 11% of the groups appeared in two or more source lists. Using this strategy, we identified 3,587 Tea Party chapters that had been active at any time between 2009 and 2014. Once we had compiled our final list of Tea Party groups, we identified the location of each organization based on its description, event locations, and any other available information that helped us spatially locate each chapter. We geocoded the location of each group at the county level allowing us to create the key features of the local communities' evolving environments.

Building Dynamic Measures of Material and Status Threats

Our focal dependent variable was the *survival time* of each Tea Party chapter. We considered a chapter to be active once it appeared on any of the listings maintained by Tea Party umbrella groups. Since our database of listings for each umbrella group was updated once every 24-hour period, we were able to identify and collect data on any group within a day of its founding. Identifying organizational mortality was substantially more complex, as few (if any) groups formally announced their dissolution on websites maintained by the umbrella organizations.[1]

We used a multifaceted approach to estimate the date that a group became inactive. If an organization disappeared entirely from the listings posted across each of the umbrella groups and Meetup, we concluded that the group had dissolved. This proved to be relatively rare, as the groups were not purged for inactivity. To provide a more accurate estimate of organizational mortality, we used evidence of organizational growth or other activity linked to a specific group. Specifically, this research design allowed us to identify when new members joined each group within a 24-hour window. We also collected listings of protest events, meetings, speaker events, or other gatherings, as well as web posts under the name of the group to gauge whether it was active. Finally, we cross-referenced each group and our database of newspaper coverage of the Tea Party, which contained the 70,834 newspaper articles we used to track Tea Party events described in Chapter 5. We specifically looked for media coverage of the events staged by each organization as a signal that it remained active. Collectively, these indicators of activity allowed us to create estimates for the last day that each chapter appeared to show any life. To estimate mortality, we took the latest date of any demonstrable activity for a group. Importantly, the organizational listings for the Tea Party Patriots and the Patriot Action Network were removed entirely in February and November of 2014, respectively. We attempted to account for this in our statistical analysis by right-censoring the effected groups.[2]

Four clusters of independent variables were used in our analysis. The clusters mimic the conceptual categories and operationalization that we used in Chapter 3 to account for the emergence of Tea Party groups and Tax Day rallies.[3] To minimize repetition, we only briefly describe each variable used previously. Measures updated for this chapter are described in more detail. Since we geocoded each Tea Party group to its county of operation, some

---

[1] We found only two cases where a group formally announced its dissolution.

[2] Right-censoring describes the situation where a group is no longer tracked, and hence is not at risk of dissolution, and has not been designated as inactive based on its activity pattern.

[3] The exception is our variable of Americans for Prosperity chapter activity at the state-level. Since few Tea Party chapters received direct assistance from conservative advocacy groups, we omitted the measure from this analysis.

variables draw from multiple years of the American Community Survey (ACS), the Local Area Unemployment series, the Department of Housing and Urban Development, and the US Religion Census Religious Congregations and Membership Study. Last, since our analysis tracks Tea Party groups over multiple years, we updated our measures as new waves of data were released. For instance, the variables drawn from the ACS are updated annually.[4]

The first set of variables includes five measures of *material threats*. They comprise the change in percent unemployed, the housing foreclosure concentration for each county between 2007 and 2009, the Gini coefficient of income inequality, the percentage of the population receiving retirement income, and the annual change in median income. Since the estimates of foreclosure concentration were only available for the 2007 and 2009 period, the variable is static in our analysis. The other variables were updated annually to capture new waves of data for each year between 2009 and 2014, giving us a precise way to account for the lingering effects of the Great Recession and the variable pace of the economic recovery in each county. We expected that Tea Party organizations located in counties that were slower to recover from the Great Recession, as well as areas with a higher proportion of residents at risk of economic precarity, such as retirees, would persist longer relative to counties where the recovery proceeded at a faster pace.

Second, we employed four measures to capture the level of *status threats* present in each county. The first is the dissimilarity index of racial segregation. The next variable captures the annual change in the percentage of White people in each county. Third, we used the percentage of households receiving benefits from the Supplemental Nutrition Assistance Program (SNAP). Last, we drew from the Religious Congregations and Membership Study to measure the number of evangelical Christian congregations in each county. The variable for evangelical congregations is based on the 2000 (for 2009) and 2010 waves of the Religious Congregations and Membership Study. The natural log of evangelical congregations is used in our analysis to reduce skewness. Following Parker and Barreto (2014), Parkin et al. (2015), and others, we expected that the racial dynamics of a Tea Party group's local context to be an important motivator for sustaining activism. Measures of racial segregation and the changes in the proportion of Whites assess these threats directly. The variable measuring the number of SNAP recipients is more indirect. We used it as a proxy to capture the conservative movement's distorted but longstanding belief in a linkage between "underserving" poor and welfare expenditures. White Christians' concerns about retaining the social power are associated with Tea Party support (Parker and Barreto 2014), so we expected that groups

---

[4] Since the annual changes may only weakly test the status threats variables, we also used change scores between the ACS values and the 2000 Census of population. The results were substantively equal.

would have a longer lifespan when situated in counties with more intense status threats.

The third variable cluster contains four measures of local *political context* surrounding Tea Party groups. The first is the county-level percentage of support for the Republican candidate in the 2008 and 2012 presidential elections. Next, we determined whether a Tea Party group was located in an electoral district represented by a member of the Tea Party Caucus. To create this indicator, we used the Internet Archive to locate members on the Tea Party Caucus' governmental webpage combined with House member-level internet searches on Republican representatives' affiliation with the Tea Party Caucus. We identified 71 politicians who aligned themselves with the Tea Party Caucus. We also coded whether a Tea Party group was in an electoral district held by a Republican who was not a member of the Tea Party Caucus. As with our other measures, this variable was updated following the outcome of each House electoral cycle between 2010 and 2014, as well as the 2008 and 2012 presidential election contests as appropriate.

Finally, we included three county-level demographic controls. These were the percentage of residents who were college educated, the median income for households, and the population size of the county. For population size, we used the natural logarithm to reduce the impact of skewness. These variables were updated annually using each successive wave of the ACS.

Since our focus was on the survival and mortality of Tea Party groups, we used event-history models for our statistical analysis. These models provide a flexible framework for data where the key element of interest is the period of time elapsed before a specific event takes place (Hosmer, Lemeshow, and May 2008), here the onset of inactivity. We used mixed-effects Cox proportional hazards regression in our analysis, nesting Tea Party organizations in states to account for any unobserved state-level heterogeneity. The analytic strategy can also readily incorporate time-varying independent variables, which was necessary given our dynamic approach to operationalization.

Explaining Tea Party Organizational Survival and Decline

We began by estimating the number and perseverance of local Tea Party organizations over time. Figure 6.1 tracks the daily size of the Tea Party's complete local chapter system, distinguishing between the cumulative count of groups ever active and the number of groups that remained active each day. It is essential to make the distinction between the cumulative number of groups and the number of active groups because the organizational listings on the Tea Party umbrella groups continued to contain hundreds of groups that no longer showed signs of activity. For example, the Tea Party Patriots listed 1,743 Tea Party groups before deleting their public listings in February 2014, but only 266 of them then showed any recent signs of activity. The organizational listings alone, therefore, were deceptive indicators of the number of groups

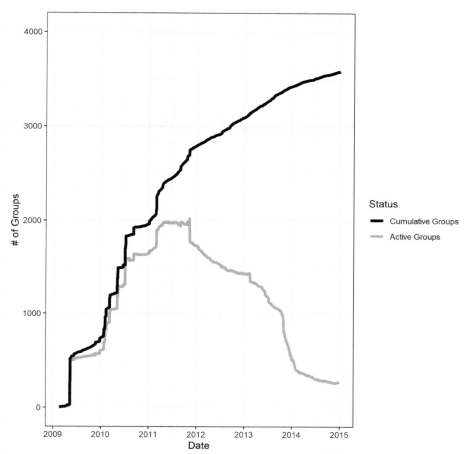

FIGURE 6.1 The density and status of local Tea Party groups, February 19, 2009–December 31, 2014 (*n*=3,587).

composing the Tea Party insurgency at any point in time. The umbrella groups typically added new, but rarely removed existing, local chapters. No doubt this was also partially because few local groups communicated news of their dissolution to the umbrella groups.

What were the dominant patterns of growth and decline in the population of local Tea Party groups? There is a strong correspondence between active and listed Tea Party groups between 2009 and mid-2010 evident in Figure 6.1. At the peak of insurgent activity, between 2011 and 2012, there were approximately 2,000 local Tea Party chapters active, with a maximum of 2,021 active groups in existence on November 6, 2011. After late 2011, however, there began a slow but stable decline in the number of active groups though mid-2013, followed by accelerated slump in the number of active groups through the start of 2014. Overall, there was a rapid rise of local Tea Party groups through 2012, with an equally rapid decline until the end of 2014. Of the 3,587 Tea Party organizations that were ever active at some point between 2009 and 2014, only 274 still showed any signs of activity by December 31, 2014, the end of our analytic period. Put another way, of the 3,587 Tea Party groups, less than 8% remained active by the end of 2014, underscoring the widespread demobilization among the insurgency's local chapters. This timeline clearly mirrors the rapid cessation of Tea Party events we identified in Chapter 5.

The trends seen in Figure 6.1 provide a bird's eye view of the count of local Tea Party chapters over time, but it is useful to go further by establishing typical survival patterns as well. The average Tea Party group remained active for only 646 days, with extensive variability around that mean. Figure 6.2 shows the

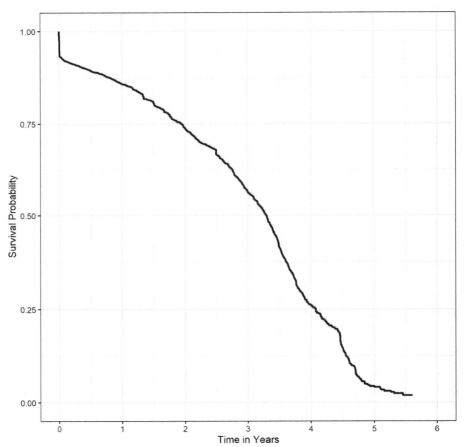

FIGURE 6.2 Survival curve of local Tea Party groups, February 19, 2009–December 31, 2014 (*n*=3,587).

survival probabilities for Tea Party groups over time. The survival calculation for a group is based on the dissolution of a group or when it was right-censored.

There are several notable implications about the trajectory of Tea Party groups shown in Figure 6.2. First, approximately 10% of Tea Party groups did not survive beyond the first few weeks of their founding, which can be seen in the steep vertical slope in the upper-left quadrant of the plot. Based on this evidence of Tea Party events, such groups likely attempted to hold an initial planning meeting or protest but quickly ceased additional activity, or alternatively managed to hold a first gathering without leaving traces of any subsequent activity. Most groups did survive beyond this initial period, after which the survival probabilities decreased at a much slower pace. There was a 50% probability that a group survived until its third year and a 25% probability of survival until its fourth year. There is a relatively sharp drop in the likelihood of survival between the fourth and fifth year of a chapter's lifespan, with only a small number of groups expected to survive beyond their fifth year. The relatively long survival estimates for some groups is meaningful in that they increasingly engaged in less publicly facing activities over time. Nonetheless, this evidence tells us that most of the local Tea Party chapters had ceased to exist by the end of 2014, as the likelihood of survival by then was less than 10%.

Local Contexts and Tea Party Group Dissolution

To better understand how local environments influenced the lifespan of local Tea Party groups, we turn to the Cox regression analysis, summarized in Table 6.1. The variables measuring the impacts of material threats and the slow economic recovery are strongly related to the durability of Tea Party activism, consistent with our expectations. Tea Party organizations located in communities where unemployment more slowly recovered, with high income inequality, and with higher numbers of people receiving retirement income – a group of citizens disproportionately affected by the sharp drop in the stock market – exhibited longer survival times. For example, each additional percentage point increase in the unemployment rate decreased the likelihood of Tea Party chapter mortality by just over 2%, holding other variables constant.[5] Organizations located in a county with an average level of income inequality had a 9% higher chance of survival. The estimates for foreclosure concentration and annual change in median income, on the other hand, are not statistically significant.

---

[5] These percentages are based on the hazard ratios for the coefficients in Table 6.1. These can be calculated by exponentiating the coefficients in the table.

TABLE 6.1 *Mixed-effects Cox proportional hazard models predicting Tea Party organizational mortality, February 19, 2009–December 31, 2014 (n=3,587).*

	Estimates
Material Threats	
Change in % Unemployed	−0.024*
	(0.011)
Foreclosure Concentration	0.148
	(0.125)
Income Inequality	−1.632***
	(0.405)
% Receiving Retirement Income	−0.016*
	(0.008)
Change in Income	−0.022
	(0.040)
Status Threats	
Racial Segregation	−0.729***
	(0.113)
% Change in White	−0.003
	(0.002)
% Receiving SNAP Benefits	−0.009*
	(0.003)
Evangelical Congregations	0.035*
	(0.015)
Political Context	
% Republican Votes	−0.002*
	(0.001)
Tea Party Caucus Representative	0.046
	(0.033)
Republican Representative	0.039
	(0.025)
Demographic Controls	
% College Graduate	−0.013*
	(0.006)
Median Income	0.086
	(0.096)
Population Size	−0.098***
	(0.014)
State-Level Variance	0.126

Note Standard errors in parentheses. Tea Party organizations are nested in states. *p<0.05, **p<0.01, ***p<0.001; All estimates excluding foreclosure concentration are time-varying.

Overall, the lingering effects of the Great Recession appear to have served as contributing factors, increasing the longevity of Tea Party groups in areas with a slower economic recovery. The material threats so important in spurring the Tea Party insurgency then, also, appear to have been instrumental in maintaining its momentum. An important caveat: our data do not allow us to speak to the individual decision-making processes of the individuals participating in Tea Party groups themselves, or whether they personally continued to experience effects from the slow economic recovery. Personal experiences may influence an individual's decisions to remain an activist in a local chapter, but our data only speak to the potential mobilizing impact of high concentrations of individuals at heightened economic risk which may, in turn, have been a catalyst for engagement.

Status threats are also associated with Tea Party chapter survival, though not always in the ways expected. Estimates for racial segregation and the percentage of residents receiving SNAP benefits are both negative, while the estimate for changes in the percentage of White residents is not statistically significant. This tells us that Tea Party groups survived longer in more racially segregated communities and those with concentrations of residents that conservatives considered to be the "undeserving" poor. Not only do these racialized dynamics help explain the emergence of the Tea Party, they are also important in understanding the continuity of activism. The estimate for evangelical congregations is statistically significant, as we expected, but the relationship is not in the expected direction. The model suggests that more evangelical congregations increased the likelihood that a Tea Party would become inactive by 3.6%. The density of evangelical congregations was positively associated with both Tax Day rallies in 2009, as well as the formation of early riser Tea Party groups, as we showed in Chapter 3. The finding suggests the importance of making a distinction between social structural factors related to the emergence of collective action and those that help sustain it. A high density of congregations may provide the infrastructures for initial mobilization, but prove insufficient to keep activism going once other facilitating conditions have waned. In summary, the overall impact of our measures of status threats on survival is largely consistent with our expectations, and also corroborates other work on the Tea Party (e.g., Parker and Barreto 2014).

Tea Party groups survived longer in communities with a higher Republican vote share. The association between organizational survival and higher Republican support is intuitive and unsurprising. Despite widespread criticism and skepticism of the Republican Party by many Tea Party activists, the GOP was the only viable political party home for the American right. High levels of Republican support in a community signaled a large pool of conservatives who were more likely to be sympathetic to the Tea Party. This likely produced a larger critical mass of activists willing and able to maintain the viability of local groups. The estimated impact for Republican support is relatively small however – a 10% increase in the percentage of Republican votes corresponded to a 2% decline in organizational mortality, holding other variables constant.

Turning to the indicators of political representation, our results indicate that groups active in an area where a Tea Party Caucus member was the Congressional representative did not influence organizational survival. There is a similarly null relationship between a chapter's longevity and its presence in a community represented by a Republican who did not join the Tea Party Caucus. This surprising finding is inconsistent with the expectation that a central path to the demise of local Tea Parties was their incorporation into the Republican Party. Instead, we see that the longer surviving groups were more likely to be disconnected from their congressional representatives in the House of Representatives, a finding that held even when the representative explicitly aligned with the insurgency. Hostility toward the GOP was common among Tea Party activists (Blum 2020), with many participants viewing the insurgency's role as a watchdog for perceived excessive spending or compromise by congressional Republicans (Skocpol and Williamson 2011). The finding again reinforces the stark disconnection between Congressional Tea Party identifiers and grassroots Tea Party groups.

The final set of variables accounts for the community demographic context surrounding local Tea Party groups. First, a higher concentration of college graduates increased the lifespan of chapters. As the percentage of college graduates in a county grew by 1%, organizational mortality declined by 1% overall. Higher levels of educational capital may have provided the resources necessary to maintain the more monotonous work required to ensure that local chapters survived for more extended periods. The estimate for the log of population size is also statistically significant, indicating that for each unit increase in population size organizational mortality decreased by 10%. Because densely populated areas had larger pools of individuals eligible to join a Tea Party group, this pattern is not surprising. Finally, the median income of each county was not associated with Tea Party organizational survival. This is most likely the case because Tea Party chapters generally required only modest budgets to sustain their activities.

CONCLUSION

This chapter summarizes the most comprehensive existing analyses of the trajectory and lifecycle of local Tea Party chapters. Using a unique database tracking 3,587 Tea Party chapters between 2009 and 2014, we can answer important questions about what became of the local groups that collectively comprised the insurgency. Our strategy emphasized the local political, economic, and social contexts where Tea Party groups thrived and declined. Consistent with our central theoretical emphasis about how contextual features shaped the origins and timing of the Tea Party, our main findings here suggest that such factors are also related to organizational vitality. Local chapter survival was shown to be associated with two primary community contextual features. First, a set of suddenly imposed material threats stemming from the

Great Recession increased the likelihood that Tea Party groups would form. Not only did these material threats help explain the emergence of Tea Party activism, but the slow, uneven economic recovery from the Great Recession helps explain the wide variation in organizational survival across the country. Second, status threats also played an important role in explaining local organizational longevity. These status threats were the product of several decades of racialized conservative discourse. Specifically, following work by McVeigh (1999) and Parker and Barreto (2014), the belief that White, Christian social power was in decline appears also to have been linked to variation in the lifecycle of Tea Party chapters.

We see little evidence that local Tea Party groups were subsumed by local Republican Party organizations. Groups active in electoral districts represented by politicians who explicitly chose to align themselves with the insurgency were no more likely to survive, and the same is true for groups in districts held by non-Tea Party Republicans. Instead, our analysis suggests that both material and status threats have greater explanatory power in accounting for the insurgency's organizational decline.

Collectively, the foregoing analyses provide the first comprehensive assessment of what happened to the Tea Party's local chapters. Prior scholarship has focused on the political capture of the Tea Party (Blum 2020; Gervais and Morris 2012, 2018), at the expense of a more systematic analysis about patterns of grassroots activism that underpinned the Tea Party insurgency. Linking the trajectory of local Tea Party groups to theoretically motivated indicators of community characteristics has helped us to substantially thicken an understanding of the Tea Party's organizational demobilization by late 2014.

7

Moving Off Message

The Discursive Demobilization of the Tea Party

The Tea Party rose to prominence on a platform emphasizing fiscal restraint, a reduction of taxation, and harsh criticism of the newly minted Obama administration's stimulus package aimed at minimizing the impact of the Great Recession. The Tea Party viewed itself as representing a silent majority of Americans who had been left behind by the economic upheaval of the Great Recession, as well as broader demographic changes eroding the power of White conservative Christians. The insurgency's claims widely resonated across the conservative media ecosystem, and rapidly came to influence the American political conversation. The Tea Party's rhetoric played an important role in shaping the Republican Party's platform for the 2010 electoral cycle (Blum 2020; Skocpol and Williamson 2011), which, at least in part, contributed to the decisive Republican victory in the House of Representatives. The Tea Party also secured steady positive, albeit sometimes distorted, attention from Fox News and other conservative media sources (Rafail and McCarthy 2018; Street and DiMaggio 2015).

Much of the research on the Tea Party's main claims, grievances, and policy positions, however, has emphasized its earliest period of mobilization, with almost no attention to the rise and fall of local activism documented in Chapters 5 and 6. The middle and later periods of Tea Party mobilization are particularly important because, following the 2014 election, Republicans controlled both the Senate and the House of Representatives. The period between 2016 and 2018, covering the first two years of the Trump administration, was marked by single-party Republican rule of Congress. As Blum (2020) argues, Tea Party activists were critical of establishment Republicans and more than willing to attack the Republican Party (or "Grand Old Party" [GOP]) from the inside if it meant achieving their policy goals. Some excellent research does indicate that a larger and more flexible set of demands eventually emerged from the Tea Party. Gervais and Morris (2018), for instance, describe how the insurgency came to endorse a broader set of conservative policies on issues such as immigration, the Second Amendment, and affirmative action. Similarly, other work has pointed to the fruitful relationship that developed between Tea Party activists and the broader evangelical Christian movement (Brody 2012).

In this chapter we analyze the claims made by the Tea Party between 2009 and 2018. The near singular branding of the Tea Party as patriotic grassroots resistance to government spending and taxation during the early wave of Tea Party mobilization was unique within conservative discourse at the time. Its novelty was important in the insurgency's early successes. The Tea Party's major policy preferences were the product of decades of elite-driven conservative activism, which had not until then achieved a credible groundswell of grassroots support. After the early wave of mobilization, remaining Tea Party activists abandoned public protest, most local groups disappeared, and the ever-present weak organizational centralization of the Tea Party network undermined the insurgency's ability to coordinate on issue messaging. As a result, the Tea Party's initially sharp criticisms became unfocused, scattershot, and otherwise unremarkable within the broader conservative movement. We refer to this process as the *discursive demobilization* of the Tea Party, and document this evolution by analyzing 91,874 blog posts published by the five leading Tea Party umbrella groups between February 19, 2009, and December 31, 2018.

FRAMING THE INSURGENCY AND THE PERFECT INTERPRETIVE MOMENT

The emergence of the Tea Party during the perfect interpretive moment was a central factor in its success. The Tea Party's elite facilitators drew from decades of conservative mobilization, and were able to situate longstanding policy demands on taxation and spending within the economic downturn of the Great Recession and the overflow of status threats that followed the election of Barack Obama. The Tea Party was able to cultivate a unique grassroots niche within the larger conservative movement through its singular focus on issues of spending and taxation that quickly lost the appearance, as well as the reality, of top-down facilitation. In short, the insurgency emerged during a massive economic upheaval and was able to promote longstanding conservative policy preferences with plausible grassroots authenticity. Such good timing was rare for conservative activism and advocacy, as we discussed in Chapter 2 (see also Martin 2013). We proceed by first introducing the framing perspective, and then turn to research, emphasizing the importance of finding a discursive niche for social movements to maximize their discursive impact.

Social Movement Framing

Scholars have long recognized the importance of how social movements frame their core issues and grievances. The framing perspective has been central in creating synergies between analyses of ideologies, claims, and mobilization processes. Framing influences organizational composition, leadership strategies, and movement outcomes (Cress and Snow 2000; Oliver and Johnston 2000; Snow 2004; Snow et al. 1986). The construction of collective action frames describes the process through which activists and organizations create shared meanings by constructing realities that challenge existing social processes (Benford and Snow 2000). Building collective action frames is a delicate process, involving careful decisions and deliberations among social movement participants and leaders. In many cases, leaders have a considerable influence on the content of the frames adopted by a movement, though emphasis on one frame over another can often itself be the source of considerable contestation (Benford 1993). One of the most important tasks for activists is constructing and maintaining *resonant* frames that link the social problems identified by activists with their preferred set of structural and policy solutions.

A vital area of research on social framing revolves around how well a particular frame resonates for both movement actors and the broader population of potential sympathizers that a movement aims to reach (Benford and Snow 2000). Effective and resonant framing aims to highlight the problems identified by a movement as dire, while simultaneously emphasizing how a movement's proposed remedial courses of action are necessary. Movements rely on what Benford (1993) refers to as diagnostic and prognostic frames, which describe the identification of problems by a movement and the specification of concrete steps needed to ameliorate them.

A weakness in previous framing research has been a lack of attention to the identification of meso- and macro-level factors that shape framing practices (Benford 1997), though recent research has attempted to address this issue directly (e.g., Gaby and Caren 2016). To that end, work by McVeigh, Myers, and Sikkink (2004) unpacking successful mobilization by the Indiana Ku Klux Klan in the 1920s provides strong evidence that the effectiveness of a specific movement frame is linked to the structural conditions in communities where mobilization occurs. In essence, they find that a frame is more likely to be resonant in a community where there is high structural congruence, coupled with high political support (see their table 1, p. 658).

The Role of Discursive Niches in Movement Impact

Social movement mobilization typically occurs within a broader set of contentious political issues and activity in a society (Hilgartner and Bosk 1988; Meyer and Tarrow 1998). In western democracies, the raw volume of activism is vast, making it difficult for an emergent social movement to effectively differentiate itself within the cacophony of ongoing framing contests. One strategy for emergent movements is to identify a less highly populated or, even better, an empty niche where its activists can promote their claims. Hannan, Carroll, and Pólos (2003:309) define niches as "the region of resource space in which an entity can persist in the absence of competition."[1] Organizational researchers have found that unpopulated niches facilitate organizational founding, while substantial overlap among organizations occupying a particular resource space heightens organizational mortality (e.g., Baum and Singh 1994a, 1994b). The concept of discourse niches applies readily to social movement organizations (McCarthy and Zald 1977; Zald and McCarthy 1980), which compete for finite resources and attention among issue categories.

The Tea Party Niche

The Tea Party emerged during the Great Recession, under conditions that powerfully motivated the insurgency's emergence. As 2009 began, economic issues were at the forefront of concern for many Americans. Drawing on decades of conservative advocacy, the Tea Party adopted a simple, clear message emphasizing the role of government and the "underserving" poor as the perpetrators of the Great Recession. This was fundamental in facilitating both a prognostic and diagnostic framing to distinguish the insurgency from long-standing conservative talking points about government expenditures and taxation.

Of course, the broad public policy issue niche about the evils of taxation and high rates of government spending was a relatively, but not wholly, empty one within conservative discourse. As we have shown in Chapters 2 and 3, it was a niche that had been cultivated for decades by elite movements with some success, including, prominently, the professional social movement led by Grover Norquist, President of Americans for Tax Reform. That group had succeeded by convincing the vast majority of Republican US senators and congresspersons to sign a "Taxpayer Protection Pledge" agreeing to vote against any federal tax increase. The group was part of a long tradition of elite movements advocating anti-tax and limited spending messages (Martin 2013). What made the Tea Party unique, however, was the strategic coupling of *mass grassroots mobilization* with a well-articulated frame of *anti-tax, anti-spending discourse*. These two components were knit together to fill an empty niche at the beginning of the Great Recession. Together they were effectively leveraged by Tea Party activists as the insurgency found its footing.

The Strategy of Tea Party Discourse

The obvious importance of structural issues and discursive niches was evident from the early stage of Tea Party mobilization. As the insurgency geared up for the 2009 Tax Day Tea Party rallies, activists were careful to link the Great

---

[1] Hannan et al. (2003) use this definition to refer to a *fundamental niche*, following earlier work in organizational theory (see Freeman and Hannan 1983; Hannan and Freeman 1977).

Recession to the policies of the Obama administration. Their claims were clearly revealed in the content available on the main organizing website for the 2009 Tax Day Tea Party rallies. As well, similar content appears in the earliest discussions on the websites for Tea Party umbrella groups such as the Tea Party Patriots and the 1776 Tea Party.

The prognostic framing employed during the initial wave of Tea Party mobilization was grounded in the ameliorative power of free-market capitalism. Examples of such framing abound on the Tax Day Tea Party website used to organize the 2009 rallies. For instance, image templates designed for use on placards, included slogans such as "Remember Real Hope & Change?" accompanied by a picture of Ronald Reagan. Another slogan linked the decline of the financial markets to the slogan of the Obama administration, suggesting "I used to have a 401k NOW I HAVE CHANGE." The Tax Day Tea Party website also contained numerous statements criticizing the "Tax and Spend" policies of the Obama administration, that activists accused of embracing socialism.

The prognostic frames deployed by the Tea Party organizers also directly associated the economic recession to the policies of the Obama administration. The early Tea Party websites made such connections explicitly, stating:

> The Tea Party protests, in their current form, began in early 2009 when Rick Santelli, the On Air Editor for CNBC, set out on a rant to expose the bankrupt liberal agenda of the White House Administration and Congress. Specifically, the flawed "Stimulus Bill" and pork filled budget. (taxdayteaparty.com; accessed April 15, 2009).

The Tax Day Tea Party website also provided a toolkit for organizers containing a series of policy prescriptions outlining the Tea Party's elite facilitators' vision for repairing the US economy. These steps were drawn from the conservative advocacy group American Solutions, led by former House Speaker Newt Gingrich, and consisted of:

1. Abolishment of "death tax," referring to the estate tax
2. The elimination of congressional earmarks and strict limitations to government spending
3. Reduction of the business taxation rate to 12.5%
4. The implementation of a flat-tax rate of 15%
5. A tax credit designed to offset 50% of payroll taxes
6. Abolishment of any capital gains taxes.

Together, these representative snippets of Tea Party discourse point to their firm adherence to the principles of free-market capitalism along with a more specific agenda emphasizing fiscal restraint and the minimization of taxation. This framing also illustrates how the insurgency borrowed heavily from previous framings of their central issues by conservative advocacy groups and elite actors. Despite this, the claims made by the Tea Party were personalized and individualized, with the goal of signaling mass grassroots support for the movement's grievances and policy solutions.

The economic messages prevalent in Tea Party discourse were embedded within an exclusive vision of patriotism. The websites built by Tea Party leaders were awash with American flags, Gadsden flags,[2] and other symbols of patriotism. Activists proclaimed themselves as representing "real" Americans, arguing that they gave voice to a silent majority who had been left behind. Such claims about representation are commonly invoked by activists and have been used to both legitimize and dismiss contentious political activity (Gillion 2020). The brand of patriotism adopted by the Tea Party was grounded in the status threats and racial resentment motivating White conservatives. Drawing on work by Parker and colleagues (2009), we argue that the Tea Party adopted a form of symbolic patriotism that treated Whites as the ideal typical representation of patriotic Americans. The vision of patriotism extends beyond one's legal status as citizen, and creates an implicit hierarchy of who can claim to represent the interests of American citizens, placing Whites at the top. Such sentiments add important context to the Tea Party's reaction to the election of Barack Obama in November 2008, which we characterized in earlier chapters as creating a spillover of White conservative racial resentment.

A main component of Tea Party discourse, then, was its bridging of patriotism, representation, and race. While manifest claims about the insurgency having represented "real" Americans were facially race neutral, they were inexorably enmeshed in a vision of White, Christian conservatism that excluded other social groups. A consequence of the Tea Party's brand of patriotism, then, was to distinguish the "real" Americans participating in the insurgency from the "undeserving" others, many of whom were subsidized by White conservatives. Parker and Barreto (2014) have made similar claims, though they focus on Tea Party supporters, rather than the discourse of the insurgency itself.

Whither Conservativism?

A main implication of our discussion thus far has been the original emphasis by Tea Party activists on fiscal and economic issues as well as political representation. The Tea Party described itself as conservative rather than Republican (Rafail and McCarthy 2018) and openly distrusted GOP leadership (Blum 2020). The early framing adopted by the insurgency only overlaps a small fraction of issue space then occupied by the larger conservative movement. The size and breadth of the conservative movement is vast (Gross, Medvetz, and Russell 2011). That said, there were relatively stable patterns of both noninstitutionalized and institutionalized political mobilization within its full policy agenda as the Tea Party emerged. A significant part of conservative grassroots mobilization, for instance, consisted of Pro-Life activism (Munson

---

[2] The Gadsden flag was used during America's war of independence. The yellow flag features a snake and the text "Don't tread on me."

2010), yet most Tea Party groups avoided explicit mention of abortion issues. Similarly, evangelical Christians were long a core component of the conservative constituency generally, and the Tea Party specifically, after making significant inroads into government, politics, and policymaking (Lindsay 2007, 2008). Despite this, claims about religious freedom or other common issues raised by conservative Christians were rare in Tea Party discourse.

The absence of a focus on the broader conservative agenda in early Tea Party discourse was especially notable given the dominance of hard-right conservatives in the rank-and-file of the insurgency. The Tea Party was ideologically diverse (Haltinner 2018), but tended to be more religious (Braunstein and Taylor 2017), Whiter, and disproportionately male (Fisher 2015). It also favored color blind racial policies meant to minimize racial disparities (Haltinner 2016) and reactionary conservatism (Parker and Barreto 2014). Given the overlapping policy preferences of Tea Party activists and supporters with conservatives in general, the insurgency's issue focus reflected a deliberate choice at the onset. Some evidence already exists that the political preferences articulated by Tea Party sympathizers, over time, came to mirror those of conservatives more broadly (Perrin et al. 2014). The narrower framing initially adopted by the Tea Party through its early successes did not persist for long.

Summary

The Tea Party insurgency occupied the grassroots space in a key issue niche in American political discourse during its relatively short early phases of mobilization. The insurgency's framing was grounded in the perfect interpretive moment: emphasizing opposition to taxes and fiscal restraint in government spending that fit squarely within popular concern about the impact of the Great Recession, along with previous elite efforts to mobilize within that narrow issue niche. These claims were embedded within a racialized vision of patriotism and representation, where Tea Party activists claimed that their own efforts were aimed to benefit real Americans, implicitly to the exclusion of non-Whites and non-Christians. This framing strategy distinguished the Tea Party from the larger conservative movement and was instrumental in the insurgency's rapid success. Prior research has indicated that over time Tea Party activists and supporters came to focus on the more general set of issues that occupied the conservative movement (Brody 2012; Gervais and Morris 2018; Perrin et al. 2014). Some of our own prior work on the Tea Party (Rafail and McCarthy 2018) found that media outlets across the political spectrum treated the insurgency as an extension of the GOP, while activists framed the movement as conservative but not necessarily Republican. Yet, there has been no systematic research on the insurgency's own discourse. We argue that direct engagement with *what*, *how*, and *when* Tea Party activists discussed policy issues is crucial to understanding the larger trajectory of the insurgency. To address this, we now analyze the evolution of Tea Party discourse through (and beyond) its effective grassroots lifespan. Doing so provides a dense and convincing portrait of the evolution of the content of the insurgency's discourse.

THE EVOLUTION OF TEA PARTY DISCOURSE

Building a defensible sample of the Tea Party's claims was not a simple task. Mass media attention to social movements filters the claims made by activists, often undermining or otherwise altering their intended messages (Gitlin 1980; Smith et al. 2001). To minimize media biases, we instead focused on collecting discourse produced directly by Tea Party activists and leaders. We used blog posts that were published on the websites for the major Tea Party umbrella groups, which provides a contemporaneous way to collect information on what activists were discussing at any particular point in time.

As mentioned at the beginning of this chapter, we identified 91,874 blog posts published between February 19, 2009, and December 31, 2018. This period captured the effective lifespan of the Tea Party, beginning with posts published during its infancy in 2009, during the insurgency's maturation between 2010 and 2012, and to its eventual demobilization starting in 2013. Our findings from Chapters 5 and 6 indicate that grassroots Tea Party activism had largely dried up by late 2014. However, we continued to track Tea Party blogs for several more years to determine whether the insurgency's framing changed after the election of Donald Trump. The blogs were collected from 1776 Tea Party (n=15,306), FreedomWorks (n=7,566), Patriot Action Network (n=51,283), Tea Party Nation (n=14,875), and Tea Party Patriots (n=2,846). As best as we can determine, these posts represent an exhaustive enumeration of all blog posts published on these main Tea Party websites. Given our theoretical aims in this chapter, blogs provided us with an optimal data source to track and analyze Tea Party discourse. The umbrella groups followed a bridge blogging form (Karpf 2008) that allows any registered user to contribute content.[3] Rather than focusing solely on the discourse of Tea Party leaders, then, we have also generated a large enumeration of content contributed by activists throughout the (thin) organizational hierarchy of the insurgency.

We wrote several web crawlers to collect and store the blog posts published by each umbrella group. The web crawlers were run quarterly to capture and preserve all posted content over time. This was an important step, as the websites for the 1776 Tea Party, Patriot Action Network, and Tea Party Patriots underwent extensive redesigns during our monitoring, resulting in a deletion of older content. Other websites, such as Tea Party Nation, repeatedly

---

[3] The exception to this was the Tea Party Patriots, who did not provide an open platform for members. The ironic consequence of this choice was that the national umbrella group with the widest reach into the grassroots of the insurgency did not create a blog vehicle that allowed their constituent local groups and activists to participate.

went offline only to reappear later, while the website for the Patriot Action Network no longer exists. Our collection of blog posts includes material written by leaders of the Tea Party insurgency as well as by rank-and-file members, maximizing the breadth of opinion in our sample. Along with the text of each post, we collected metadata on the author, date of publication, and any subsequent comments posted in response to the original blog post.

We applied several sample selection criteria. First, we omitted blog posts that did not contain any textual content. Such posts were primarily embedded videos without any other textual material, placing them beyond the scope of our analysis. Second, we identified authors who contributed spam posts or advertisements, eliminating those posts. Last, we omitted content posted outside the analytic time period. FreedomWorks and its blogs existed before the Tea Party insurgency, any post published prior to the Santelli rant in February 2009 was excluded.

Capturing the main thematic content of the Tea Party blog posts as they evolved over time was our analytic goal. To do so, we used topic models[4] which are a statistical technique that can identify themes in large volumes of text by identifying word patterns that cluster around latent topics. Topic models are less useful for more nuanced analyses of textual content. However, since we focus on major trends in Tea Party discourse, the tradeoff of breadth for depth is reasonable in this case. We conduct a more detailed qualitative analysis of blog posts about the Tea Party activist's reaction to Donald Trump in Chapter 9.

Our analytic strategy involved fitting a series of models with between 2 and 20 topics. We then interpreted the results for each model specification paying particular attention to the uniqueness and coherency of the topics returned by each round of estimation. Our aim was to identify a final model that maximized the breadth of the thematic content of the Tea Party blogs while at the same time ensuring that the resulting set of topics was substantively meaningful, with each unique from one another. After reviewing the results, we selected a final model that included nine topics. This specification provided an optimal balance of coherency and diversity.

The Trajectory and Content of Tea Party Discourse

Temporal trends in the Tea Party's blogosphere are shown in Figure 7.1. The overall pattern shows a steep decline in the volume of Tea Party blogging over the life of the insurgency. Tea Party leaders and activists published an average of 71 blog posts during a typical day during 2009. The rate fell to a mean value of 51 posts per day during 2010, and was reduced further to 38 posts per day by

---

[4] Topic models were developed by Blei, Ng, and Jordan (2003) and are widely used tools to summarize large volumes of textual information (see e.g., DiMaggio, Nag, and Blei 2013).

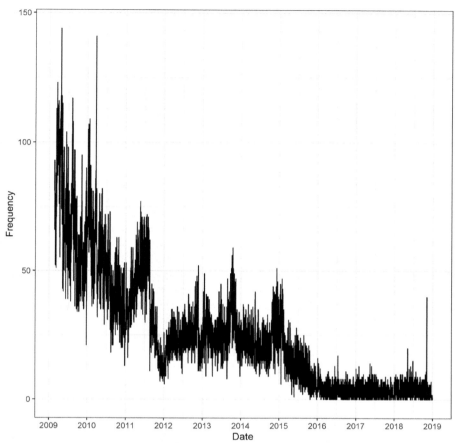

FIGURE 7.1 The daily counts of Tea Party blog posts.
Note: Values are based on 91,874 posts.

2011. An even more significant trend in the insurgency's discursive demobilization began in 2015, with a mean of 15 posts per day, and ended in 2016, where just 4 blog posts were published on the average day. Both 2017 and 2018 also saw averages of just 4 posts a day across all the Tea Party umbrella groups. Of the 91,874 blog posts, 45%, were published between 2009 and 2010. Nearly 60% of the posts were published during the first three years of the insurgency; in contrast, 5% of the total volume of posts appeared between 2016 and 2018, another stark indicator of the Tea Party's widespread demobilization. A noticeable spike in blogging occurred immediately after the 2018 midterm elections, but that minor surge was atypical and dissipated quickly.

The temporal trends in Figure 7.1 highlight an important dynamic for the Tea Party's overall pattern of discursive demobilization: a negative association exists between the rate of Tea Party blogging and Republican control of the federal government. That is, as the Republican Party came to secure first the House of Representatives, and eventually the Senate and the Presidency, the Tea Party's rate of blogging declined to the point where it was almost invisible within the broader conservative discourse, including print media, talk radio, television, social media, and other sources. This pattern of decline is also consistent with the larger tactical and organizational demobilization of the Tea Party we have shown in earlier chapters.

The Population of Tea Party Bloggers

How extensive was participation in the Tea Party blogosphere? Figure 7.2 shows the cumulative number of unique authors over the insurgency's lifespan. Except for the Tea Party Patriots, all the other umbrella groups opened up their blogging platforms to all members and to local Tea Party groups. The pattern in Figure 7.2 supports our contention that a wide variety of activists connected with the insurgency produced the content we examine in this chapter. A total of 8,545 unique authors produced blog posts between 2009 and 2018, though few new authors began blogging after 2015 as the curve shown in Figure 7.2 becomes effectively flat. In 2009, 3,051 individual authors contributed at least one post, which grew to 5,180 unique authors by the end of 2010, and then 6,453 posters by the end of 2011. By 2012, the growth in new bloggers became quite modest, increasing to only 7,255 unique authors.

Despite the large number of individual bloggers who created content for the Tea Party, we also identified a small number of quite prolific contributors who mainly were leaders of the insurgency or were identified as the web-master for an individual umbrella group. Judson Phillips, founder of the Tea Party Nation published nearly 4% of all blog posts included in our database. The administrators of Tea Party Patriots were credited for publishing 3% of the posts in our sample, though did not claim individual authorship. The overall distribution of posts by author was highly skewed to the right, with a median of 1 and a mean of 11. Nearly 54% of posters contributed a single post, while at the 75th percentile, authors contributed just three posts. Taken together, the blog data capture the content produced by a large and diverse set of activists, despite the disproportionate representation by the insurgency's leaders.

What explains the decline in the volume of Tea Party blog posts and the number of unique content creators? Perhaps the most obvious explanation lies in the Republican Party's electoral victories. That is, activists determined that blogging was no longer necessary after achieving political representation. Reading the blog posts suggests, however, that this was not so. The more likely alternative, we argue, was that the reduction in blogging activity was due to the insurgency's more general demobilization. As the insurgency's extent of activism shrank, the volume of its public discourse declined in tandem.

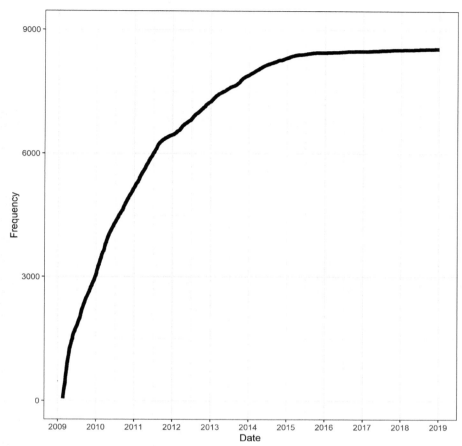

FIGURE 7.2 The daily cumulative number of unique authors posting Tea Party blog posts.
Note: Values are based on 8,545 unique authors.

While the raw volume of blog material produced by activists might speak to the overall vitality of the insurgency, it does not attend to how issues were framed. We therefore turn to our analysis of the content of the insurgency's blog posts. We emphasize whether and how the Tea Party's framing evolved over time.

The Evolution of the Tea Party's Framing

Table 7.1 summarizes the results of our topic model analysis. We organize the table around nine prominent themes that appeared in Tea Party blog posts. Examining the results synthetically, we recoded the nine topics around three

TABLE 7.1 *Major categories and topics appearing in Tea Party blog posts.*

Major Category	Topic Name	Interpretation	Representative Keywords	% of Sample
Classic Tea Party	Regular Americans	The Tea Party represents the views and interests of regular Americans	People, just, like, America, think, need, good, really, believe, conservative	32.68
	Spending & Taxation	Discussion of fiscal responsibility, particularly related to healthcare spending	Health, government, tax, Obamacare, budget, debt, plan, pay, million, reform	12.22
	Obama Administration	Criticism of the policies of the Obama administration	Obama, President, Barack, white, house, court, health, IRS, legal	8.55
			Total	53.45
Conservative Positioning	Foreign Policy	Commentary on US foreign policy, particularly concerning the Middle East and Israel	Muslim, Islamic, Iran, military, Israel, Clinton, world, security, attack	8.95
	Christianity	The role of Christianity in the conservative movement	God, life, people, America, Christian, nation, Jesus, schools, Lord, faith	7.84
	Energy & Environment	Federal policies toward renewable energy, climate change, and oil production	Energy, oil, economic, global, climate, EPA, power, gas, green, China, reserve, industry	7.13
			Total	23.92
Political Events and Legal Processes	Legal Rights	The constitution, court decisions, gun control policy, and issues related to the judicial branch	Law, constitution, power, court, Amendment, freedom, gun, control	8.30
	Elections	Discussion of federal elections, primaries, and related political maneuvering	House, senate, party, vote, Republican, GOP, Democrats, district, senator	7.25
	Information Sharing	Sharing of articles, videos or other information relating to ongoing events	Watch, YouTube, video, article, Fox, news, link, decide, Soros	7.08
			Total	22.63

Note: Keywords were unstemmed for clarity. Total sample size is 91,874.

aggregated thematic clusters: *Classic Tea Party, Conservative Positioning,* and *Political Events and Legal Processes.* We use these clusters to organize our discussion of the Tea Party's discursive demobilization. The first cluster, Classic Tea Party, contains blog posts emphasizing fiscal restraint, the Tea Party's representation of "real" Americans, and criticism of the Obama administration. More than 53% of all posts emphasized these issues, indicating that this substantive cluster captures the larger initial agenda of the Tea Party identified by much of the early scholarship (e.g., Barreto et al. 2011; Parker and Barreto 2014; Skocpol and Williamson 2011; Street and DiMaggio 2015). The first component of this cluster includes the posts discussing the Tea Party's claims that its views and policy positions represent real American values, the primary theme of 33% of all blog posts. The posts emphasized the silent majority in America: that extensive group of individuals who were purported to believe that government spending and taxation had spiraled out of control, justifying a view that a substantial reduction of the tax burden for individuals and businesses was the only viable policy solution. This topic is consistent with the early Tea Party talking points, described above, and provides supporting evidence that the insurgency extensively emphasized its role as a megaphone for the interests of regular Americans, which we argue should be understood to mean White, conservative Christians.

The second component of the Classic Tea Party theme emphasized issues of spending and taxation, which were the dominant theme in 12% of blog posts. Third, these posts emphasized a theme expressing critical commentary of the Obama administration, present in 9% of blog posts. The relative frequency of these topics is unsurprising, and is largely consistent with the initial discursive thrust of the Tea Party, one which was grounded in attacking key Obama priorities such as the economic stimulus package of 2009 and the Affordable Care Act of 2010. Keywords predicting this topic, such as Obamacare, health, and reform, emphasized how Tea Party activists worked to seamlessly couple healthcare reform to a larger pattern of excess government expenditures.

We call the second aggregate cluster of topics Conservative Positioning, as it touches on social and economic issues that were present in the conservative movement, but not necessarily early Tea Party discourse. We coded 24% of blog posts as belonging to the Conservative Positioning thematic cluster. These blog posts focused on a larger set of issues than prior research on the insurgency suggested. For example, nearly 9% of these posts emphasized foreign policy. The posts did not emphasize fiscal issues, such as the economic costs of Bush, Obama, or Trump administration foreign policy practices. Rather, these blog posts expressed solidarity with Israel and criticized Muslim-majority countries as undermining global peace. Similarly, 8% of posts included Christianity as a major theme. Activists outwardly emphasized the centrality of the Christian religion in American life and political culture, the importance of prayer in public schools, and perceived attacks on individuals of faith by liberals. The explicit promotion of Christianity departs from the more latent emphasis on race, religion, and social power prevalent in the Tea Party's earlier economic discourse. More than 7% of posts focused on energy policy and environmental issues. Many of these blog posts embodied critiques of green energy production, questioned climate science, or were generally supportive of the fossil fuel industry. When considered collectively, these topics expanded the original Tea Party discourse into a broader set of conservative talking points.

We coded the final aggregate cluster of topics to capture blog posts about Political Events and Legal Processes, which constituted the remaining 23% of all posts. These topics were generally connected to major political events of the day or to legal cases, and were more reactive in scope. They are akin to kibitzing about current events. A common pattern across these blog posts was detailed commentary on issues of the day rather than more abstract political or policy positions that were more common in the other aggregate clusters we have discussed. The remaining three topics fell into this aggregated group, starting with 8% focusing on legal rights and 7% of posts emphasizing electoral issues. Just over 7% of these posts were written by activists sharing information with the broader Tea Party blogsphere.

Our discussion so far has captured the major themes embodied in Tea Party discourse. It is incomplete, however, because it lacks the temporal context necessary for understanding the evolution of the insurgency's messaging. Figure 7.3 shows the temporal trajectory of each aggregate topical cluster, providing a clearer picture of which messages the Tea Party emphasized as the insurgency evolved. The values, shown in Figure 7.3, were calculated by combining the daily count of posts falling within each of the three aggregated categories included in Table 7.1. Percentages were calculated using the total number of blog posts appearing each day. In cases where no Tea Party blog posts were published, all values were set to 0. As the number of blog posts declined, the daily percentages became substantially more volatile. To aid

(a)   (b)   (c)

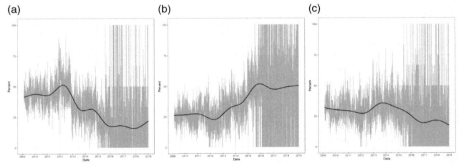

FIGURE 7.3 Temporal trends in the content of Tea Party blog posts: a) classic Tea Party; b) conservative positioning; c) political events and legal processes.
Note: Values are based on daily percentages of blog posts about each major theme. Gray lines are the observed daily values and the black line is an additive smooth.

interpretation, we presented both the daily percentages (in gray) along with a smooth of the overall trend (in black). Together, the plots in Figure 7.3 describe the content of the Tea Party blogosphere from the insurgency's beginning through its decline. The trends seen in Figure 7.3 indicate a radical shift in the content of Tea Party discourse over time.

Starting with the thematic cluster of Classic Tea Party claims in Figure 7.3a, blog posts about the Obama administration, the Tea Party's claims that it represented regular Americans, and spending and taxation were dominant between 2009 and 2012. The start of 2012, however, marks the beginning of what became a continuing decline of emphasis on the issues that had launched the Tea Party to the forefront of American politics. Starting in early 2012 through the middle of 2015, blogs emphasizing Classic Tea Party themes ultimately stabilized at between 25% and 50% of all posting activity, which then fell to between 15% and 25% after 2015 until the end of 2018. The reduction in Tea Party attention to issues of spending, taxation, and fiscal restraint is particularly noteworthy, as the first two years of the Trump administration produced near trillion-dollar deficits. The blog posts also do not show any coordinated effort to support the tax cuts for the Trump administration.

While classic Tea Party discourse declined over time, the opposite was true for blog posts about Conservative Positioning. Figure 7.3b points to a steady increase in posts about more traditional conservative issues over time. This content ultimately came to surpass the Tea Party's emphasis on its core themes by early 2012 and continued on an upward trajectory until the start of 2016. Between 2016 until the end of 2018, we see relative stability in the percentage of posts emphasizing conservative issues, despite the striking decline in overall blogging activity over the same time, as evidenced in Figure 7.1. This pattern is consistent with our expectations: we argued that over time the Tea Party's grassroots activist's emphasis on populism, government spending, the Obama administration, and taxation eroded and came to be replaced by more trad-itional conservative talking points. The niche carved out by early Tea Party activist discourse was left behind as the insurgency evolved and demobilized.

The final cluster capturing Political Events and Legal Processes seen in Figure 7.3c points to a modest decline in emphasis of these issues between 2009 and 2018. Similar to the temporal trends in Figures 7.3a and 7.3b, as the raw volume of Tea Party blogging dissipated, the latter three years of these blogging trends were marked by extensive volatility. The steady stream of com-mentary on electoral issues, legal rights, Christianity, and other conservative policy issues produced by Tea Party activists may have been intended to comple-ment its broader framing of issues, whether using Classic Tea Party or more strictly conservative talking points. For example, a review of the original blog content suggests that activists often linked events of the day to broader Tea Party messages, including populism, spending and taxation, or other conservative messages.

Overall, the temporal trends in the blog posts point to a dramatic discursive shift by Tea Party activists. While in the early phase of the insurgency bloggers disproportionately focused on the themes of spending and taxation or the Obama administration that were grounded in Americanism and populism, those emphases faded and were ultimately crowded out by a broader and more generic bundle of conservative issue foci. By the end of our analysis, the Tea Party's original message became rarer, inconsistent, and variable, as the blog posts oscillated rapidly among issues in all three topical clusters. It is especially important to ground this latter volatility in the low volume of blog content. These trends are consistent with our major claims about the eroding niche that the Tea Party had occupied in the larger conservative movement. Our evidence suggests that as the Tea Party activist's core message became increasingly diluted as the bulk of the insurgency's discourse, then contributed by only a small remnant of die-hard Tea Partiers, it became indistinguishable from that of the broader conservative movement. Indeed, the blog posts appearing at the end of our analytic period were largely indistinguishable from commentary available on right-wing talk radio and other conservative media.

CONCLUSION

This chapter addressed the evolution of Tea Party discourse from its emergence to the end of 2018. To summarize, our central argument is that during the Tea Party's early and middle phases of mobilization the insurgency occupied an important niche in conservative discourse because it was located within the perfect interpretive moment. The emphasis on spending and taxation, drawing on decades of conservative activism and advocacy, was placed within a widely resonant frame of grassroots populism and symbolic patriotism that facilitated the Tea Party's rapid initial success. Over time, the Tea Party became increasingly decentralized, and demobilization began. This led to an accompanying discursive shift in the issues discussed by activists in their blog posts. What we call the Classic Tea Party talking points were superseded by more traditional conservative issue frames, with the former fading in emphasis over time. Evidence from 91,874 blog posts published by Tea Party activists over nearly a decade supports this characterization. These findings have implications for our understanding of the Tea Party and social movement mobilization more broadly.

Our results underscore the fragility in the Tea Party's framing strategy, and the insurgency more broadly. Activist insurgencies like the Tea Party that anchor themselves in specific issue frames may experience difficulty adapting them to larger changes in their political environments. While we have noted that economic issues were a widely resonant point of concern in 2009, such intense apprehension did not last. By 2018, a national random sample of American adults indicated that less than 20% expressed concern about the state of the economy (Gallup 2019). As the economic recovery progressed, Tea Party activists appeared to have broadened the scope of their issue claims, perhaps in hope of remaining relevant to the national political conversation.

The Tea Party's message, crafted during its emergence amidst the perfect interpretive moment made such broadening difficult without losing the insurgency's distinctive voice. Once the Tea Party abandoned its narrow focus in favor of a broader set of conservative policies, the insurgency lost the niche that had brought it to power and prominence. Over time, the Tea Party's commentary became indistinguishable from other conservative media and activist rhetoric. The shift in priorities was particularly important given the narrow ferocity of early Tea Party discourse at its beginning. While criticism of Obama-era budgeting was a rich target for activists, during the first two years of the Trump administration the federal deficit grew substantially. This was not a significant cause of concern for many conservatives, including politicians elected to the House of Representatives in the Tea Party wave of 2010, or senators such as Ted Cruz who similarly adopted Tea Party talking points in their earlier campaign platforms.

It is necessary to place Tea Party rhetoric within the larger demobilization of the insurgency. The Tea Party was initially a hybrid movement, with a strong grassroots element that developed after an initial push from established elite conservative advocacy groups such as Americans for Prosperity and FreedomWorks (Lo 2012; Martin 2013; Skocpol and Williamson 2011). These actors carefully and strategically crafted the Tea Party's original message, which became highly resonant in light of the Great Recession and election of Barack Obama. However, the bridge-blogging format adopted by most Tea Party umbrella groups was almost completely unmoderated, allowing bloggers complete freedom to craft their own individual messages. As both popular and activist issue consciousness moved away from a central focus on exclusive patriotism, economics, and fiscal restraint and steered back toward the broader set of issues that concerned conservatives, it is not surprising that the rank-and-file membership of the Tea Party followed suit in their own discourse. Lacking a centralized organizational structure to police the boundaries of the insurgency's messaging, such a shift was perhaps inevitable, even as it appeared to have played a major role in the Tea Party's demobilization.

8

How Tea Party Activism Helped Radicalize the House of Representatives

The Tea Party insurgency's rapid, aggressive, and definitive reshaping of the Republican Party (the "Grand Old Party" [GOP]) has become a central claim of recent scholarship on political parties and social movements. Scholars have concluded that the insurgency profoundly shaped both the policies and trajectory of the GOP (Blum 2020; McAdam and Kloos 2014; Skocpol and Williamson 2011; Tarrow 2021). Indeed, Skocpol and Williamson's excellent book on the emergence of the Tea Party asserts in its title that the insurgency had remade the Republican Party. Perhaps the most visible consequence of the Tea Party's impact on the GOP occurred in 2010, when a group of politicians in the House of Representatives, led by Minnesota Representative Michele Bachmann, formed the Tea Party Caucus. The Caucus was a major achievement for the fledgling insurgency, solidifying an institutionalized version of the Tea Party in Congress. Tea Party Caucus members were primarily from conservative districts with high unemployment (Gervais and Morris 2012); however, the reach of the Tea Party spread far beyond the caucus itself. Sustained engagements also developed between Tea Party Caucus members and elected Republicans (Gervais and Morris 2018), creating a powerful legislative presence.

Only recently have protest and mobilization come to be seen as playing an important role in political parties and institutionalized politics (Gillion 2020; McAdam and Tarrow 2010, 2013), despite researchers highlighting the centrality of such connections (e.g., Andrews 2001). Social movements sometimes develop strong alliances with political parties (Heaney and Rojas 2015) and may come to serve as political anchors for parties by providing a base of voters (Schlozman 2015). Nevertheless, we know little about how the efforts of the grassroots faction of the Tea Party – the array of local groups which largely independently staged protests, hosted meetings, or did publicly invisible organizational work – interacted with electoral politics after emerging in 2009.

It is especially important to illuminate these mechanisms because the Tea Party largely lacked any semblance of centralized organization or coherent collective agenda as the insurgency evolved. How, then, did a series of largely disconnected groups overtake a major political party so rapidly and so effectively? We argue that the impact of the Tea Party insurgency on American political processes is highly localized and temporally contingent. However, upon accumulation, its efforts created a sea change in the trajectory of the GOP that remains pertinent to the present. We develop this argument in some detail and then evaluate it in a series of empirical tests.

This chapter provides the most comprehensive assessment to date of the impact of the grassroots Tea Party on institutionalized politics generally and the Republican Party particularly. The assessment relies heavily on our granular data of Tea Party activism described in detail in earlier chapters. We emphasize local spatiotemporal patterns of grassroots activism as it intervened and disrupted existing political processes. We aim to answer four questions. First, how did Tea Party activity shape the Republican primaries in the 2010 election cycle for the House of Representatives? Second, what role did Tea Party activism have on securing electoral victories in the 2010 election for the House? Third, what was the trajectory of the wave of Tea Party-affiliated politicians elected to Congress in 2010? Finally, is there evidence that Tea Party activism had a durable impact on the political behavior of the GOP more broadly?

First, we theoretically situate these analyses within the larger literature on social movements, protest, and political parties. We focus on the 2010 Republican primaries, the results of the 2010 election, and the aftermath of these events, using evidence of how local patterns of Tea Party activism and the institutionalization of the insurgency together intervened in the political process. We show that a combination of *mobilization effects* – protests and other public events – and *movement infrastructure effects* – organizational formation – both impacted political processes. The 2010 Republican primaries and subsequent electoral contests were transformative for the Tea Party insurgency, but were only the first stage of its broader impact. Once the Tea Party identified an opening to the halls of power, activists kept up the pressure on the GOP, hastening a rightward shift and deepening political radicalization. Much of the research on the Tea Party's impact on politics has emphasized politicians aligned with the insurgency, what we call the institutionalized Tea Party, while grassroots mobilization has received comparatively less attention. We show that the grassroots faction of the Tea Party *intervened and disrupted* the political process and, by doing so, altered the trajectory of the Republican Party by influencing both affiliated and unaffiliated politicians, pushing the GOP further toward ideological extremism.

SOCIAL MOVEMENTS IN THE POLITICAL PROCESS

Research has traditionally treated social movement mobilization and institutionalized politics as loosely connected, but largely independent realms of activity. Tilly's (1978) influential polity model, for instance, treated social movements as outsiders attempting to influence insiders, including political decision-makers. Over time, such sharp contrasts have softened, with most scholars now accepting that noninstitutionalized behavior like protesting has a strong, reciprocal relationship with institutionalized political action such as voting, as noted by Meyer and Tarrow 1998. A recent synthetic analysis of social movements and political parties by Tarrow (2021) argues that the relationship between social movements and political parties has thickened considerably over time in the US, due in part to the normalization of party–movement hybrids such as the Tea Party. While theoretical boundaries between political parties and social movements still remain, they are increasingly permeable with activity flowing between the two (Goldstone 2003, 2004).

This is not to suggest that scholars have ignored the impact of protest and social movements on political processes. Indeed, they have not. A large body of work has emphasized the political consequences of social movements (Amenta et al. 2010). The segment of that literature which focuses primarily and directly upon protest and activism, most relevant to our concerns here, heavily emphasizes its effects on legislative agenda setting, short-term legislative attention, and legislative outcomes (Johnson, Agnone, and McCarthy 2010; King, Bentele, and Soule 2007; McAdam 1999; Olzak and Soule 2009; Walgrave and Vliegenthart 2012). There is an underlying hydraulic logic to much of this research, in that protest strength is generally assumed to influence outcomes. Typically, the political party in power in the US House and US Senate is included in analyses rooted in the assumption that a party's stance on an issue – e.g., environment, civil rights – will result in variability in its attentiveness and sympathy. But for the most part, these analyses ignore the role of protest in influencing internal party processes. In this chapter we theoretically ground our discussion of the Tea Party's engagement with the political process, addressing two related strands of work. The first emphasizes the institutional dynamics of social movements and political parties. The other examines how movements remain outsiders to the political process while pressuring politicians and influencing the electoral process. Institutional dynamics and institutional distance were interrelated, and together explain the Tea Party's remarkable success at altering the course of the GOP. The role of grassroots activism was notably disruptive to the Republican Party's agenda by not only securing the election of a slate of politicians adverse to compromise, but also by creating an activist core of watchdogs willing to fight long primary battles for secure seats in Congress.

Social Movement Infrastructures: Organizations, Hybridity, and Social Movement Partyism

The partial integration of the Tea Party into the Republican Party represented a fundamental shift in the tone and tenor of American politics; one not so different from Donald Trump's later remaking of the GOP in 2016. Tarrow (2021) demonstrates how the Tea Party and Republican Party came to represent a blended hybrid formation, as the Tea Party and GOP worked together on common projects with common goals – a horizontal hybrid in Tarrow's conceptualization. At the same time, well-established national advocacy groups such as FreedomWorks aimed to use the grassroots elements of the insurgency as a vehicle for policy reform, along the lines of what Tarrow calls a vertical hybrid formation. A consequence of the blended hybridity was that the Tea Party rapidly turned constitutional conservatism and uncompromising fiscal responsibility into a central policy plank of the Republican Party. Following work by Andrews (2001), we emphasize the role of local Tea Party groups that were spread across the country, who often either built bridges with their local Republican politicians or more aggressively attempted to bend them to the insurgency's will. Andrews conceptualizes the role of organizations, leaders, and resources as *social movement infrastructure* effects (pp. 71–72), which are crucial in understanding the Tea Party's role in the political process.

The fragile coalition between grassroots Tea Party activists, Republican Party structures, and organized conservative interests was highly consequential. While this process unfolded, a group of Republican politicians, most of whom had long served in Congress, aligned themselves with the Tea Party. Blum (2020) and Gervais and Morris (2018) highlight the hardball tactics pursued by Tea Party–affiliated politicians, especially in the House of Representatives. The Tea Party embraced obstruction and encouraged Republicans to vote against what had traditionally been fairly routine, albeit sometimes contentious, governance issues, such as raising the debt ceiling or funding the operations of the Federal government. Such tactics were directly responsible for shutting down the Federal government from October 1 to October 17, 2013, after the newly emboldened GOP refused to approve funding without the simultaneous defunding of the Affordable Care Act of 2010. Almeida (2010; Almeida and Van Dyke 2014) characterizes this maneuver as an instance of social movement partyism, in that it describes a scenario where a political party adopts tactics generally preferred by outsider groups.

Schlozman (2015) highlighted how shared priorities of social movements and political parties create stable alliances between them. These alliances are based, in part, on the party dependably representing the views of the movement in return for the movement delivering large groups of motivated voters during election cycles. Schlozman's examples include the linkages between the newer alliance of the Republican Party and Christian Right, and the older one of organized labor and the Democratic Party. Social movement tactics, for example bloc recruitment (Oberschall 1993), were used as voter registration drives and turnout operations during major waves of contention, such as the civil rights movement, to put pressure on politicians (Andrews 1997; McAdam 1999). Tea Party activists were an important bloc of Republican voters, in that they were highly motivated, willing to buck party conventions, and uncompromising in their policy objectives.

Mobilization Effects: Protests and Elections

Election cycles provide routinized, predictable pathways for social movements to shape political processes using outsider tactics like protests, demonstrations, and other gatherings. The vast number of federal, state, and local legislative elections in each cycle provide ample targets for activists. Research has been slow to embrace the interrelationships between elections and movements (McAdam and Tarrow 2013), but a growing body of work has emerged to provide a logic for when, how, and why social movements and protest influence electoral processes. McAdam and Tarrow (2010) point to several mechanisms through which social movements become linked to political actors through elections, including joining or building electoral coalitions and increasing intraparty polarization. Social movement groups are strategic in their electoral activities, taking cues from perceived opportunities, threats, or constraints in a specific electoral cycle (Blee and Currier 2006). Importantly, social movement engagements with election cycles are best understood as spatially contingent (legislative district) and temporally specific (election cycle), rather than fixed and aggregative.

Politicians are aware of, and responsive to, protest activity, which we call *mobilization effects*. Though social movement actors are sometimes dismissed as "loud minorities" by politicians (Gillion 2020), they often represent important elements of a political party's base and thereby may draw the disproportionate attention of either incumbents or electoral challengers. Voters may also connect the grievances articulated by social movements to political parties. Bremer and colleagues (2020) show, for instance, that mass protests expressing economic grievances during the Great Recession in 30 European nations amplified grievances and influenced voting behavior.

Social movement mobilization can influence election outcomes through symbolic communication as well. Politicians are responsive to social movement tactics in general (Wouters and Walgrave 2017), but several caveats apply. A study of the ability of the women's movement to influence policy by Fassiotto and Soule (2017) suggested that clear messaging is most likely to have the greatest effect, and other work shows that large, unified protests are more likely to catch the attention of politicians (Wouters and Walgrave 2017). Large, visible street protests may also communicate disagreement with incumbent politicians or existing political arrangements (Gillion and Soule 2018). Such large protests then, may have two potential impacts on elections: they first create a political opportunity for social movements to pressure incumbent candidates running for reelection in primaries to adopt movement goals in hopes of increasing their likelihood of victory; second, they create an opening for aspiring candidates to run against incumbents by signaling that there exists a mass of dissatisfied voters. Both political opportunities are pertinent to understanding the impact of the Tea Party insurgency.

The Interplay between the Grassroots and Institutionalized Tea Party

The preceding discussion grounds the scope of our analysis. For institutionalization, we attend to the formation of the Tea Party Caucus, its trajectory, and the larger ideological spillover of the Tea Party's tactics on sitting members of Congress. We also emphasize how grassroots Tea Party activism – specifically organizational formation and hosting events – intervened in the political process in 2010 and onward, starting with the primaries for the House of Representatives. Our discussion distinguishes between mobilization effects, or the impact of protest, and movement infrastructure effects, based on fragile coalitions between the Tea Party and GOP. The primaries were the first major test of whether and how the street-level activism, popular support, and upward trajectory of the Tea Party insurgency could upend electoral politics. Tea Party activists were critical and skeptical of GOP leadership (Blum 2020; Rafail and McCarthy 2018), so greater influence, or even a takeover of the party, would require either replacing incumbent politicians with challengers sympathetic to the Tea Party movement, or alternatively, forcing sitting politicians to adopt the goals of the insurgency; ideally both.

We emphasize, particularly, the disruptive intervention of the Tea Party over time and across space, heeding Skocpol and Williamson's (2011) emphasis on how grassroots activists played a watchdog role for Republicans. A major aspect in the interplay between the institutionalized and noninstitutionalized factions of the Tea Party was the latter's willingness to drive moderates from electoral politics through long primaries and sharp criticism, thereby hastening ideological radicalization in the GOP.

VOICING DISAPPROVAL: THE 2010 PRIMARIES
AND TEA PARTY ACTIVISM

Competitive primaries were widely adopted in American politics early in the twentieth century (Lawrence, Donovan, and Bowler 2013), replacing a system where candidate selection was controlled entirely by party elites.[1] Political

---

[1] Despite the movement toward democratizing political primaries, the process for presidential nominations remained largely in the control of political parties for several more decades. An example is the 1968 Democratic primary, when Hubert Humphrey secured the nomination without running for a single party primary.

primaries serve several purposes during elections. The primary system is intended to provide predictable, institutionalized opportunities for citizens to affirm their support for an incumbent candidate, or, alternatively, to replace incumbent elected officials who are no longer perceived as adequately representing their constituents. Voters in primary elections tend to be highly motivated members of a party's base, and even open primaries (i.e., those not requiring party membership to participate) do little to moderate the extreme positions of candidates (McGhee et al. 2014). While incumbency is a strong predictor of electoral success (Gelman and King 1990), primaries do, nevertheless, provide an institutionalized pathway for social movements to intervene in the electoral process, potentially altering existing political opportunity structures. McAdam and Kloos (2014) reiterate the fact that primaries, particularly those following the caucus format, have low turnout. As a result, they provide ideal opportunities for the movement wings of a political party.

Incumbent politicians are particularly sensitive to the concerns of primary voters. For example, the fear of backlash by primary voters decreases a legislator's willingness to compromise (Anderson, Butler, and Harbridge-Yong 2020). Protest activity can send a strong signal to an incumbent that a primary challenge may be imminent. Extensive protest signals to challengers indecisive about running that a motivated group of voters exists whose support may prove vital in deciding a tight election. Highly visible protest activity may therefore create strategic opportunities within the electoral process by encouraging political outsiders to run for office. We hypothesize that congressional districts with extensive Tea Party activity saw more challengers, which in turn publicly signaled underlying dissatisfaction with the incumbent's party.

We begin our analysis of the 2010 US House congressional primaries by looking at trends in who ran for office. We use databases maintained by the Federal Elections Commission (FEC) listing all candidates running for office. These data also include key characteristics of each candidate, including whether they were incumbents, challengers, or running for an open seat, and whether they raised more than $0 to support their run for office.[2] A remarkable, but unnoticed facet of the 2010 electoral cycle was the surge of candidates who ran in the Republican Party primaries, coinciding with the growing wave of Tea Party activism. The temporal trend in Republican challengers is shown in Figure 8.1. Since running for office only requires filing minimal paperwork with the FEC, we distinguish between all candidates who filed to run, and the subgroup of candidates who were able to raise at least some funding to support their candidacy. Controlling for at least some fundraising eliminates the least serious candidates but does not change the overall trend in the figure. To contextualize the atypical pattern in the 2010

[2] The data are freely available at fec.gov/data/candidates (accessed January 18, 2022).

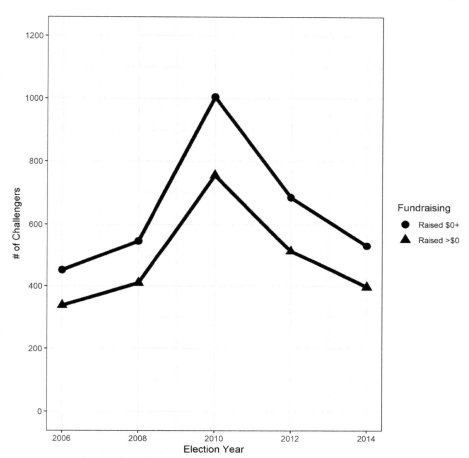

FIGURE 8.1 The number of challengers in the Republican primaries, 2006–2014.

primaries, we also include challenger numbers for the two prior and two subsequent election cycles.

Across both temporal trends in Figure 8.1, the 2010 primaries show a significantly larger number of challengers to incumbent Republicans. In the 2006 and 2008 electoral cycles, there were just 451 and 547 challengers who filed to run in the Republican primaries, respectively, while 338 and 410 candidates were able to secure at least some financial backing. In contrast, the 2010 primaries had an 84% increase in challengers, with 1,005 candidates filing to run. Of these, 76% raised at least some money. The number of challengers in the 2012 election cycle further underscores the atypical number of challengers in 2010, as only 686 challengers declared their candidacy (514 of whom had no funding), while by 2014, there were just 532 Republican challengers to incumbents, and only 398 challengers had raised money.

The Impact of Tea Party Activism on the 2010 Primaries

So far, we have shown the aggregate surge of 2010 primary challengers occurred during the most elevated period of Tea Party activism. Not all Republican primary challengers were likely to have been associated with the Tea Party, however, and those that were may not necessarily have chosen to run in districts that had seen high levels of Tea Party activism. To systematize our claims about the impact of the Tea Party on the 2010 primaries, we analyzed whether the extent of Tea Party activism in a congressional district was associated with more Republican primary challengers. We used a negative binomial regression analysis to account for the number of Republican challengers in the primaries for each of the 435 seats in the House of Representatives in 2010.

Our key independent variables captured two different forms of Tea Party activity, those we call mobilization effects and movement infrastructure effects. Our proxy for mobilization effects was the cumulative count of Tea Party events that took place in a congressional district between February 2009 and June 2010. A total of 3,796 events took place during that time. The event counts were developed from the analysis described in Chapter 5, and combined all meetings, protests, rallies, and other Tea Party gatherings. Second, to assess movement infrastructure effects, we took the cumulative count of Tea Party organizations that were ever active in each congressional district between February 2009 and June 2010, using our database of Tea Party groups described in Chapters 4 and 6. A total of 1,939 Tea Party groups were active during this period. We used a cutoff of June 2010 for our estimate of Tea Party activism since the primaries took place across many races and were resolved at multiple points in time during 2010. Using June as a threshold avoids potential reverse causality. An initial inspection of both variables pointed to a strong skew to the right during the period. Consequently, we used the natural log of each variable in our analysis, adding a constant of 0.1 to congressional districts without any Tea Party events or organizations before June 2010.

We controlled for the political context of each electoral district using two measures. The first is simply the percentage of votes for the Republican candidate in the 2008 election (logged to minimize skew). As we demonstrated in Chapter 3, Tea Party activism found its footing in areas with higher concentrations of Republican voters, so this variable allowed us to account for baseline levels of Republican support that may have attracted primary opponents from the political right. Second, we added a variable for the number of challengers in the district Republican primaries in 2008. This was important to control for congressional districts where primary challengers running for office had been observed in the prior election cycle.

Finally, we used five contextual and demographic control variables. Four of these measures were drawn from the 2010 five-year estimates of the American Community Survey (ACS). We used census tracts as our initial unit of analysis,

TABLE 8.1 *Negative binomial regression of the number of challengers in the 2010 Republican primaries (n=435).*

	Model 1	Model 2
Tea Party Activism		
# Tea Party Events	0.119**	0.156***
	(0.044)	(0.043)
# Tea Party Organizations	−0.032	0.020
	(0.045)	(0.043)
Political Context		
% Republican (2008)		0.304***
		(0.052)
# Challengers (2008)		0.214***
		(0.029)
Control Variables		
% White		0.011
		(0.052)
% Unemployed		−0.001
		(0.031)
Income Inequality		0.004
		(0.004)
% College Educated		−3.243
		(2.059)
Foreclosure Rate		0.007
		(0.133)
Intercept	0.658***	1.983*
	(0.079)	(0.876)
Overdispersion Parameter	2.212***	3.517**

Note: *p<0.05; **p<0.01; ***p<0.001 (two-tailed tests).

which were cross-referenced with congressional districts to create our final values. The variables included the percentage of residents in an electoral district who identified as non-Hispanic White, the percentage unemployed, the percentage of residents over 25 with a college degree or higher, and the Gini Index of income inequality. The fifth variable used the data on foreclosure rates for each congressional district in 2009 produced by the Department of Housing and Urban Development's Neighborhood Stabilization Program described in earlier chapters. Similar to our approach for the ACS data, we started with census tract-level estimates that were aggregated by district to build our final measure.

Our regression analysis is summarized in Table 8.1. The first model, which contains only our measures of Tea Party activism, shows that the number of Tea Party events is linked to an increase in the count of challengers. In contrast, the impact of the density of Tea Party organizations was not statistically significant. Once the full set of variables is included in Model 2, there is a similar pattern of estimates for our two Tea Party activism variables. Even after controlling for the political context of each electoral district and our control variables, each unit increase of Tea Party events increases the expected count of primary challengers. While the magnitude of the effect is small, its cumulative impact on the expected count of challengers is quite pronounced. Districts without Tea Party events had approximately one challenger. The average congressional district had approximately five Tea Party events, which translated to a prediction of two challengers choosing to run in the 2010 primary. Even modest levels of Tea Party activism, therefore, served to put incumbent Republicans on notice that their seats were viewed as potential targets for capture by local Tea Party activists and Republican voters. The impact of Tea Party events on districts with the highest level of Tea Party activism was quite pronounced. Congressional districts with between 40 and 60 Tea Party events, the most active areas in our data, had about three challengers run in the primaries.

The measures capturing the political context of each congressional district add important information to better understand the impact of Tea Party activism on the 2010 election. The coefficients for both variables are positive, indicating that challengers in the 2010 primary were most prevalent in highly Republican areas. Further, our assumption that congressional districts with more challengers in prior cycles would carry over to the 2010 primary is supported. The number of challengers in the 2008 election is positively associated with the number of challengers in 2010.

Overall, the 2010 primary season was clearly atypical compared to the standard electoral process in other years for the Republican Party. This had several consequences for the tone and tenor of the 2010 electoral cycle overall. First, the Tea Party's extensive dislike and mistrust of the GOP highlighted by scholars (Blum 2020; Rafail and McCarthy 2018) was likely linked to efforts at unseating incumbent Republicans in the house. Higher levels of Tea Party activism were signals to incumbent politicians, even those serving safe Republican districts, that disapproval existed within the GOP's base. Second, the core economic variables including unemployment, income inequality, educational attainment, and foreclosures shown earlier to be so important to understanding the emergence of the insurgency did not carry over to create a general dissatisfaction with incumbent politicians. None of our control variables were statistically significant, indicating the crucial factors driving which incumbent GOP representatives were primaried was a mixture of the political context of each district and the extent to which the Tea Party activists staged events.

To summarize, we have shown a strong relationship between mobilizing effects and the number of challengers who ran in the 2010 Republican primaries. Not only did the 2010 primaries produce a large spike in challengers for Republican seats in the House, but patterns of Tea Party activism appear to have intervened in the political process. As Tea Party events increased in a congressional district, so too did the number of challengers. Tea Party organizational strength, our proxy for movement infrastructures, was not a significant predictor of district level incumbent challenge. It is one thing to run as a challenger, but quite another for a challenger to emerge victorious in a general election. We now turn to a detailed discussion of the 2010 general election itself and the Tea Party insurgency's role in shaping its outcomes.

INSTITUTIONALIZED INROADS: THE 2010 MIDTERM ELECTIONS

The 2010 midterm elections were a watershed moment for the Republican Party. After two years of unified Democratic control of the presidency and Congress, the GOP seized the House of Representatives with a net gain of 63 seats, and considerably narrowed the Democratic majority in the Senate to a buffer of just 4 seats. The 2010 election did not just secure the Republican majority in the House, but it also cemented the Tea Party's influence through the creation of a block of affiliated Representatives in the House. How did Tea Party activism intervene in and influence this process?

Our analysis focuses on the relationship between Tea Party activism/organizational formation and electoral outcomes in 2010 for the House of Representatives. We follow work by Gillion (2020) and Gillion and Soule (2018), who have linked patterns of protest activity to electoral outcomes, and McAdam and Tarrow (2010, 2013) and others (Bremer et al. 2020; McAdam and Kloos 2014), who emphasize the sometimes radicalizing effects that social movements can have on political parties. Our central hypothesis is that local Tea Party activism in a congressional district in the 2010 midterm election increased the likelihood that a Republican candidate won. Importantly, our argument is more general than simply suggesting that the Tea Party worked to elect Tea Party candidates. As Skocpol and Williamson (2011) pointed out, local Tea Party groups situated themselves as watchdogs for all Republicans. The Tea Party's emphasis on ideological purity and unwillingness to compromise put even the most secure, traditional Republicans in a precarious position – they risked facing the wrath of their base by taking any cooperative action with the Democratic Party. To the degree that the Tea Party could flex its muscles at the local level, we expect that the probability of Republican victory, Tea Party aligned or not, increased.

As before, we examine the role of mobilization effects and movement infrastructure effects using our variables of Tea Party events and organizations as proxies. Our dependent variable is the outcomes of the 2010 elections for the House of Representatives, again using congressional districts as the unit of analysis. Our dependent variable includes categories for whether the winning candidate was a member of the Tea Party Caucus, the Republican Party, or the Democratic Party. Given this operationalization, we use multinomial logistic regression. Our independent variables largely recycle the measures employed in our earlier analysis of primary challengers. In brief, we used the count of Tea

Party organizations founded by November 1, 2010, before the elections, and the number of unique Tea Party events occurring during that period. In both cases, we took the natural logarithm to correct skewness. We also controlled for the political context of each congressional district using the vote share for the Republican Party in 2008 and the total number of challengers in the 2010 primary. Finally, we controlled for the percentage White, percentage unemployed, percentage of residents with at least a college degree, the Gini index of economic inequality, and the foreclosure rate. These variables were constructed using the operationalizations described in our analyses of the primaries.

The results of our regression analysis are summarized in Table 8.2. We use two models: the first contains only our measures of Tea Party activism, while the second is the full model with the complete set of independent variables.

TABLE 8.2 *Multinomial logistic regression predicting the outcome of the 2010 midterm election in the House of Representatives (n=435).*

	Model 1		Model 2	
	Republican	*TP Caucus*	*Republican*	*TP Caucus*
Tea Party Activism				
# Tea Party Organizations	0.788***	0.905***	0.495*	0.657**
	(0.157)	(0.180)	(0.209)	(0.221)
# Tea Party Events	0.179	0.323	−0.122	0.024
	(0.149)	(0.167)	(0.199)	(0.197)
Political Context				
% Republican (2008)			2.801***	2.675***
			(0.323)	(0.345)
# Challengers (2010)			−0.156*	−0.177*
			(0.069)	(0.084)
Control Variables				
% White			0.573**	0.198
			(0.211)	(0.233)
% Unemployed			−0.232	−0.246
			(0.140)	(0.157)
Income Inequality			−4.141	−0.418
			(9.084)	(10.184)
% College Educated			−0.054***	−0.067***
			(0.016)	(0.019)
Foreclosure Rate			0.493	0.088
			(0.564)	(0.642)
Constant	−0.011	−0.984***	5.395	4.283
	(0.114)	(0.153)	(3.931)	(4.455)

Note: *p<0.05; **p<0.01; ***p<0.001 (two-tailed tests). The base category is that a Democratic Party member won the election.

In both cases, the presence of Tea Party organizations is linked to an increased likelihood of both Republican and Tea Party Caucus victory in the election, relative to congressional districts won by the Democratic Party. In model two, a logged increase of one organization increases the probability of victory by 6% for both Republicans and Tea Party Caucus members relative to Democratic victories (holding other variables constant at their means). This supports the importance of movement infrastructure effects. Tea Party events were not associated with either GOP or Tea Party Caucus members winning a seat in the House, a finding contrasting with the earlier analysis of the 2010 primaries. In other words, these results do not support the role of mobilization effects on electoral outcomes in 2010.

Congressional districts with high levels of GOP support in the 2008 election were most likely to elect members of the Republican Party, a finding consistent for both Tea Party and non-Tea Party–affiliated candidates. Republican primary contests with more challengers did ultimately depress the likelihood of victory for Tea Party Caucus members and Republicans more broadly. Our control variables have mostly inconsistent impacts when we compare the estimates for Tea Party Caucus members with other Republicans. A higher concentration of educated residents in a district lowered the likelihood of victory for both Republicans and Tea Party Caucus members, but none of the other variables are consistently significant. We note that districts with more White residents were more likely to elect Republicans (but not Tea Party Caucus members) relative to districts won by Democrats.

This analysis has several important implications for understanding the 2010 election, as well as how different forms of activism can disrupt institutionalized political processes. First, the presence of Tea Party organizations is associated with an impact on the electoral outcomes in 2010, even after controlling for prior Republican vote share. This increases confidence that the Tea Party effects we identify support our contention that the grassroots insurgency intervened directly in the 2010 electoral cycle. The positive association between Tea Party organizations and members of the GOP who were not affiliated with the Tea Party Caucus also apparently sent a strong signal that Tea Party activists were a crucial block of potential supporters. Given the sensitivity of politicians, both incumbents and candidates, to their base, it is possible that the heavy presence of Tea Party organizations may have incentivized members of the GOP to shift rightward. This finding is particularly interesting, given the weakness of individual Tea Party organizations. In accumulation, however, the national network of Tea Party groups appears to have had powerful movement infrastructure effects.

Second, Tea Party activism was not strictly linked to the electoral victories of Tea Party Caucus members. Instead, the intervention of the insurgency was consistent for both Tea Party–affiliated Republicans and other Republicans. Overall, even though visible street-level activism may have affected the primary process, it did not necessarily carry over to electoral success for politicians aligned with the movement. If anything, highly contentious primaries marked by multiple challengers may have lowered the probability of Tea Party victories in the general election. Such a conclusion is consistent with Blum (2020), who emphasized that Tea Party activists were more than willing to harm GOP candidates to achieve their policy ends.

We conclude that the impact of social movement mobilization on elections is not uniform. Different forms of activism intervene more effectively at specific points in an election cycle. Visible, street-level protests appear to facilitate challengers, while more invisible organization work is associated with electing candidates. As we documented in Chapter 5, many Tea Party organizations had slowly started shifting away from staging protests after the 2010 Tax Day rallies, and instead were hosting meetings. Many of the meetings involved speakers who were either members of the House of Representatives or candidates for office. These linkages between the local Tea Party groups and their representatives may have secured blocks of voters whose members were highly motivated to turn out on election day. In sum, there are important tactical implications about how social movements may shape elections. Different forms of activism create alternative routes of influence for social movements and insurgencies.

THE POLITICAL LEGACY OF THE TEA PARTY INSURGENCY

After the remarkable Tea Party push to victory in the 2010 midterm elections, the new Republican majority in the House faced the task of governing. The insurgency's uncompromising positions on fiscal restraint and taxation left few options for working with Democrats who still controlled the Senate and presidency. How did Tea Party activism shape the agenda of the Republican House of Representatives? We approach this question in two ways. First, we show that much like the trajectory of the insurgency itself, the Tea Party Caucus lost ground almost as quickly as it emerged. Second, despite the disappearance of formal representation of the Tea Party that occurred along with the larger demobilization of grassroots activism, our evidence shows that the most durable consequence of Tea Party activism in the House GOP was a push toward ideological extremism.

The Disappearance of the Tea Party Caucus

Membership in the Tea Party Caucus peaked after the 2010 midterm elections, with 66 representatives joining the caucus during the 112th session of Congress that followed. Most of those caucus members were incumbents who joined with freshman Tea Party members. The Republicans held 242 seats in the House, giving the Tea Party Caucus outsized influence with a membership spanning more than 27% of the full House Republican Conference. The surge of Tea Party politicians was fleeting, however. McNitt (2014) shows that by 2012, electoral success for candidates affiliated with the Tea Party was not tied

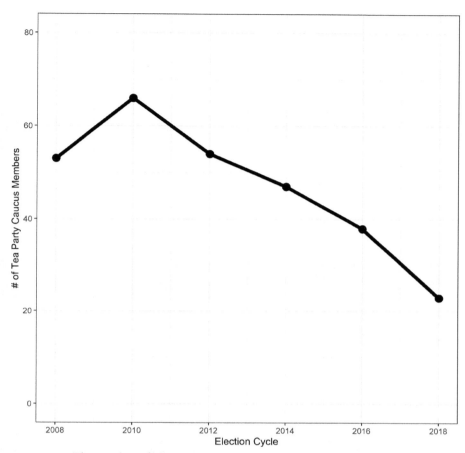

FIGURE 8.2 The number of Tea Party Caucus members in Congress, 2008–2018.

to their affiliation with the insurgency, but instead to more conventional factors like incumbency. Following the 2010 midterm elections, the number of House members who had ever been affiliated with the caucus declined after each subsequent electoral cycle. The count of House of Representatives members who were ever affiliated with the Tea Party Caucus between the 2008 and 2018 election cycles is summarized in Figure 8.2. After the 2012 election, the number of Representatives affiliated with the Tea Party caucus declined to 54, then 47 after the 2014 election, 38 in 2016, and just 23 by 2018. Much like the grassroots Tea Party mobilization, then, the institutionalized faction of the insurgency came and went quite quickly, despite its impact. We note, too, that there was a temporal coincidence between the decline of Tea Party activism – both in events and active chapters – and the declining membership of the Tea Party Caucus.

TABLE 8.3 *Trajectory of 71 politicians affiliated with the Tea Party Caucus, 2010–2018.*

Outcome	Frequency	Percent
Still in House	23	33.39
Retired	18	25.35
Lost Senate Race	7	9.86
Lost General Election	7	9.86
Resigned	5	7.04
Lost Governor Race	4	5.63
Lost Primary	4	5.63
Won Senate Race	2	2.82
Won Governor Race	1	1.41

What became of the Tea Party Caucus? Table 8.3 summarizes the trajectory of Representatives who joined the Tea Party Caucus between the 2010 and 2018 election cycles. We found a total of 71 Republicans who were ever affiliated with the Tea Party Caucus since its formation in the summer of 2010. By 2018, 68% of caucus members no longer remained representatives, while 32% were still in office. The most common reason that Tea Party Caucus members left the House was retirement, the case for 25% of members, including Michele Bachmann, its founder, who left Congress in 2015. Many Tea Party Caucus members held aspirations for higher office, including senate and governorships. Few were successful in these pursuits. Approximately 10% of Tea Party Caucus members went on to lose a bid for a senate seat and another 6% lost a race for governor. Just two members of the Tea Party Caucus – Bill Cassidy of Louisiana and Jerry Moran of Kansas – were able to pivot from the House to the senate, and one – Mike Pence of Indiana – from the House to a governorship. Tea Party Caucus members who ran for reelection in the House largely faced defeat at different stages of the electoral process. Four members (6%) lost their primary and another seven members (10%) lost in a general election. Finally, an additional 5% of the Tea Party Caucus members resigned from the House. Some, like Tom Price of Georgia, resigned to take a position in the Trump administration after the 2016 electoral cycle, while several others resigned due to their involvement in scandals or allegations of illegal conduct. For instance, Blake Farenthold of Texas resigned from the House in April 2018, after allegations that he used taxpayer funds to settle a sexual harassment lawsuit filed by a former staffer. The Tea Party Caucus never formally disbanded, but became inactive by early 2015 with members no longer holding regular meetings. By then, the grassroots Tea Party largely ceased staging events and many local chapters disbanded during this same period. Some House Republicans, including a few former Tea Party Caucus members, joined the similarly hard-right Freedom Caucus. However, there was little continuity in membership between the Tea Party Caucus and Freedom Caucus, as Green's (2019) detailed analysis shows. He found that only seven Tea Party Caucus members joined the Freedom Caucus (p. 9). Even if the critical mass of politicians affiliated with the Tea Party shrank as quickly as it had expanded, we will show that the legacy of grassroots Tea Party activism had a durable impact on the Republican Party, and on American democracy more broadly.

Political Radicalization as a Consequence of Tea Party Activism

By 2014, the grassroots Tea Party showed strong signs of demobilization, described in Chapters 5, 6, and 7. At that point, the Tea Party Caucus had also ceased as an organized faction in the House. Despite the aggregate decline of activity, the legacy of the Tea Party, we argue, remains long-lasting and fundamentally important to understanding the state of current American politics. In this final section of our analysis, we analyze the longer-term impacts of the Tea Party on the GOP. Our evidence suggests that Tea Party activity is linked to the increasing ideological radicalization in the Republican Party, which not only paved the way for Donald Trump's presidency but further eroded American democratic institutions.[3] In short, we show the importance of the Tea Party's legacy in hastening the process of radicalization.

We begin by showing how the trajectory of political ideology evolved in the House using the mean political ideology of House of Representative members over all electoral cycles between 2008 and 2018. The results are shown in Figure 8.3. This period captures the rise and fall of the Tea Party, both its institutionalized and grassroots factions. We separate the political ideology scores for Tea Party Caucus members from other Republicans and Democrats using the Nokken-Poole multidimensional scaling scores, also referred to as the DW-Nominate scores. These scores were proposed by Nokken and Poole (2004) based on patterns of roll-call voting as a barometer of underlying political ideology. The values are bound between −1 and 1 and are scaled so that higher values indicate heightened conservatism. Other scales have been proposed to capture political ideology, but the DW-Nominate scores offer several advantages for our purposes (see also McCarty 2016). In particular, the DW-Nominate scores are updated for each congressional session rather than by tracking individual politicians over their careers, allowing us to capture the individual and aggregate changes taking place in the House in a manner that is temporally and contextually specific. This operationalization is necessary for us to link Tea Party activism to changes in voting behavior.

The trends in Figure 8.3 indicate that of the three factions we examine, the Tea Party Caucus displayed the most conservative voting record, followed by

---

[3] We prefer the term radicalization to polarization, since the growing ideological gap between parties is largely a consequence of the Republican Party drifting to the right, while the Democrats remained largely stable. See Figure 8.3.

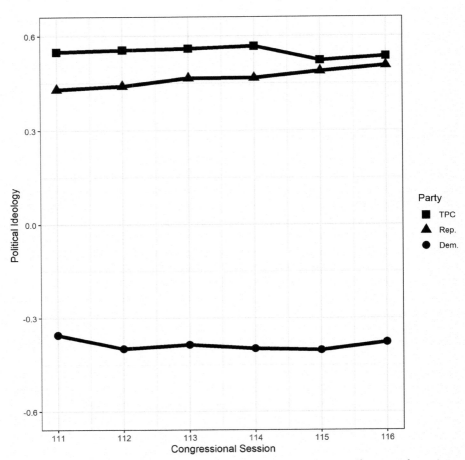

FIGURE 8.3 Political ideology in the House of Representatives, 111th to 116th sessions of Congress.
Notes: Estimates are based on the mean DW-Nominate scores.

the GOP.[4] The gap between Republicans writ large and Democrats was pronounced over our analysis, and only widened over time. While the rightward shift in political ideology for the Republican and Tea Party Caucus members might appear slight, it is salient and consequential. We estimated an Analysis of

---

[4] A parallel analysis by Vann (2021), using an alternative operationalization of Tea Party association, emphasized only the economic portion of the DW-Nominate scores. His results show little impact of grassroots Tea Party activism. Vann's measures of Tea Party activity come from the Institute for Research and Education on Human Rights (IREHR) database of Tea Party activity in 2010, and do not account for the more granular spatiotemporal activity patterns that we do here. Both time and space are essential to accurately estimate the impact of Tea Party activism.

Variance model designed to assess whether the overall trajectory seen in Figure 8.3 is statistically significant. The overall model, main effects, and interactions are statistically significant at the 95% level of confidence. Substantively, the results indicate that 1) there are statistically significant differences in political ideology between the Tea Party Caucus members, Republicans, and Democrats; 2) the differences grew over time; and 3) the gap between these groups also increased over time.

The initial finding of increased conservatism in the House by political faction is temporally consistent with the rise and fall of the Tea Party insurgency, but far from a systematic relationship. We now turn to a statistical analysis that more rigorously contextualizes the growth in more radical ideology. As before, we emphasize the mobilization effects and movement infrastructure effects, and argue that Tea Party activism might influence the behavior of House members beyond the Tea Party Caucus for two reasons. First, many Republicans flirted with the Tea Party, even if they did not directly join the Tea Party Caucus or otherwise align themselves with the insurgency. Gervais and Morris (2018) show that a significant portion of the Republican conference were "Tea Party adjacent," meaning they may have praised the Tea Party's ideology or tactics, spoken at rallies, or attended meetings without joining the Tea Party Caucus itself. As a result, such politicians are inclined to vote consistently with the preferences of the Tea Party. Second, Skocpol and Williamson (2011) document how the Tea Party served as an ideological watchdog of the Republican Party, working to ensure high levels of conformity on matters of policy. Such informal oversight was directly responsible for pushing the GOP to the political right. In both cases, then, we expected that Tea Party activity increased radicalization.

Our statistical analysis used the DW-Nominate scores for each House member as the dependent variable.[5] We used multilevel linear models, with congressional district years nested in congressional districts. The dependent variable was updated every two years for each congressional district to match the electoral cycles in the House. The analysis included the 111th through 116th sessions of Congress, generating a total of 2,610 cases (from 435 seats x 6 sessions). Overall, this analysis is ideal for examining the rise of political extremism more directly relative to localized spatiotemporal patterns of Tea Party activity, net of other key covariates.

The independent variables follow our earlier analyses of the 2010 primaries and general election described previously in this chapter. The key independent variables were, again, two measures of Tea Party activity, proxies for mobilization effects and movement infrastructure effects. First, we used the cumulative number of events, and second, the cumulative number of organizations. As in

---

[5] Our analysis includes all political parties since activism took place in Democratic, Republican, and Tea Party Caucus districts. Retaining all districts also helped us control for swing districts that might vary by party across congressional cycles.

TABLE 8.4 *Multilevel linear regression of the ideological position of members in the House of Representative, 111th to 116th sessions of Congress (n=2,610).*

	Model 1	Model 2
Tea Party Effects		
# Tea Party Orgs.	0.150***	0.097***
	(0.009)	(0.008)
# Tea Party Events	0.016*	0.019**
	(0.007)	(0.007)
Control Variables		
% Republican		0.006***
		(0.0003)
% White		0.007***
		(0.0005)
% Unemployed		0.006**
		(0.002)
Income Inequality		−2.095***
		(0.341)
% College Educated		−0.002***
		(0.0005)
Constant	0.063***	0.290
	(0.017)	(0.149)
Level-2 Variance on Intercept	0.121	0.060

Note: Ideological position is based on the DW-Nominate scores. Congressional sessions are nested in districts. *p<0.05; **p<0.01; ***p<0.001 (two-tailed tests).

previous analyses, these variables were operationalized to avoid temporal spuriousness by updating our cumulative counts after each congressional session. There were a total of 19,758 events and 3,587 organizations by the end of our analytic period. Importantly, we controlled for the Republican vote share for the prior election, as more conservative areas would have elected politicians with more conservative policy positions. We also included the percentage of non-Hispanic Whites, the percentage unemployed, the Gini index of income inequality, and the percentage college educated, using operationalizations described in our analysis of primary challengers and the 2010 election. The variable on foreclosures is omitted since it was based on data collected between 2007 and 2008 – the height of the Great Recession – that we did not expect to have remained relevant by the end of our analytic period.

Table 8.4 summarizes our statistical analysis using a partial model containing our Tea Party covariates and a full model with the Tea Party variables and all other controls. In both cases, our estimates of Tea Party activism point to substantively important roles in the growing Republican radicalization in

Congress by pushing politicians to adopt increasingly conservative positions. Though we control for Republican support and several other factors, each additional logged increase in local Tea Party groups is associated with a 0.097 growth in the DW-Nominate score. Similarly, each additional logged increase in local Tea Party events produced an estimated 0.019 increase in political conservativism, net of other variables. Since the DW-Nominate score is bound between −1 and 1, this is a notable effect size, suggesting that Republican politicians were at least partially reacting to the extent of Tea Party activism taking place in their district when casting votes. The vote share for Republicans further increased the estimated ideology score, yet does not moderate the Tea Party effect. Notably, each of our control variables is also a statistically significant predictor of the DW-Nominate scores, but they also do not eliminate the association between Tea Party activism and voting behavior.

The impact of Tea Party activism on the GOP has not been systematically examined by researchers, locally or over a long period of time. These results, therefore, fill an important gap in the literature and contextualize the larger impacts of the Tea Party insurgency on American politics. In short, the analysis indicates that even after controlling for a variety of contextual and demographic factors, Tea Party activism was positively associated with Republican House members shifting to the political right. This shift remained intact even after Tea Party activism declined and local groups ceased operating. The Tea Party served as an ideological watchdog for the GOP: from our analysis of the 2010 electoral cycle, the Tea Party followed through on its threats to politicians not deemed appropriately conservative by mounting challengers or intervening in elections themselves. We suggest that this common state of affairs nudged Republicans, regardless of their support of the Tea Party and its tactics, to move further to the political right in hopes of avoiding critical scrutiny.

CONCLUSION

This chapter raises some important, but largely unexamined questions about the Tea Party and its legacy in American politics. In summary, we have convincingly shown that Tea Party activism disrupted three important aspects of the political and electoral processes after its emergence: first, it disrupted the 2010 Republican primaries by signaling grassroots disappointment with the many incumbents; second, the Tea Party's role as an uncompromising watchdog coupled with its rapid ascendency was strongly linked to the election or reelection of a bloc of politicians affiliated with the insurgency; last, we show that both forms of Tea Party activism – events and organizational presence – played an important part in driving radicalization in the Republican Party. That impact continued even after the Tea Party Caucus ceased activity and the grassroots Tea Party demobilized. These findings have several implications.

First, mobilization effects, or widespread public protest, can put incumbent politicians on notice through the primary process. A surge in challengers during primaries may communicate to incumbents that a faction of the party's base is dissatisfied with their performance. We suspect it likely that politicians respond to such signals by modifying their positions to stymie future challenges. Though there are important spatiotemporal contingencies in the effectiveness of social movement mobilization, following McAdam and Kloos (2014), we show that primaries are an important way for social movements to shape the trajectory of political parties.

Second, social movement infrastructures can have differential impacts on institutionalized, and especially electoral, politics. While Tea Party events, especially protest, were associated with the emergence of primary challengers, organizational density was linked to electoral outcomes in 2010, consistent with Andrews' (2001) analyses of the civil rights movement and anti-poverty programs. We suspect this reflects the tactical evolution of the Tea Party, described in Chapter 5. The widespread use of public protest early in the Tea Party insurgency's lifecycle signaled a political opportunity to incumbents and aspiring politicians. As local Tea Parties turned their focus to holding meetings and semipublic events, they laid the groundwork for mobilizing the most conservative voters, especially those who, while identifying with the GOP, were seriously disaffected from the Republican status quo.

Third, the Tea Party's impacts were relevant long after the insurgency effectively demobilized as a grassroots movement and political faction. During the height of its power, both the grassroots and institutionalized factions of the Tea Party rejected compromise, and ultimately pulled both incumbent and new members of the House of Representatives to the political right. This is not to say that political radicalization started with the birth of the Tea Party insurgency in 2009; it certainly had begun earlier – witness the incumbent House members who jumped at the opportunity to join the Tea Party Caucus. Our work began with the question of whether increasingly partisan voting took root in geographical areas where the Tea Party prospered. Our evidence indicates that it did, and that the course it set for the GOP did not change even as the Tea Party's impact waned. The enduring influence of the Tea Party also appears to have carried on even as the volume of events dwindled, and local chapters disbanded. It is highly plausible that the activists who took part in the insurgency remained motivated to vote, participate in primaries, and otherwise hold politicians to account even after the demobilization of the grassroots Tea Party.

We close this chapter noting two limitations of our analyses. First, our focus has been primarily on the House of Representatives because it is the most localized branch of the federal government. The larger dynamics we have illuminated no doubt extends beyond the House to the GOP as a whole. For instance, work by Medzihorsky and colleagues (2014), using textual analysis of Republican rhetoric during primary debates between 2008 and 2012, points to a notable shift in discourse toward Tea Party talking points. GOP candidates, in short, quickly fell in ideological line, much like they did a few years later after

Donald Trump's successful bid for the Republican nomination for President and victory in November of 2016.

Finally, it is widely understood that elite political radicalization – or voting patterns by political leaders – has been increasing in US politics for several decades (Baldassarri and Gelman 2008). This rapid shift toward radicalization on the right may be less true for individual citizens (Fiorina and Abrams 2008). However, our results suggest that when highly partisan voters adopt social movement tactics, they may further exacerbate the ideological gap between the political parties. Had the Tea Party insurgency been smaller or fizzled out soon after its inception, the march toward political radicalization would probably have continued, though perhaps with less force. However, our analysis suggests that the Tea Party's grassroots activism not only hastened this process, but did so through localized political processes that created accessible political opportunities for citizens. The march toward increasing radicalization in the House characterizes the Republican Party, in general, and its base more broadly. In our final empirical chapter, Chapter 9, we extend this claim by arguing that the Tea Party's influence on the GOP's political identity had an unexpected consequence: it laid the groundwork for the election of Donald Trump as president.

9

From Ridicule to Unbridled Enthusiasm

The Tea Party's Slow Embrace of Trumpism

As the 2016 presidential election approached, the Tea Party had largely ceased to exist as anything resembling an insurgency. Compared to its peak mobilization only a few groups remained active, protests were rare, and the Tea Party's messaging had become unfocused. While the institutionalized wing of the Tea Party had entered Congress in 2010, most of the politicians affiliated with the insurgency were voted out, had retired, or otherwise left office. The radicalization of the larger Republican Party (the "Grand Old Party" [GOP]) that we linked to Tea Party activism in Chapter 8 created an opening for a brash, unapologetic candidate such as Donald Trump to capture the party and bend it to his own vision of conservatism.

The candidacy and eventual victory of Donald Trump in the 2016 presidential election appeared, at first, to be a continuation of the populist, hardline conservatism espoused by the Tea Party. Despite the apparent resemblance, as Rohlinger and Bunnage (2017) note, little research has been designed to systematically uncover such purported direct connections between the Tea Party and Donald Trump's political candidacy. The most comprehensive effort to demonstrate such connections to date is Gervais and Morris' (2018) analysis linking the Tea Party to Trump using a concept the authors call reactionary republicanism. Reactionary republicanism emphasizes feelings of resentment among White, religious conservatives who came to be strong supporters of the Tea Party, paving the way for the Tea Party surge in the House of Representatives. This in turn provided the fertile ground for the election of Donald Trump. Gervais and Morris' important analysis clarifies how the institutionalized, congressional, segment of the Tea Party was linked to Trump's rise, a conclusion similar to our emphasis throughout this book on the importance of status threats in motivating Tea Party activism. However, there is only scant, if any, research examining these connections that existed between the grassroots elements of the Tea Party and Trump's candidacy. One study by Westermeyer (2022) also emphasizes White identity as a bridge between Trump and the Tea Party, arguing that activists slowly and reluctantly came to support Trump's movement. We trace the evolution of Tea Party assessments of Donald Trump from 2009 to 2018 and integrate those trends with an analysis of the extent to which Tea Party strength in local communities during its heyday was predictive of support for Trump in the 2016 primary and general elections.

We focus on how the Tea Party assessed Trump's evolution from a private citizen to a GOP leader between 2009 through 2018. The Tea Party's eventual embrace of Donald Trump followed a quite different path than earlier work has suggested. The trajectory of the Tea Party is markedly distinct from that of the larger GOP in several important ways. From its beginnings through the 2012 election, the Tea Party embraced, applauded, and adopted Trump's birtherism, a campaign to cast doubt on Barack Obama's eligibility to serve as president based on a conspiracy theory that he was born in Kenya and thus not a natural-born American citizen. Few in the Republican leadership endorsed the birther conspiracy, much to the chagrin of Tea Party activists. With respect to Trump's viability as a political candidate, the Tea Party was sharply critical of the prospect, and activists steadily maintained this position until Trump became president-elect. The Tea Party questioned Trump's commitment to conservatism, and ridiculed his past financial contributions to Democratic politicians. Activists also derided Trump's earlier prior presidential aspirations, which were widely viewed as attention-seeking.

Our analysis of these trends led us to hypothesize, against the tide of social and political analysis, that communities with greater Tea Party activism would be less likely to support Trump in the 2016 primaries and general election. As we expected, Tea Party activism had little discernible influence in predicting support for Trump in both the primary elections and 2016 general election. Tea Party activists did eventually embrace Trump, much like the rest of the GOP, but only after his early decisions as president-elect made it clear he planned to pursue many of the policy preferences of conservatives. By then, their earlier criticisms of Trump were largely forgotten.

We proceed by summarizing the research on the rise of Trumpism as a political movement providing a broader theoretical context for our analyses. Then, we denote three periods marking the evolution of Tea Party's views on Trump and Trumpism: 1) the early engagement period through the 2012 presidential election; 2) the uneven embrace period lasting through the Republican National Convention in 2016; and finally, 3) the period of unbridled enthusiasm when the Tea Party mounted a full-throated defense of Trump's America First platform.

THE RISE OF TRUMPISM

Donald Trump's electoral victory in 2016 generated an extensive social science literature. While our goal in this chapter is to analyze how the Tea Party engaged with Trump over the insurgency's life course, we begin by grounding our discussion in the larger literature on the rise of Trumpism. A widely cited account of Trumpism characterized it as a populist movement spurred by Donald Trump's emphasis on nationalism, the mistrust of experts, and anti-elitism (Oliver and Rahn 2016). Trumpism was further seen as characterized by a departure from existing free trade orthodoxy and Western diplomatic norms, restrictions on immigration, and the aggressive enforcement of immigration law. Scholars of Trumpism have produced two explanations of his candidacy as he ascended to the presidency (Manza and Crowley 2018). The first emphasizes the role of *status threats* while the second focuses on the role of *material threats*.

Status Threats

The central argument of the status threat explanation speculates that Trump's rise was linked to a slow and steady chipping away of existing hierarchies of race and gender coupled with rising levels of anti-immigrant sentiment, authoritarianism, and nativism within the electorate. Crucial here was Trump's unapologetic advocacy for White, male, Christians, whose societal dominance was perceived as being diluted because of demographic shifts that occurred over several decades. Trumpism, in short, appeared to provide a path to reclaiming and retaining a socially superordinate status for its supporters, which resonated with a large group of voters who felt left behind by Republican Party leaders (MacWilliams 2016). The emphasis on status threats can help explain apparent ambiguities in Trump's electoral coalition. For example, evangelicals were overrepresented among Trump supporters despite tension between Trump's record of personal behavior and the values important to evangelical Christians (Margolis 2020).

Mutz (2018) provides one of the most comprehensive studies conceptualizing and empirically assessing the role of status threats in predicting Trump support by analyzing patterns of presidential voting in 2016. Her analyses compare variables capturing material and economic factors to a second set of indicators constructed to gauge status threats. Mutz concludes that economic and material concerns had a limited impact on voting for Trump in the 2016 election, while attitudes toward China, views about social dominance, and other status threats had substantial explanatory power. Additional research has corroborated the linkages between Trump support and authoritarianism (Sherman 2018; Womick et al. 2019), sexism (Ratliff et al. 2019), and anti-elitism (Grossmann and Thaler 2018).

Material Threats

Material threat explanations for the rise of Trumpism center, instead, on the role of economic anxiety and changes to the organization of work that increasingly disadvantaged the White working class (WWC). The central thesis here is that Trump secured the support of the WWC as a result of his emphasis on undoing social, structural, and economic changes that had undermined job growth, depressed wages, and reduced economic opportunities. These material threats disproportionately affected the WWC, who as a result were motivated to support Trump's campaign. This absorption of the WWC expanded the traditional GOP base and was instrumental in Trump's razor-thin margins of victory (Morgan and Lee 2018).

Several studies have found support for the material threat hypothesis. Patenaude (2019) showed that economic anxiety predicted support both for the Tea Party in 2010 as well as Trump in 2016. Work by Morgan and Lee (2017) also suggested that the rate of electoral participation by the WWC did increase in the 2016 election, consistent with expectations of the material threat hypothesis. Rothwell and Diego-Rosell (2016) confirmed that Trump support was disproportionately high among blue-collar workers, with the caveat that those supporters, in fact, commanded greater socioeconomic resources than working class nonsupporters, a pattern also shown by Manza and Crowley (2017).

From the Tea Party to Trump?

Neither of these two explanations for the rise of Trumpism has received consistent support in subsequent research, nor do researchers discuss the role of the Tea Party much at all, despite its previous outsized influence on the congressional Republican Party. On the first point, Morgan and Lee (2017) show that while the turnout of WWC voters did increase in the 2016 election, there is little evidence that Trump's campaign activated racial animus or anti-immigration sentiment to any degree that had not already been present among those voters. Morgan's (2018) careful reanalysis of Mutz's (2018) data also suggests that the support for status threats may be an artifact of modeling rather than a genuine empirical relationship, casting doubt on the overall veracity of the status threat explanation. As we have noted, it is almost certainly the case that status threats are linked to Tea Party activism (see also Barreto et al. 2011; Parker and Barreto 2014). There is also obvious overlap between the Tea Party's vision of itself representing "real" Americans and Trump's emphasis on taking back America. Others have questioned the degree to which Trump's supporters were members of the working class, based on their comparatively high levels of material resources. Manza and Crowley (2017) analyze primary voters and conclude that, while Trump supporters had lower median income and educational attainment compared to non-Trump Republicans in the 2016 primaries, Trump voters were in aggregate above state averages in both income and education.

The accumulation of ambiguous evidence carries over to research seeking strong and widespread connections between the Tea Party and Trump's political movement. Parker and Barreto (2014), Skocpol (2020), Blum (2020),

Gervais and Morris (2018), and Westermeyer (2022) emphasize the importance of grievances in motivating both the Tea Party and Trump, especially the role of racial resentment and ethnonationalism, and there is little doubt that such sentiments motivated support for Trump's candidacy. In contrast, Rohlinger and Bunnage (2017) emphasize the Tea Party's dissatisfaction with GOP leadership, suggesting that such dissatisfaction created a vacuum that Trump filled with his campaign. As we showed in Chapter 4, participants in the Tea Party were disproportionately at risk of being affected by the Great Recession and were located at the margins of the middle class compared to the more working-class constituency that defined Trump's electoral coalition. It is unclear why seamless transitions from the Tea Party to Trumpism should have been expected other than the fact that the two each fundamentally transformed the status quo of the GOP. The core positions of the Tea Party, at least initially, were inconsistent with the hardline populist policies defining Trump's campaign (McVeigh and Estep 2019:90). Thus, there remains a significant gap in evidence for firmly establishing whether the Tea Party had any direct role in the rise of Trumpism, and the degree to which the two constituencies overlapped.

THE TEA PARTY'S UNEVEN ADOPTION OF TRUMPISM

The Tea Party's interactions with Donald Trump stretch back to the birth of the insurgency. Prior to his victory in 2016, Trump had actively courted the Tea Party in an earlier, quickly abandoned, bid for the presidency in 2012. Understanding how the Tea Party, or what was left of it by 2016, came to embrace Trump requires describing the slow evolution of what began as a total dismissal of Trump that evolved into unconditional support. We use a mixed-methods research design to develop a more detailed, process-based, understanding of how the Tea Party engaged with Trump over time.

The analyses are anchored in three periods that define the Tea Party's changing relationship with Donald Trump. First, we focus on the *early engagements* with Trump from February 19, 2009, through the presidential election held on November 6, 2012. During that period, Tea Party activists supported Trump's campaign to question the eligibility of Barack Obama to serve as President, but few supported Trump's broader political aspirations. Next, we describe the Tea Party's pivot toward an *uneven embrace* of Trump from November 7, 2012, until he became the Republican nominee for the presidency on July 21, 2016. During that period, Trump actively courted the Tea Party while at the same time most Tea Party activists remained critical of his candidacy and doubtful of its viability. The final period began at the conclusion of the 2016 primary and continued through the end of our analysis in 2018. By then, the few remaining Tea Partiers, the insurgency's remnant, expressed *unbridled enthusiasm* in their support for Trump as the Republican nominee and eventually as president. Importantly, our blog data cover the lifespan of the insurgency, allowing us to capture the varying reactions to Donald Trump

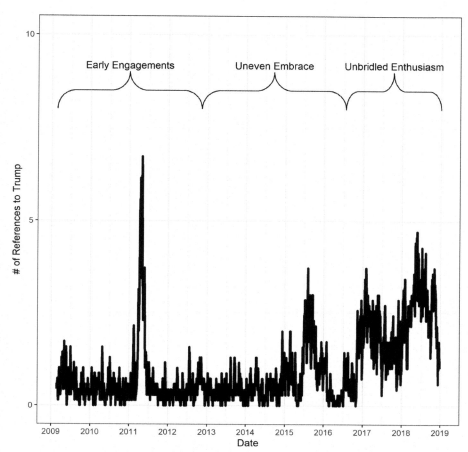

FIGURE 9.1 Tea Party blog posts mentioning Donald Trump, 2009–2018.
Note: Estimates are based on seven-day moving averages; *n*=1,494 posts mentioning Donald Trump.

across the origins, maturation, and decline of Tea Party activism. Since these data were collected contemporaneously, there is less risk of the survivorship bias that comes with relying on the Tea Party's remnants who continued blogging despite the larger decline of grassroot activism.

These periods are marked by major developments in the evolution of the Tea Party and Trump's takeover of the Republican Party. The temporal ebb and flow of Tea Party bloggers' discussion of Trump is plotted in Figure 9.1. The values are based on keyword searches identifying 1,494 blog posts referencing Donald Trump published during three periods. These posts were drawn from our corpus of 91,874 blog posts analyzed in Chapter 7, which represented a census of all blogs posted on the websites of core Tea Party umbrella groups including the 1776 Tea Party, FreedomWorks, Patriot Action Network, Tea Party Patriots, and Tea Party Nation. Individual posts were aggregated to produce daily counts. Figure 9.1 shows how the Tea Party's engagement with Trump as a subject was not constant over time, but instead is better understood to proceed in fits and starts. The substance of the Tea Party's reaction to Trump changed dramatically through these periods. Throughout this chapter, we use illustrative quotations from activists discussing Trump. These are presented verbatim, including the many typographical errors present in the original material. We have left such material intact to more accurately capture the tone of the discourse circulating on Tea Party websites. Numerous statements are drawn from posts authored by rank-and-file Tea Party members, so we avoid listing author information or the originating webpage to preserve some level of confidentiality for authors.

These blogs are an ideal source of evidence to understand the Tea Party's contemporaneous reactions as Trump's role as a GOP leader crystallized over nearly a decade. The posts were written by Tea Party actors, including both those in leadership positions and rank-and-file members. This rich blog archive forms the backbone of our analysis in this chapter. For the uneven embrace and the unbridled enthusiasm periods, we supplemented our analyses of the blog posts with statistical modeling of electoral data from the 2016 Republican primary and the 2016 presidential election. Doing so allowed us to assess the associations between hotspots of Tea Party activism and support for Trump.

Early Engagements: Birtherism, CPAC 2011, and the 2012 Presidential Election

The 265 blog posts written by Tea Party leaders and activists that directly mentioned Donald Trump in some capacity serve as our primary data for characterizing the early engagements period. We used summative content analysis (Hsieh and Shannon 2005), where we iteratively read the full text of each blog post to develop coarse codes, which were then refined over several iterations. Two primary themes emerged from that analysis: first Tea Party discussions of Trump's endorsement of the birther conspiracy, and second discussion of Trump's viability as a political candidate in the 2012 election. We discuss each theme in detail along with the more refined codes that emerged from our analysis.

By far the dominant theme in Tea Party blog posts referencing Trump was uniformly positive reactions to Trump's advocacy for the false birther conspiracy theory, which was overwhelmingly accepted as factual by Tea Partiers. Under Article 2 of the Constitution, it is a requirement that presidents have been born in the US. Birthers referred to this as the "eligibility issue" and argued that Obama was likely born in Kenya, sometimes citing fraudulent evidence that he had registered as a foreign student while attending Columbia University. Though baseless, the birther conspiracy gained rapid traction, especially among the political right and Whites holding anti-Black views (Jardina and Traugott 2019). Birther views became sufficiently mainstream that Obama released his long-form birth certificate in 2011, though many birthers claimed the document to be a forgery, remaining steadfast in their claims that Obama was not a natural born citizen.

Of the 265 blog posts we examined for this period, 37% referenced the birther conspiracy at least once. Tea Party activists lauded Trump's efforts to push the birther conspiracy to the national stage; one poster emphasized the role of Trump's celebrity status: "Donald Trump had the celebrity firepower to bring the eligibility issue to the public consciousness" (Blog ID: #10715). Other posters noted that Trump's financial resources would allow him to mount a thorough investigation of Obama's birth. Typical commentary included statements such as: "I am sure Trump has enough money to get Odinga to turn on his half-white illegitimate cousin here in the states! I bet for $500 K Odinga would turn on his grandmother let alone his bigamy-created-Muslim-cousin Barack! At any rate, MY THANKS GOES TO DONALD TRUMP!" (Blog ID # 18854). Another widespread theme was Trump's relentlessness about the birther issue, which they believed was what forced Obama to eventually release his long-form birth certificate:

The fact that you [Barack Obama] would demean the voters of America by calling their demand for your "long form" birth certificate as "silliness" is an insult an obscenity to these tens of millions of voters. It was not until we the people, the tens of millions of us, had a fearless leader named Donald Trump who was able to take the lead on this important constitutional issue that you came forth with your "long form" birth certificate. (Blog ID # 5716)

In summary, the Tea Party emphasized the mythos of Donald Trump as a resourceful, ruthless, obscenely wealthy businessperson who was willing to ignore political orthodoxy to unravel the issue of Obama's "true" place of birth. This fit neatly with the Tea Party's wholesale rejection of not just Obama's policies, but of his personhood too, emanating from their exclusive vision of patriotism that we have emphasized previously. Trump's advocacy of the birther position filled a void created by the reluctance of GOP leadership, especially Speaker John Boehner, to discuss the issue, which was a complaint repeatedly voiced by Tea Party bloggers.

The embrace of birtherism also provided a useful foil for the Tea Party, which had mostly adopted race-neutral rhetoric in its policy positions on big government, taxation, and spending (Lowndes 2012). This is consistent with the larger conservative movement, which understood spending on welfare and other entitlement programs as disproportionately benefiting non-Whites (Skocpol and Williamson 2011), thereby converting anti-minority sentiments into broader opposition to government programs (Lowndes 2012). Birtherism was an opportunity to use racially coded rhetoric as a dog whistle – sometimes a bullhorn – to motivate the fringes of the conservative movement, while framing these issues around the more innocuous issue of constitutional eligibility. The birther issue allowed the Tea Party insurgency to find a fictitious, but prima facie race-neutral, pathway to challenge the legitimacy of Obama rooted in a larger cultural understanding that conflated Whiteness and citizenship (Hughey 2012).

Obama's Otherness coupled with racialized commentary was widely present in discussions of Trump and birtherism. Posters regularly referenced Barack *Hussein* Obama, adding his Middle Eastern middle name (often in capital letters) to further underscore his Otherness in contrast with White America. Many posts also referred to Obama as Barry Soetoro, which they erroneously claimed was his Kenyan birth name. Most frequently, however, was the claim that Obama was a practicing Muslim, a point, importantly, that was immaterial to his eligibility to serve as president. One representative post claimed that "Obama is a Kenyan Born Muslim who hates America" (Blog ID # 1426), while another stated that "Trump is ready to boil those Arabs in their own oil, bring those arrogant Chinese back to realty [Obama was] not born in America and a true Muslim and a communist all negatives to any real American patriot" (Blog ID #3153).

While the blog data suggest that Trump quickly came into the good graces of the Tea Party by moving the birther issue into the national conversation, the party's support for Trump as a political candidate reflected an entirely different tone. By 2011, Trump was actively attending Tea Party events and secured a speaking slot at the 2011 Conservative Political Action Committee (CPAC), a bona fide credential for viable conservative Republican candidates planning a presidential run. The speech itself largely spoke to the themes that would dominate Trump's candidacy in 2016, emphasizing issues of trade, the need for strong leaders to negotiate with other world powers, an opposition to Obama's signature healthcare reform, and his own accomplishments. Trump performed well in early polling for the 2012 election, but his support rapidly declined. He ultimately announced that he would not run for president in the 2012 electoral cycle.

The blog posts for that period indicate that the Tea Party did not take Trump's candidacy seriously, nor did they treat it as desirable or viable. Criticisms of Trump as a political candidate, the second-most frequent theme, appeared in 24 of the blog posts. Several rationales were offered to buttress their criticisms. Most commonly, Tea Party activists believed Trump was not a conservative, did not understand conservative policy positions, and was not committed to conservative values. A representative example is a post arguing "Trump is NOT a conservative and does not deserve our votes, even if he would be better than Obama" (Blog ID # 964). Activists consistently pointed out that Trump had routinely donated to Democratic candidates and that Trump Organization executive Michael Cohen, who later achieved notoriety for his role in paying off Stormy Daniels, a pornographic actress, to remain quiet about her alleged relationship with Trump, had a previously "impressive political background in Democratic politics" (Blog ID # 10930).

Other bloggers suggested that Trump's belabored final decision about whether he would run was a direct result of his vanity. One argued that:

Donald Trump is a shameless self-promoter. His prowess as a developer and business-man has been greatly exaggerated … He is an outsized egotist (about on a par with Obama) whose passion for self-congratulation is the only reliable thing we know about him. And that his future candidacy for president may soon be taken seriously owes to no one so much as it does Barack Obama, whose own candidacy seriously eroded the standards for presidential qualification. (Blog ID #17436)

Many comments were driven by Trump's repeated claims that he would run for higher office dating back to the 1980s, only to withdraw after making new headlines. Such decisions were widely viewed by Tea Partiers as tactics to increase attention for the Trump Organization generally, and to boost ratings for Trump's reality television show *The Apprentice* particularly. One Tea Party blogger discussed Trump's claim that Obama had been a weak student, saying "Trump, who is pretending to mull over a run at the GOP Presidential nomin-ation in 2012, offered no proof for his claim [about Obama's academic per-formance], other than the fact that it would generate a lot of media coverage for his tedious reality show" (Blog ID # 12889).

A less frequent, but nonetheless consistent, theme was the claim that Trump was a stooge candidate who was feigning a presidential run, perhaps at the direction of the Obama campaign. One blogger noted that "as for Donald Trump, he is the definition of a fraud. He's in bed with more Democrats and is probably in the race to serve the Democrats" (Blog ID # 53282). Another blogger similarly noted that "Trump is the next usurper the next egomaniac who is bought and sold by Progressive Democrats. It is no accident Trump shows up days before Egobama launches his campaign. Trump is playing upon Conservative angst" (Blog ID # 6545). Other common themes emphasized Trump's flip-flopping on core conservative issues such as abortion, gun control, and healthcare reform. Overall, Tea Party activists were interested in 2012 can-didates like Michele Bachmann and Sarah Palin, who were widely regarded as allies favorable to the Tea Party and its agenda, and most likely to implement conservative policies if elected.

Even though most of the early opinions expressed about Trump's political aspirations were critical and dismissive, a few Tea Partiers were a bit more optimistic about his candidacy. The common thread among those with more positive views was his outsider status and willingness to challenge Republican leadership. One blogger wrote "so what's the appeal Donald has for the Patriot Movement? It's not difficult to figure out. All you have to do is look at the prevaricating hogwash we're getting out of our leadership" (Blog ID # 48963). Even among those favoring Trump's candidacy, support was conditional and often only treated Trump as a viable candidate relative to Obama or on a small number of policy issues. One Tea Party activist, discussing negotiations about the national debt, said "I have my doubts about Donald Trump, but this would be a good issue for him to lead on" (Blog ID # 3967). The reasoning was based on Trump's background in business, hoping his policies would minimize government spending.

Overall, the early engagement period elicited two major reactions from the Tea Party activists about Trump: one congratulatory and the other largely critical. On the issue of birtherism, Tea Party support for Trump was effectively unequivocal. However, when it came to Trump's aspirations in politics, most Tea Partiers believed that Trump was not genuine in his views and as a result they preferred other candidates. Since Trump abandoned any serious intentions of running for president in 2012 early in the race, the fissures did not expand beyond the occasional reference to Trump in the blogs. The initial skepticism, however, carried over to the second phase to which we now turn.

An Uneven Embrace: From 2012 to the 2016 Republican Convention

Following Trump's withdrawal from the 2012 election and the reelection of Barack Obama to a second term, the blog discussions largely turned to other matters. Most notably, Tea Partiers aimed at pressuring the Republican-controlled House of Representatives and, by 2014, the Senate, to stymie Obama's agenda. We label this the uneven embrace period because most of the Tea Party blog posts were harshly critical, even as it became clear that Trump would become the Republican nominee for president. At the same time, Trump actively continued courting the Tea Party, consistent with his approach during the 2012 presidential primary. For instance, Trump spoke at the 2016 Tea Party convention held in Myrtle Beach, SC, and had joined several elite-facilitated Tea Party events in 2015. A few blogs indicated some level of openness to Trump, even though his affection for the insurgency was not widely reciprocated. This warming resulted, in part, from Trump's endorsement by politicians like Sarah Palin who were admired by grassroots Tea Party activists (Zoorob and Skocpol 2020:82).

We reinforce this point with two complementary data sources. First, we again draw on qualitative coding of 328 blog posts from the period. These posts establish the Tea Party's uneasiness about Trump as a viable political candidate and what a Trump win might mean for the insurgency and for the conservative movement generally. We also deploy a county-level regression analysis of primary voting patterns. We focus on whether the local strength of the Tea Party predicted support for Trump in the primaries. In short, were hotspots of Tea Party activity positively or negatively associated with Trump support? Together, these two analyses demonstrate the Tea Party's continuing ambivalence and sometimes outright hostility to Trump's candidacy, policies, and possible takeover of the Republican Party.

Three major findings emerged from our qualitative analysis of the uneven embrace period. First, the absences in the blog posts compared with the earlier period are worth underscoring. While birtherism dominated the Tea Party's early positive assessments of Trump, the issue effectively disappeared after 2012. Of the blogs published during the uneven embrace period, just 10 referenced Trump's advocacy for birtherism. Of these, four posts mentioned Trump's questioning of whether his main primary competitor, Ted Cruz, was eligible to be president. Absent were discussions of Trump's extensive criticism of the healthcare reform package passed by the Obama administration, which had been a regular target of Tea Party activists' earlier ire. Second, there is clear continuity with the Tea Party blogger's earlier criticisms of Trump's commitment to conservatism across several policy areas. Of the 328 blog posts we examined, more than 30% of them were explicitly critical of Trump's candidacy. Third, of the positive assessments of Trump, present in just 9% of posts, most were conditional and emphasized his positions on immigration, Islam, and willingness to defy political conventions and GOP leadership. Only a few blog posts were unequivocally positive about Trump's candidacy. We expand on the latter two themes, using representative quotations from our data.

Blog posts criticizing Trump as a candidate emphasized two subthemes: Trump's lack of commitment to conservatism and his inability to be a viable candidate on the national stage. Some posters were terse in their assessment of Trump, claiming that "Donald Trump will be problematic for conservatives, if he wins. He is not a social conservative" (Blog ID # 5159). Others questioned his commitment to the Constitution, stating "have you EVER heard DONALD TRUMP talk about the CONSTITUTION? I haven't. And I've got serious questions about his fidelity to the document all Tea Partiers REVERE" (Blog ID # 2003).

As in the early engagement period, many bloggers focused on Trump's prior history of financial support for Democratic politicians. During the early phases of the 2016 primary season, one poster argued that "Trump is the circus sideshow, a lifelong liberal Democrat with New York values, a reality TV star and casino mogul supposedly without a chance of winning the more conservative Southern states – an absolute must for any Republican" (Blog ID # 39185). One blogger highlighted Trump's lack of deference to the core conservative principle of small government: "Whether you like him [Trump] or don't like him, pay attention to what he is saying. He is not even giving lip service to the idea of shrinking the government" (Blog ID # 13553). This uneasiness grew as it became clear that Trump's intention to run in the Republican primaries was genuine, rather than mimicking his prior rapid withdrawals after making headlines.

Several balked at the idea that Trump would even have enough support to be a viable candidate in the Republican primary. One representative remark summarizing the broader reaction was "If Donald Trump is the best we, as Conservatives, Republicans, Tea Partiers or Teapublicans can come up with as a candidate for the presidency we have set the bar far, FAR too low in fact we have made that bar subterranean as that is where moles reside" (Blog ID #

14179). The expression of such sentiments continued through to the GOP convention, with many Tea Partiers either refusing to support Trump or lamenting the sea change taking place in the GOP. An illustrative example, written by the founder of a major Tea Party umbrella group on the final day of the Republican Convention in 2016, emphasized the death of conservatism in the GOP if Trump became the nominee:

> For conservatives in the Republican Party, the end has come. The Party is splitting because of Donald Trump. Perhaps the Party could have survived a little while longer if Trump wanted to make an effort at unity. He doesn't. He wants to crush anyone who disagrees with him and that means conservatives no longer have a home in the GOP. (Blog ID # 14419)

For this Tea Party leader, Trumpism meant abandonment of the conservative movement's commitment to the Constitution and to limited government.

   While most blog posters categorically rejected Trump, a minority of activists were more optimistic. This latter group of Tea Partiers focused on recurring themes to ground their support of Trump: restrictive immigration policies, a ban on Muslims entering the United States, and his willingness to buck established GOP leadership. One post addressed several of these themes when evaluating Trump's performance at the first primary debate: "Donald Trump declared that he will build the fence/wall at Mexico's expense and the RINO's stampeded" (Blog ID # 16686). This poster used the pejorative acronym RINO (Republican in name only) to describe the other candidates who were unwilling to adopt Trump's hardline immigration stance. Notably, the poster also included Ted Cruz who entered the Senate in 2012 after aligning himself with the Tea Party. Trump's early emphasis on curbing undocumented immigration and deporting all undocumented immigrants already in the US received high praise. One blogger applauded Trump's willingness to welcome critical media coverage and wrote that "with Donald Trump under fire from all sides, no matter what you think of him he is one of the few who has spoken out about this devastating invasion of illegals" (Blog ID #1425).

   These examples highlight the Tea Partiers appreciation of Trump's willingness to ignore existing norms of contemporary politics. As we have noted, anti-Muslim views were common in the Tea Party and many believed that Barack Obama was a practicing Muslim. Trump's adoption of what had hitherto been fringe positions bought him significant political capital among Tea Partiers and was directly responsible for expanding his support among the rank-and-file activists.

   The blog posts, it must be emphasized, were written by a small number of leaders and activists among the hundreds of thousands of local activists who joined the grassroots Tea Party. Consequently, the largely critical reaction to Trump we have summarized, may not have broadly characterized Tea Party activists. We evaluate this possibility in the following analyses by assessing ecological patterns of support for Trump during the presidential primaries.

We ask whether hotspots of Tea Party activism were associated with aggregate voting patterns in 2016 by analyzing county-level patterns of primary support for Donald Trump and Ted Cruz. The percentages of voters supporting each candidate are our dependent variables. To control for unobserved state-level heterogeneity, we use multilevel linear regression with counties nested in states. Our analysis includes only competitive state primaries, which comprised solely those contests that occurred prior to Ted Cruz's decision to suspend his campaign following his loss in Indiana. We include competitive primaries from 37 states and Washington, DC.[1] These began with the Iowa caucuses on February 1, 2016, and concluded with the Indiana primary on May 3, 2016. Ultimately, we had an analytic sample size of 2,433 counties.

The comparison between Trump and Cruz is compelling for several reasons. First, Cruz won election and joined the Senate in 2012. During his first campaign, he rode to victory after aligning himself with the Tea Party, and was endorsed by the Tea Party Express (Anonymous 2012). In 2012 and onward, Cruz remained an advocate for Tea Party policy goals. Reflecting that advocacy, he received endorsements from the Tea Party Patriots Citizen's Fund in 2016 (Anonymous 2016), and several local Tea Party leaders and organizations (Garrison 2015; Svitek 2015). Second, of the slate of Republican primary candidates in 2016, Cruz was by far the most competitive after Trump. Cruz suspended his campaign after winning 551 delegates. In comparison, Marco Rubio, who was also widely identified as Tea Party adjacent, withdrew from the primaries in third place with just 167 delegates. Finally, as we have argued, the Republican coalition established by Trump differed from the traditional base of the party. Comparing the performance of a Tea Party Republican who was also attractive to the traditional base, such as Cruz, to a political outsider like Trump allowed us to assess empirical support for our claims.

We employed three measures of Tea Party activity as our independent variables. First, we used the cumulative count of Tea Party groups that ever existed in each county based on the organizational listings we compiled daily, and described in Chapter 6. Second, we measured the cumulative number of Tea Party protests, meetings, rallies, and other events occurring in each county between 2009 through 2014, drawing on the database of all Tea Party events described in Chapter 5. Last, we included an indicator (1=Yes; 0=No) of whether any member of the Tea Party Caucus was elected in a congressional district overlapping each county for our analytic period, as outlined in Chapters 6 and 8. The first two variables allow us to assess the cumulative

[1] We omitted four states: Colorado, Kansas, North Dakota, and Wyoming. These states only made data available for congressional districts, or did not have a voting procedure comparable to that of the rest of the country, or the primary processes were either spread over several days or decisions were made without a popular vote. Our data includes votes in AK, AL, AR, AZ, CT, DC, DE, FL, GA, HI, IA, ID, IL, IN, KY, LA, MA, MD, ME, MI, MN, MO, MS, NC, NH, NV, NY, OH, OK, PA, RI, SC, TN, TX, UT, VA, VT, and WI.

impact of grassroots Tea Party activity in a community and how such activism may have shaped primary voting decisions, while the last variable emphasizes the impact of the institutionalized wing of the Tea Party. Using multiple measures to capture the institutionalized and grassroots factions of the Tea Party is essential, we argue, due to the lack of synchronicity between the different actors of the insurgency.

We also built three additional sets of variables to control for other factors potentially linked to primary support patterns. We combined data from the five-year estimates of the American Community Survey, the Bureau of Labor Statistics' Local Area Unemployment program, the US Department of Housing and Urban Development's Neighborhood Stabilization Program, the Religious Congregations and Membership Study, and prior electoral data. These variables and sources have been discussed extensively in earlier chapters, so we will be brief to avoid repetition. The first group of variables is designed to collectively capture *material threats*, which, as discussed earlier in this chapter, may have spurred higher levels of support for Trump. We built measures of the change in unemployment rate between 2009 and 2015, the unemployment rate in 2015, the foreclosure concentration index described in Chapter 3, and the percentage change in manufacturing jobs between 2009 and 2015. Second, we used three measures of *status threats*, which also have been linked to Trump's level of primary support. We built several variables to account for the demographic groups that prior research has shown were most vulnerable to status threats. These included the percentage of residents who were non-Hispanic White, the change in percentage White between 2009 and 2015, and the percentage of residents with high school education or less. Last, we included six control variables. These were county-level support for the GOP in the 2012 presidential election, the number of evangelical congregations in 2010, the natural log of the median income in each county, the percentage of households receiving Supplemental Nutrition Assistance Program (SNAP) benefits in 2015, and the natural log of the population size in 2015. We also included a dichotomous measure indexing whether the primary process in a state was open (1=Yes; 0=No), that is, allowing voters to cross the party lines when voting.

The regression analysis is summarized in Table 9.1. The first model specification contains only the Tea Party–related variables to predict Trump's vote share, while the second model adds all the other variables. There is little evidence that Trump support was higher in areas with higher levels of both forms of Tea Party activism; nor was it higher in counties represented by a Tea Party Caucus member in the House. In fact, Model 1 shows that the three variables aimed at tapping Tea Party activity are each negative. These effects are not robust, however. Once the full array of variables is included in Model 2, the two measures of grassroots activism become statistically insignificant, while the estimate for Tea Party Caucus membership reflects, contrary to expectations, a decrease in Trump support across the county primary elections. This is

TABLE 9.1 *County-level primary support for Donald Trump and Ted Cruz, 2016 (n=2,433).*

	Support for Trump		Support for Cruz	
	Model 1	*Model 2*	*Model 3*	*Model 4*
Tea Party Activism				
# Tea Party Groups	−0.496***	−0.035	−0.286***	−0.141
	(0.079)	(0.084)	(0.066)	(0.083)
# Tea Party Events	−0.019***	−0.002	−0.007	−0.002
	(0.005)	(0.004)	(0.004)	(0.004)
Tea Party Caucus Representatives	−1.946***	−1.210***	0.834**	0.534
	(0.396)	(0.323)	(0.329)	(0.318)
Material Threat				
Unemployment Rate		1.198***		−0.709***
		(0.113)		(0.111)
Change in Unemployment		−0.130		−0.071
		(0.108)		(0.106)
Foreclosure Concentration		1.756		−0.884
		(1.018)		(1.004)
Change in % Manufacturing Jobs		−0.020		−0.045
		(0.041)		(0.041)
Status Threat				
Percentage White		0.138***		−0.071***
		(0.013)		(0.013)
Change in Percentage White		0.039		0.015
		(0.042)		(0.041)
Percentage with High School or Less Education		0.292***		0.035
		(0.019)		(0.019)
Other Controls				
Republican Support (2012)		−0.033*		0.120***
		(0.015)		(0.015)
Evangelical Congregations		−1.985***		1.189***
		(0.264)		(0.260)
Median Income		2.472*		1.358
		(1.043)		(1.030)
% of Households Receiving SNAP		0.201***		0.012
		(0.035)		(0.034)
Population Size		2.111***		−1.569***
		(0.288)		(0.284)

(continued)

TABLE 9.1 (*continued*)

	Support for Trump		Support for Cruz	
	Model 1	*Model 2*	*Model 3*	*Model 4*
Open Primary		3.793		−0.178
		(3.465)		(3.674)
Intercept	43.602***	−0.486	28.250***	25.379***
	(1.824)	(4.894)	(1.947)	(4.901)
County-Level Variance	45.160	29.130	31.160	28.350
State-Level Variance	122.970	111.700	141.680	125.650

Note: Estimates include competitive primaries between February 1, 2016, and May 3, 2016.
*p<0.05, **p<0.01, ***p<0.001 (two-tailed tests).

an important association that bears repeating: communities represented in Congress by a Tea Party Caucus member were significantly less likely to support Donald Trump in the 2016 primaries.

The additional variables included in Model 2 show partial support for both the material threats and the status threats arguments, as expected. Counties with higher unemployment had higher Trump support, likely the result of his emphasis on job creation and trade restrictions. Trump had substantially higher support in counties that were Whiter and where more residents had lower levels of education. The control variables also reveal several associations relevant to Trump's base in the primary elections. In Model 2, each additional 1% of support for Romney in the 2012 election was associated with a small decrease in support for Trump. Similarly, each additional evangelical congregation present in a county decreased support for Trump.

The comparison of these results with those for support for Ted Cruz in Models 3 and 4 illustrates a lack of any important impact of local Tea Party mobilization in shaping the results of the 2016 primary. In Model 3, the cumulative number of Tea Party groups is negatively associated with support for Cruz. On the other hand, however, the existence of a Tea Party Caucus member representing any part of a county increases support for Cruz. None of the estimates remains statistically significant in Model 4. The comparison between Trump and Cruz in Models 2 and 4 reveal several important clues about Trump's weaker support from the GOP establishment and its traditional base. Counties with more Republican support in 2012 as well as areas with more evangelicals saw higher levels of support for Cruz. The comparison strongly suggests that Trump and Cruz appealed to two different clusters of GOP voters in the 2016 primary elections: Trump captured greater proportions of White working-class voters facing high unemployment; Cruz's base was more reflective of traditional Republicans.

When considered jointly, during the uneven embrace period our two sources of evidence show deep concern among the Tea Party activists about a Trump candidacy, which remained largely in place even after he became the presumptive nominee and ultimately secured the nomination. This main finding is consistent with the qualitative analysis of the blog posts. While Trump understood that the Tea Party was important to his credentials as a conservative, the blog evidence makes it clear that the sentiment certainly was not mutual. Trump's expansion of the Republican base moved beyond the typical Tea Party member, who was White, but also more highly educated and possessing greater socioeconomic resources. Importantly, our regression analyses also indicate that the legacy of Tea Party activism in a county had a negligible role in shaping the primary election in 2016. We suggest that this is most likely a direct consequence of the insurgency's broad demobilization by then.

Unbridled Enthusiasm: The 2016 Election and Trump Presidency

The Tea Party's skepticism of Trump's commitment to conservatism remained mostly intact during the remainder of the 2016 campaign up to the election. Soon after Trump became president-elect, there was a rapid change in the tone of the blogs. Activists expressed a newfound enthusiasm after securing Republican control of the presidency, Senate, and House. The remnant of Tea Party activists, at this point mostly leaders of the umbrella groups, quickly became rabid defenders of Trump's policies and administration. To ground these claims, we rely on a qualitative content analysis of 901 blog posts published from July 22, 2016, through December 31, 2018. We supplement the blog evidence by analyzing county-level support for Trump in the general election to assess whether the Tea Party's cumulative level of local mobilization, which we showed had no consequence in the primaries, continued to show muted effects in the contest for the presidency.

Between the GOP convention and the early aftermath of the 2016 presidential election, the tone of Tea Party blogs referencing Trump remained largely critical, and echoed sentiments widely shared in the prior two periods. Bloggers questioned Trump's adherence to conservative policy positions, with one noting that "I find Donald Trump's moral behavior offensive and disgusting but that is not why I do not plan to vote for him, I do not trust him and find nothing in his record to cause me to trust him" (Blog ID # 14240). Other Tea Partiers claimed that Trump's candidacy was part of a larger push by the Republican Party to extinguish the influence of true conservatives. A representative example comes from a blogger who stated:

This is a time unique in politics: each of the major parties has presented us with an abhorrent candidate … The Republicans had a true conservative running for the first time since Reagan, Ted Cruz. The Party couldn't bear the nomination of someone who would undo their years of work extinguishing conservatism becoming more like Democrats and nullifying the Constitution. So they sandbagged him with a flock of shill candidates and the help of Fox News. We wound up with Trump. (Blog ID # 14377)

Such claims, made without evidence, are consistent with large swaths of distrust among Tea Party activists of the GOP and its leadership.

While more positive assessments of Trump's candidacy remained a minority voice during the uneven embrace period, after Trump secured the presidency there was a large transformation in discourse, indicating a strategic shift in the remaining Tea Partiers' assessments of the incoming Trump administration. Bloggers particularly emphasized the importance of Republican unity despite any prior misgivings about Trump. For example, a Tea Party leader said:

During the campaign, there were serious divisions in the Republicans, conservatives and Tea Party activists. Some people supported Donald Trump whole heartedly. Some were never Trump because they simply did not believe he would govern as a conservative. He is now the President-elect and now we will find out. It is time for everyone to unify. (Blog ID # 14266)

The gradual acceptance of Trump remained present in only a minority of blog posts after the election but foreshadowed the larger shift in opinion that would come to dominate Tea Party activists' discourse.

Advocacy for Trump diffused outward from the Tea Party blogs to build a broader post-election media strategy. One striking example of the tone shift is evident in comments made by Jenny Beth Martin, one of the founders of the Tea Party Patriots, in March 2016 and November 2016. Speaking at a conservative summit on March 4, Martin argued that "Donald Trump has no business thinking that he is Tea Party" since "Trump is about love of himself. But the Tea Party is about love of country and the love of our Constitution" (these quotes are reported by Kamisar 2016). By November 16, Martin (2016) published an op-ed in *Politico*, arguing that "with the victory of Donald Trump, the values and principles that gave rise to the tea party movement in 2009 are finally gaining the top seat of power in the White House." While the op-ed does note that the Political Action Committee run by the Tea Party Patriots endorsed Trump only after he became the presumptive nominee, the earlier criticisms and concerns remained entirely unaddressed.

On balance, then, Trump did not elicit widespread excitement in the Tea Party, even if a growing number of activists were warming to his candidacy by the dawn of the election. Our analysis of county-level support for Trump in the 2016 election provides corroborating evidence that previous levels of Tea Party activism did not translate into support for Trump in the general election. We mimic the multilevel linear regression models used previously to examine patterns of primary support for Trump in the uneven embrace period. We again employed the percentage of support for Trump in the general election as our dependent variable, along with identical variables and operationalizations to assess the impacts of previous levels of Tea Party activism, material threats, status threats, and other control variables seen in analyses in Table 9.1. The results of the regression analysis examining the general election results are given in Table 9.2.

TABLE 9.2 *County-level support for Donald Trump in the 2016 presidential election (n=3,141).*

	2016 Election	
	Model 1	*Model 2*
Tea Party Activism		
# Tea Party Groups	−0.990***	−0.041
	(0.130)	(0.046)
# Tea Party Events	−0.127***	−0.007
	(0.017)	(0.005)
Tea Party Caucus Representatives	2.655***	−0.054
	(0.673)	(0.182)
Material Threat		
Unemployment Rate		0.169**
		(0.059)
Change in Unemployment		−0.058
		(0.060)
Foreclosure Concentration		−1.505**
		(0.496)
Change in Manufacturing		−0.030
		(0.023)
Status Threat		
Percentage White		0.211***
		(0.006)
Change in Percentage White		0.164
		(0.217)
Percentage High School Educated or Less		0.345***
		(0.010)
Other Controls		
Republican Support (2012)		0.809***
		(0.007)
Evangelical Congregations		−0.106
		(0.174)
Median Income (ln)		1.003
		(0.544)
% of Households Receiving SNAP		0.039*
		(0.019)
Population Size		−0.063
		(0.187)
(Intercept)	59.392***	−23.569***
	(1.525)	(2.257)
County-Level Variance	158.700	11.220
State-Level Variance	109.000	10.630

Note: Estimates are based on county-level votes for Donald Trump. *$p<0.05$, **$p<0.01$, ***$p<0.001$ (two-tailed tests).

Similar to our analysis of the primary elections, the pattern for the 2016 presidential election shows that previous Tea Party activism had neither a positive nor a negative impact on the vote share for Trump. Indeed, in Model 1 the coefficients for the counts of Tea Party groups and all events are both negative and statistically significant, while the election of a Tea Party Caucus member is positively associated with support for Trump. However, once the full set of variables is included in Model 2 these effects disappear and each becomes nonsignificant. The lack of impact of Tea Party mobilization in both the primaries and the general election is entirely consistent with the broad demobilization of the Tea Party.

The pattern seen in the other variables in Table 9.2 suggests that a combination of material threats and status threats was associated with support for Trump in the general election, consistent with our previous analysis of primary support for Trump. Our full model indicates that counties with higher unemployment, more Whites, lower levels of education, and more families receiving SNAP are more supportive of Trump. Of the control variables, the percentage of residents who voted Republican in the 2012 election has the strongest impact. Each 1% increase in Republican support in 2012 translated to a 0.8% increase in the vote share for Trump. There is strong consistency in voting patterns in Republican areas then, which exhibit only glacial change between 2012 and 2016.

Even though levels of Tea Party mobilization in a county did not yield a decisive block of voters in the primaries or 2016 election for Trump, enthusiasm for him among Tea Party activists grew rapidly afterwards. The turning point in the blog posts came as Trump announced nominees for his cabinet and other federal positions. He filled them disproportionately with candidates either amenable to or affiliated with the Tea Party. For example, posts regularly applauded the selection of Scott Pruitt to lead the Environmental Protection Agency, which Pruitt had repeatedly sued while Attorney General of Oklahoma. One blog noted that the selection of Pruitt was "a pick dripping with poetic justice as Pruitt has been at the forefront of pushing back on President Obama's industry-crushing emissions regulations" (Blog ID # 1543). Other notable nominees included Tea Party Caucus member Mick Mulvaney to lead the Office of Management and Budget and staunch conservative Jeff Sessions to serve as Attorney General and lead the Department of Justice. As the tone and substance of Trump's presidency solidified, one poster concisely summarized a common sentiment expressed in the blogs:

Many people in the Never Trump movement were a part of it for the same reason I was. We believed that if he were elected, Trump would immediately move hard left. But a funny thing happened on the way to the Inauguration. Donald Trump became President Elect and did not move hard left. In fact, he went far more conservative than a lot of people believed he would. (Blog ID # 14207)

Trump's conservatism was routinely questioned by the Tea Party, but his actions and decisions as the president-elect quickly created strong allies among activists. While the acceptance of Trump may have been part of a larger political strategy to secure policy change within a GOP-controlled Congress and presidency, there was little evidence of satisficing in the blog record. This is a particularly important point as Tea Partiers never shied away from aggressive criticism of Republican leaders, including Paul Ryan, John Boehner, and Mitch McConnell. The support for Trump by this time, in contrast, was ubiquitous and appeared quite genuine.

By the time that Trump assumed office, there had been a clear rhetorical shift in how the Tea Party activists engaged with the federal government. The conspiratorial posts about birtherism, Obama's religious faith, or other common topics evaporated entirely. Instead, Tea Party bloggers emphasized issues of policy, reflected in 25% of posts. One post published on December 21, 2017, lauded "the many victories since the new and improved administration took over" (Blog ID # 2258) by emphasizing tax reform, appointments to the judiciary and Supreme Court, decertifying the nuclear agreement with Iran, and the suspension of the Deferred Action for Childhood Arrivals (DACA) program. Tea Party activists were enthusiastic about Trump's widespread deregulation, approach to the environment and climate change, and America's global trade relationships. One representative blogger wrote "God bless President Donald Trump for addressing the dragon in the room (dragon seems more China-appropriate than elephant). In two years he has revamped many trade deals and reversed much of this awful job outsourcing trend" (Blog ID # 14570). Soon, the Tea Party came to adopt the rhetoric pioneered by Trump. Of the 901 blog posts published in the unbridled enthusiasm period, 34% had at least one reference to "draining the swamp" or "America First," hallmark slogans of the Trump Administration.

Trump's presidency did not deliver on all its promises, particularly when it came to healthcare reform, or durable legislative victories beyond the Tax Cuts and Jobs Act of 2017. While Republican leaders had received vitriolic criticism from the Tea Party previously for policy failures or working with the Democratic Party, Trump was not subject to such attacks. Instead, the Tea Partiers framed Trump as a political outsider and relished his willingness to battle with Republicans working against his agenda, actions they viewed as parallel to the Tea Party's relationship to the GOP. Policy failures, such as the repealing of the Patient Protection and Affordable Care Act, were not linked to Trump, but instead seen as a result of RINOs in Congress and the deep state – career bureaucrats and politicians who inappropriately used their positions and power to undermine Trump's agenda. One poster, for instance, argued that "the government bureaucracy class is the enemy of Trump" (Blog ID # 14322), with another claiming that "Trump is serious about shrinking government and Big Government is attacking back" (Blog ID # 14809). Such claims were common in the Tea Party's defense of Trump, and criticisms of his performance became rarer through the end of the unbridled enthusiasm period.

Much like the rest of the GOP, then, the dwindling embers of the Tea Party came to a full-throated embrace of Trumpism.

CONCLUSION

With the benefit of hindsight, we know that the actual policies and practices of the Trump administration sometimes conformed and sometimes deviated sharply from the Tea Party's early emphasis on fiscal restraint and big government. Trump's imprint on the federal judiciary and Supreme Court were quite in line with the Tea Party's goals. However, Trump's presidency ran large deficits each fiscal year and did little to shrink the size of the government bureaucracy that was anathema to the Tea Party. Even Trump's signature Tax Cuts and Jobs Act was panned by Tea Party leaders (Kibbe 2018) because of its astronomical costs. Despite these inconsistencies, the national Tea Party remnant became stalwart defenders of Trump's administration.

Others have linked the rise of Trump to the larger transformation of the Republican Party brought about by the Tea Party (Gervais and Morris 2018; Rohlinger and Bunnage 2017). Our analysis adds important context to such a claim. The Tea Party's embrace of Trumpism was not a natural fit. The process was more gradual, critical, and strategic than is evident in the portraits provided in the existing research literature. Rather than establishing a clear continuity between the material threats and status threats motivating Tea Party activism, support for Trump was not concentrated in hotspots of Tea Party activism. Communities with concentrations of Tea Party activists came to support Trump only after his election, and only when Trump made it clear that he intended to be responsive to the hard-right conservative base.

Our county-level analyses, rather, indicates that more extensive grassroots Tea Party activism was largely not associated with support for Trump in the 2016 election. This finding requires additional discussion given the mixed reaction to Trump that began to emerge during the uneven embrace period we identified in our blog posts, and that is also seen in other research (Skocpol 2020; Zoorob and Skocpol 2020). The electoral map for 2016 differed from that of prior election cycles. Trump flipped 230 counties from Democratic in 2012 to Republican in 2016 (just 24 counties moved from Republican in 2012 to Democratic in 2016). This broadening of the electoral map may have been a consequence of Trump's ability to mobilize White working class voters (Morgan and Lee 2018). Importantly, the counties that flipped toward Donald Trump contained averages of 1 Tea Party organization and 6 events relative to counties that remained stable Republican areas, which had respective averages of 4 chapters and 15 events. In other words, Trump's expansion of the electoral map occurred in locations with substantially less Tea Party activity.

The electoral success of Trump highlights the declining influence of the grassroots Tea Party and the end of its outsized influence on the GOP. The Republican primaries in 2016 had a candidate, Ted Cruz, who was explicitly aligned with the Tea Party, yet the insurgency failed to mobilize the voters necessary for Cruz to secure the nomination. By 2016, the material threats that had motivated the Tea Party to action in 2009 had diffused, unlike the palpable material threats that intensified during the peak of the Great Recession. The urgency of the Tea Party in 2009 and its victories in 2010 were in direct response to widely felt economic peril, which was no longer as salient by 2016. The Tea Party moment, in short, was over.

10

Conclusion

On the afternoon of January 6, 2021, approximately 10,000 demonstrators gathered at the Ellipse park in Washington, DC, adjacent to the White House. The protest, self-proclaimed as the "March to Save America" and "March for Trump," was aimed at voicing objections to the impending count of the electoral college votes in the joint session of Congress, the last step necessary to finalize Joe Biden's victory in the 2020 presidential election. Then, via Twitter, President Donald Trump encouraged his supporters to attend, using a maelstrom of false claims about ballot harvesting and biased voting machines to baselessly claim that he had won the election. As the rally unfolded, speakers including Rudy Giuliani, a former New York City Mayor and Trump's attorney, and Representative Mo Brooks (Republican, Alabama) took the stage to reiterate lies about the stolen election and rile up the crowd. Donald Trump eventually spoke too, urging his supporters to march on the US Capitol building in hopes of pressuring Vice President Mike Pence, a former Tea Party Caucus member, to reject the electoral results.

During Trump's speech, a small splinter group of the Ellipse rally broke off and breached the police lines erected to secure the US Capitol building. They were soon followed by other participants from the rally who marched to the Capitol, and together fought the police in an attempt to breach the Capitol building. As the crowd grew, the police were ultimately overwhelmed and the assault turned into a violent attack. Participants breached the police lines using weapons, chemical irritants, and physical violence, and entered the Capitol. Congressional members and Pence were forced to cease counting the electoral college votes and flee to secure locations, providing the insurrectionists a short-term success. For several hours, the rioters raged through the Capitol building, damaging property, taking photos, and searching for politicians. Law enforcement regained control of the Capitol, and by 3:00 am on January 7, Pence, after completing the count, declared Joe Biden the victor.

American democracy has so far withstood the consequences of that attack, but not without long-lasting bruises. Despite the events of that day, many congressional Republicans remained undeterred, formally objecting to the results in Arizona, Georgia, Michigan, Nevada, Pennsylvania, and Wisconsin. Ultimately, eight Senate Republicans voted to sustain at least one objection, as did 139 members of the House Republican delegation. At least five deaths occurred during or immediately after the insurrection, along with a substantial number of injuries to law enforcement and participants. Hundreds of criminal cases were launched against the insurrectionists, with some participants, thus far, receiving sentences of multiple years of prison time.

The events of the January 6 insurrection will almost certainly trigger a vast opinion and research literature (e.g., Tarrow 2021:1–4). The roles of several extremist organizations, like the Proud Boys and Oath Keepers, have so far received outsized attention because of their leadership role in breaching the Capitol and engaging in violence. A website used to advertise the rally listed nine organizational sponsors, including several that had deep ties to the Tea Party insurgency.[1] Jenny Beth Martin, founder of the Tea Party Patriots, was one. Another was Amy Kremer, founder of the Tea Party Express and at the time a leader of Women for American First. Kremer's daughter, Kylie Jane Kremer, the executive director of Women for Trump, was listed as an applicant for the rally's permit. Following the attack on the Capitol, many sponsoring groups moved quickly to distance themselves and their organizations from the violence. A blog post by Corn (2021), published by the progressive website *Mother Jones*, noted that:

On January 6, Jenny Beth Martin, the co-founder of Tea Party Patriots, posted a photo of herself at the pre-attack rally and noted, "I am here at the Save America March to fight for President Trump. We will not allow them to steal this election!" Sometime between 4:27 p.m. and 10:49 pm on January 6 – that is, after the mob had ransacked the Capitol – the Tea Party Patriots were removed from the list of sponsors on the March for Trump's website.

In Chapter 4 we showed that the Tea Party Patriots were one of the most important umbrella groups for the Tea Party insurgency and a key organizing hub for many local chapters. The remnants of the umbrella structures of the Tea Party had become important supporters of the President Trump. Their supporting role in the insurrection and associated conspiracy theories about electoral fraud represents, it seems, an irreconcilable departure from their original beliefs in constitutional conservatism, lower taxes, and lower spending.

[1] The website used to organize the Ellipse rally is now offline. Fortunately, its contents were preserved by the Internet Archive. A capture collected on January 5, 2021, lists the nine sponsoring organizations: web.archive.org/web/20210105002211/https://marchtosaveamerica.com (accessed August 27, 2022).

While Jenny Beth Martin condemned the violence of January 6 (O'Harrow Jr. 2021), election fraud conspiracies, framed as questions about election integrity, have now become commonplace on the Tea Party Patriot's website, and are listed as one of a small number of action items for the group. To the extent that the Tea Party Patriots' remaining followers had been activists during the insurgency, we might speculate that many of them also altered their view in concert with Trump's triumphs and post-election antics. Nevertheless, searching our database of 91,874 Tea Party blog posts between 2009 and 2018 for references to "election integrity" returned only 42 posts. The major rhetorical shift we identified in Chapter 7 appears to have taken a turn to the explicitly conspiratorial after Trump's electoral loss.

What are the major theoretical lessons we can learn from our analyses of the Tea Party, from its birth to its death, and what does its trajectory tell us about the state of American politics? We end with five major insights and the implications of our work. *First* is our assessment that the grassroots Tea Party demobilized, leaving open questions about its current state. *Second* is the importance of economic grievances, and especially suddenly imposed economic grievances, in explaining explosions of collective action. Our *third* conclusion concerns the enduring importance of mobilizing structures and organization building, which is directly relevant to other contemporary social movements. *Fourth*, we outline the Tea Party's lasting consequences on American politics, which have already outlived the insurgency's relatively short life. Finally, *fifth*, we close with a strong claim that our approach to capturing the Tea Party's grassroots dynamics provides a methodological template widely applicable to the study of social movements and collective behavior. These synthetic conclusions provide answers to our motivating research questions, posed in the introduction.

HAS THE TEA PARTY DEMOBILIZED?

A recurrent finding across multiple chapters is that the once-thriving grassroots of the Tea Party insurgency has effectively vanished. We ground this claim in our major findings in Chapters 5, 6 and 7. In summary, in Chapter 5 we showed that while public events staged by Tea Party groups became rare, protests were even rarer. The insurgency also proved unable to maintain any semblance of coordinated action. The core results in Chapter 6 show a thoroughgoing demobilization and disappearance of local Tea Party groups across the country. The decision by the Tea Party umbrella groups to end their hosting services for local organizations, we believe, was likely a fatal blow to any lingering grassroots insurgency. Finally, our analysis in Chapter 7 points to the discursive demobilization of the Tea Party, spurred by its drift away from the clarity of its initial issue framing. We believe that elements of the Tea Party's national leadership's adoption of fringe conspiracy theories about election fraud were a direct extension of this drift.

Upon initial inspection, the Tea Party Patriots' participation in the January 6 rally may raise questions about one of our major conclusions. It is certainly true that some Tea Party umbrella groups still exist. As we finalize this book in the spring of 2023, the websites for the 1776 Tea Party, FreedomWorks, Tea Party Nation, and the Tea Party Patriots remain online, while the Patriot Action Network appears to have entirely abandoned its web presence. At the height of the insurgency, these websites were vibrant communities humming with extensive evidence of thick grassroots activism. There is no longer much trace of the thousands of local groups once active on *any* of the websites. Instead, op-eds and articles rife with conspiracy theories about electoral fraud, questions about the efficacy of the vaccines for the COVID-19 pandemic, and other threads of misinformation now run rampant. Conspiratorial talking points were not uncommon in Tea Party discourse during the insurgency, such as the widespread acceptance and tolerance of the racist birther conspiracy we described in Chapter 9. But such talking points are now a central feature and omnipresent in a manner they were not during the heyday of the insurgency.

Our conclusion about the trajectory of the Tea Party is directly informed by what appears to be its reversion to top-down control. As we outlined in Chapters 2, 3, and 4, the Tea Party's emergence in 2009 was not organic. Instead, it was the product of longstanding trends in White conservative mobilization in combination with an elite-driven set of policy preferences (see, e.g., Lo 2012; Martin 2013). At the same time, it is difficult to imagine that the overwhelming success of the 2009 Tax Day rallies did not surprise the insurgency's early enablers. The groundswell of grassroots support quickly overshadowed the Tea Party's elite origins, as local groups were left to their own devices with no effective national coordination. What exists of the Tea Party, in short, has reverted back to its elite-driven origins. The Tea Party's overall trajectory is best described as moving between top-down, then bottom-up, then finally settling back to a top-down structure. We find the prospect of a grassroots resurgence unlikely, unless another perfect interpretive moment reoccurs. Our claim that the grassroots Tea Party has demobilized for good, therefore, is well-rooted in evidence from a variety of sources.

Economic Grievances and Threats as Important Predictors of Collective Action

One of our most important findings is the durable explanatory power of material threats in accounting for multiple aspects of the Tea Party's trajectory. Activism emerged in areas where the Great Recession was most severe and persisted in locations where economic recovery was slower. We concluded that potential Tea Party activists perceived an enhanced risk of economic precarity as the Great Recession took hold, and this provided a powerful mechanism for activism. A looming feeling of threat can enhance the power of grievances among those on the fence about taking action (Almeida 2019). The early Tea

Party activists and elite facilitators worked hard to craft a narrative about who was responsible for their mounting sense of economic precarity.

Few scholars (exceptions being, e.g., Cho et al. 2012; Rojecki 2016) emphasized the role of economic grievances as important precursors of the Tea Party. This, we believe is the result of a general reluctance by scholars to take the material motivations of conservative activism seriously. Our emphasis on the importance of material threats, and their role in the Tea Party's trajectory constitutes another of our important contributions. We emphasize that material threats matter for social movement mobilization broadly, and that this includes conservative movements. Material considerations were necessary in explaining the timing of the Tea Party, they thickened our explanatory account of the continuity of activism, and they contextualized the Tea Party's vehement objections to Obama's stimulus proposals and his other programs aimed at minimizing the effects of the economic downturn.

The lack of attention to the role of material threats by previous Tea Party scholars mirrors the similar inattention by social movement scholars to the importance of economic threats and associated grievances in general (those that have include Caren, Gaby, and Herrold 2017). That deemphasis is in part a consequence of the routine use of resource mobilization ideas in research, which suggested holding grievances constant in analyses of social movement emergence, since they are omnipresent (McCarthy and Zald 1977). But the structural bases of threat, especially material ones, change and create opportunities for activists to mobilize grievances out of new threats.

While American scholars have mostly eschewed a broad emphasis on material and economic threats, European researchers have taken them seriously. A growing literature has emphasized protests in the "Age of Austerity" as nation-states scaled back their social safety net or related programs following the Great Recession (e.g., Bojar et al. 2021; Giugni and Grasso 2016; della Porta 2015). Importantly, the austerity measures were quite different than Obama's early policy proposals responding to the recession. As Kriesi (2016) notes, European populist groups and parties generally did not take to the street in response to austerity measures, as the Tea Party did to oppose Obama's spending policies.

Much of the scholarly work on the Tea Party emphasized the role of status threats, or perceived threats to existing power structures, as being primary motivators of activism (e.g., Parker and Barreto 2014; Parkin et al. 2015). This was for good reason: there is little question that status threats and White racial resentment were powerful motivators of Tea Party activism, particularly following Barack Obama's victory in 2008. Our findings reinforce the importance of status threats, and especially the salience of apparently race-neutral rhetoric that animated White conservative objections to government spending on the "undeserving" and unmentioned, but implied, minority group members. Subsequent work on Donald Trump's rise to power has further highlighted the importance of status threats to understanding both movement and political dynamics (McVeigh and Estep 2019). We heartily agree that acknowledging status threats, and especially the intersection of race, power, and politics, is necessary in comprehensively understanding movements like the Tea Party. But material threats cannot be ignored.

An emphasis on status threats need not be exclusive of other theoretically salient explanatory mechanisms. Our mutual emphasis on material and status threats helps to thicken our explanatory account, and render it more complete. The two components interact rather than compete with one another, and together produce a more comprehensive explanation of the Tea Party's rise and fall. As attention to the threats and grievances motivating collective action have grown in recent years (Almeida 2019; Simmons 2014), the bulk of the research on conservative movements has continued to focus primarily on status threats. This often comes at the expense of more seriously fleshing out other threats and grievances that may have equally important roles in shaping right-wing activism. While our focus has emphasized the economic threats associated with Tea Party activism, material threats include a broad category of mechanisms useful in comprehensively assessing patterns of mobilization for movements of myriad political views.

The Importance of Mobilizing Structures

The Tea Party's primary mobilizing structure was a combination of the federated and spins forms of organization building. The national Tea Party umbrella groups provided web hosting for local chapters, but not much beyond that in the way of tactical guidance, professional staff, or other resources. This mobilizing structure is increasingly common for contemporary social movements. For example, largely decentralized mobilizing structures were adopted by movements such as Occupy Wall Street (Gould-Wartofsky 2015) and the Movement for Black Lives (Oliver 2021; Woodly 2021). There are clear initial advantages to the hybrid form: it facilitates rapid growth and diffuse organizational founding. This is reflected, for instance, in the more than 740 early riser Tea Party groups that were formed in just eight months in 2009.

At the same time, it is essential to consider the weaknesses of the hybrid mobilizing structure, as it can pose extensive complications for medium and long-run mobilization. We argued that the Tea Party's demobilization was, at least partially, a consequence of its core mobilizing structure. The 2009 Tax Day rallies were nothing short of transformative, not just for the Tea Party, but also for the conservative movement more broadly. The rallies also proved prohibitively difficult to sustain. While the decline in Tax Day rallies can be attributed, in part, to the larger downward trajectory of the Tea Party that appeared to begin in 2012 and the evolving views of the activists who staged them, there were still between 1,000 and 2,000 local groups that remained active through late 2013. The disappearance of Tax Day rallies, then, temporally preceded the demobilization of local chapters. Many existing chapters made a strategic decision to avoid staging additional rallies on Tax Day. The weak network ties between groups probably exacerbated the movement away from Tax Day rallies as local activists were generally disconnected from any national or state-level Tea Party groups capable of coordinating regional or nationwide protests. The insurgency's meager response to the Internal Revenue Service (IRS) scandal is further evidence that, by 2013, the Tea Party simply lacked the collective organizational capacity to produce a mass organized, street-level rebuke of the agency's enhanced oversight of 501(c) applications from conservative groups, especially Tea Party organizations.

Strong collective identity among activists is important in producing sustained mobilization for social movements (Polletta and Jasper 2001), yet can be quite difficult to sustain in settings where the spin organizational form overwhelms any semblance of a federated structure. Given the sparse network structure of clusters of Tea Party groups, it is quite plausible that individual activists felt more affinity to their local chapters than to the Tea Party as a whole. The insurgency was also somewhat unusual in its proliferation of competing umbrella groups, each espousing ownership while capturing only weakly overlapping constituencies of activists. This state of affairs further drove an effective wedge between local groups. Despite the opportunities for complicated cross-organizational networking and collaborative campaigns facilitated by the internet and social media platforms, disconnected local Tea Party groups did not appear able to muster functional and lasting extralocal networks. An emphasis on the relative advantage of professionalized organizational forms for longer term survival, emphasized by McCarthy and Zald (1977), rings true for understanding the trajectory of the Tea Party. It is also applicable to other recent insurgent social movements like Occupy Wall Street.

The Political Consequences of the Tea Party

The Tea Party's lasting legacy has already become evident in political processes generally, and elections specifically. While our results in Chapter 9 demonstrated that the legacy of grassroots Tea Party activism, at least in the aggregate, did not appear directly associated with Trump's victory in 2016, our conclusion about the insurgency's role in elite political radicalization in Chapter 8 has broader implications for American politics. In particular, the ruthlessness and unwillingness to compromise characterizing the Tea Party now appears to be commonplace within the Republican Party. The hardening of the political right was not, of course, exclusively a consequence of the Tea Party. Newt Gingrich's Contract with America before the 1994 midterm elections and Nixon's Southern Strategy are other manifestations of a more general shift. The insurgency, however, almost certainly hastened the process nationally and locally. In short, the Tea Party's uncompromising approach to its political competition has already exceeded the insurgency's lifespan and appears to be metastasizing moving forward.

A second lasting consequence, we believe, is the Tea Party's role in normalizing a brand of conservative rhetoric lighter on factual claims and detailed policy proposals, and more grounded in combativeness, conspiracy theories, and vague talking points. This post-policy strand of conservatism is perhaps best encapsulated in an exchange that took place in the summer of 2009 during a heated town hall about the Obama administration's healthcare reform package, that was a flashpoint of mobilization for the Tea Party. During the course of the event, hosted by Representative Robert Inglis (Republican, South Carolina) one participant demanded "keep your government hands off my Medicare" (Rucker 2009). The normalization of such rhetoric was and is not exclusively a Tea Party phenomenon, nor one exclusive to the political right. Nevertheless, we see great continuity between blanket claims about lowering taxes and policies without accompanying coherent proposals grounded in evidence and claims that building a wall on the southern border will stop unauthorized crossings.

Finally, let us speculate on the impact participation in the insurgency had on the grassroots activists who participated, and perhaps the larger mass of supporters. Participation in fevered insurgent mobilization can produce transformative change for activists throughout their subsequent lives (McAdam 1990). The number of participants in the Tea Party events was substantial, and tens of millions of Americans supported their work. It is likely that for many activists, and many supporters as well, having been part of the Tea Party insurgency produced a political awakening that shaped their beliefs and behavior for many years afterwards. Evidence from our web survey and many of our qualitative interviews indicates that for many of the activists, their work in Tea Party insurgency was their first serious brush with political activism. To the extent that these Americans remain actively engaged in electoral politics, political primaries, and other activities now, more than a decade later, the Tea Party insurgency's effects on local and national politics persevere.

Capturing the Dynamics of Insurgencies and Social Movements

We conclude by calling attention to, and highlighting, the vast trove of data we assembled that allowed us to pose many of the questions we have asked and attempted to answer. Our earliest attempts at tracking the Tea Party relied on the familiar, well-worn, protest event methodology. That research design locked us in to asking a narrow set of theoretical questions about the insurgency. It was clear that a research design moving beyond a strict focus on newspaper data was needed to capture the rich diversity of the Tea Party's activities and its trajectory. Our methodological approach helped circumvent the limitations of newspaper data, and allowed us to consider a broader set of important theoretical questions. This book's appendix describes in great detail how we collected our evidence by harnessing widely applicable methodological tools that are underutilized by social movement researchers. The empirical strategies can, we believe, serve as a template for studying the temporal and spatial trajectory of future insurgencies allowing more comprehensive theoretical and empirical explanations of political activism.

Appendix

Research Design: A Data Template for Spatiotemporal Collective Action Research

This appendix provides details about the major research designs and data collection strategies we employed across the entire project, and which are reflected in one or more chapters. There exists some overlap between the descriptions of research and design methodologies in our substantive chapters, with the more comprehensive summaries offered here. The appendix is intended to provide more exhaustive descriptions of each data collection strategy used across our analyses. We limit our focus to research designs and data collection strategies. We do not include discussion of the analytic techniques used, such as multilevel negative binomial regression, as their use is generally well established within the social scientific research community. We describe the protocols we created to sample: 1) Tea Party events; 2) Tea Party chapters; 3) IRS filing status for Tea Party groups; 4) Tax Day rallies; 5) Blog posts from Tea Party umbrella groups; 6) Twitter data on the IRS Scandal; 7) Our web survey of surviving Tea Party organizations; 8) Cable news coverage of the Tea Party; and 9) Qualitative interviews of Tea Party activists.

We rely regularly on data collection strategies that are less widely used by social scientists, prompting us to provide clear definitions of the techniques for clarity. We made extensive use of *web crawlers* to collect data. Web crawlers are computer programs designed to automate data harvesting from online sources and are ideal for large-scale data collection efforts that would have been prohibitive to complete if relying only on human labor. We built customized crawlers to look for events, organizational listings, blog posts, and other important data from Tea Party groups over the life of the insurgency. We designed these programs to be as efficient as possible and implemented numerous checks to ensure that each one did not burden the servers for the target websites (e.g., requiring the crawler to sleep for five seconds between requests). Other components of our data collection used *Application Programming Interfaces* (APIs), whenever available to streamline and automate data collection more efficiently. APIs are intermediaries between computers and servers that allow developers to submit structured queries and receive predictable responses to data requests. Unlike web crawlers, APIs are highly rule-governed and necessary for using websites such as Twitter, Google, and other major platforms. For example, our research design made extensive use of the Google Geocoding API, which streamlined placing Tea Party events or organizations in their spatial context. We also used the Meetup API to identify Tea Party chapters that were unaffiliated with the major organizing hubs of the insurgency.

In several sections below, we refer to the Tea Party umbrella groups, which were the main organizing hubs of Tea Party activism. To avoid repetition, our references to umbrella groups include, unless an exception is noted, the 1776 Tea Party, FreedomWorks, Patriot Action Network, Tea Party Nation, and Tea Party Patriots. The 1776 Tea Party is sometimes referred to as TeaParty.org, and the Patriot Action Network is also referred to as ResistNet. Data was also collected on independent Tea Party groups from Meetup, a social media platform that Tea Party activists used extensively to facilitate staging events.

TEA PARTY EVENTS

Our database of Tea Party protests, rallies, meetings, and other events was the product of a triangulated research design. The goal was to assemble the most comprehensive set of events possible by combining the traditional approach entailing sampling events from newspaper coverage, with the less typical strategy of using web data drawn from Tea Party umbrella groups. The complete database of events contains 19,758 cases with information about the event type, its date, and its spatial location. We used the event data in several chapters, most notably in Chapter 5, but also to create cumulative measures of Tea Party activity in Chapters 8 and 9. Note that the discussion which immediately follows documents our general approach to sampling Tea Party events. Our methodology for sampling the Tax Day rallies required a differently tailored approach, described in some detail later. These two sources were reconciled for all of our analyses of Tea Party activism.

Sampling Events from Newspapers

We collected 70,834 unique pieces of newspaper content about the Tea Party. This included any pertinent articles, editorials, letters to the editor, or photo captions referencing the Tea Party. As a shorthand, we refer to these as articles. This sample of newspaper data was drawn from the complete US-based, English newspapers database maintained by LexisNexis, which contained a total of 785 local, state, and national newspapers. This is an atypically large number of newspapers to be included for research on social movement mobilization, which typically relies on a much smaller number of sources. We used this expanded scope of sources since researchers have consistently found a regional bias in how likely it is that newspapers report on social movement mobilization: events occurring in close proximity to an outlet's editorial office are more likely to be featured in print (Ortiz et al. 2005; Rafail, McCarthy, and Sullivan 2019).

As a consequence of the large number of newspaper sources, we used keyword searches to eliminate clearly irrelevant articles from the full database maintained by LexisNexis. After testing several search strings, we ultimately settled on '"Tea Party" or "Tea Parties" to identify candidate articles. These strings were tested and compared with several alternatives and did the best job at identifying relevant content from the complete set of articles, based on our testing. We further constrained our search dates to the period between February 19, 2009, and December 31, 2014, the period capturing the main arc of Tea Party activism.

Since our keywords returned *any* newspaper content referencing the Tea Party, extensive post-processing was necessary to identify and distinguish the protests, meetings, and other events. Our solution involved two steps. First, we ran searches for the strings "protest" and "meeting" in the full text of each article, and set aside all matches for coding. For the remaining content, we developed a classifier to determine whether there was mention of any type of event. Classification is a widely used tool in machine learning, which involves training a model to make accurate predictions when processing new information based on the completed classification (Murphy 2012). Our workflow involved, first, building a random sample of 3,000 pieces of media content from the full set of 70,834 articles These 3,000 pieces of content were manually annotated by the authors and a team of research assistants to denote whether an event was mentioned. The full 3,000 manually labeled cases were split in half to create training and testing databases, used to build our classifier. We machine coded the full-text, title, and metadata for the articles to build 33 independent variables predictive of whether events were present. Using these variables, we estimated and compared the performance of several models to predict the results of our manually annotated training and testing data. Specifically, we estimated and compared the performance of models using support vector machines, logistic regression, stochastic gradient descent, classification trees, and naïve Bayes approaches. Of these, the support vector machine exhibited the best performance, with a precision of 0.94 and a recall of 0.73. The trained classifier was then used to identify 34,929 articles suspected of containing an event.

The final step involved training a team of research assistants to review each of the 34,929 articles, identify events, and when necessary, code the pertinent details. We developed a set of coding conventions for capturing the main features of each event, such as its location, type, and claims of participants that could be coded expeditiously given the sheer number of articles. During the coding process, we implemented regular reliability checks to ensuring minimum of 90% agreement on 1) the decision to code an article; 2) the events (if any) present in each article; and 3) the variables extracted from the full-text coverage.

Sampling Events Online

The newspaper data alone provide an incomplete picture of Tea Party activism, because we know events that are violent, large, or otherwise atypical are disproportionately featured (Earl et al. 2004). This is of particular concern for the Tea Party because the insurgency quickly shifted away from protest and toward maintenance events, which were far less likely to be featured in newspapers because of their lower newsworthiness. As well, violence, arrests, or other contentious tactics were incredibly rare at Tea Party gatherings. Our second major research design was implemented to extend and complement the newspaper data by relying on internet listings of Tea Party events drawn from the main umbrella groups. Unlike the more laborious newspaper-based data collection, assembling the online listings of Tea Party events was largely automated.

We built several web crawlers to look for all events listed on the websites of the umbrella groups. The web crawlers were run every 24 hours starting in 2009 or 2010, from when an umbrella group began posting event listings. We downloaded the source code for the web pages describing each event, as well as the full set of listings to create as comprehensive a database as possible. We also used the Meetup API to identify events sponsored by independent Tea Party groups. The Meetup platform was widely used by independent Tea Party groups that were independent from the umbrella organizations. Web crawlers were run through the end of 2014, or sooner if and when an umbrella group went offline. Once we had collected events, each was sent through a second workflow to extract the time, date, place, and textual description that accompanied the event. We also removed all HTML coding and other markup.

Coding Event Type

Once we had assembled the databases of Tea Party events from newspaper and web sources, we developed a computer program to code the events into one of four mutually exclusive and jointly exhaustive categories. These included *protests* and related actions, *meetings, awareness events*, and *political events*, as we described in Chapter 5. Since we were interested in only in-person or face-to-face events, we excluded all events that took place entirely online. We identified a total of 598 events that were entirely virtual, which represents only 3% of Tea Party events overall. Virtual events never exceeded 1% of all events. Last, any of these events appearing to direct activists to online seminars were excluded.

Our computer program searched for 28 specific keywords, strings, or other terms in the title and description of each event to code its type. The coded data were then passed through a decision tree that identified patterns or combinations of keywords to make a final determination about event type. We compared our machine coded results to a random sample of 1,000 events where we manually coded the event type and found over 93% agreement.

Geocoding the Events

Each event was geocoded to place it in spatial context. After determining whether an event was face-to-face, we drew upon all available details about the event's spatial location to place it. The workflow for geocoding was contingent on the source. For events drawn from newspaper coverage, we coded the address, intersection, or landmark along with the city and state of each event from the detailed descriptions included in each article. This approach was used in prior work (Rafail 2018b) to create granular spatial data on the location of social movement mobilization. Geocoding the data from umbrella groups was contingent on how each group made the location information available. FreedomWorks embedded the latitude and longitude of each event in the page source of the HTML files that we used to capture the details of each event. This allowed us to create specific location estimates for the latitude and longitude of each event, which then could be linked to the several geographic units of analysis, counties, or congressional districts, that we used.

The other umbrella groups included textual descriptions in their event listings specifying the location of specific events. To process these descriptions, we wrote computer programs to parse the source code of the webpages to extract, clean, and geocode each description specifying where each event took place. This information was usually a specific street address or a business, a park, or another specific location. The Google Geocoding API is sufficiently flexible that it is able to process specific street addresses as well as the location of businesses, restaurants, or other points of assembly. As a robustness check, we randomly sampled our geocoded results to ensure that they matched the locations provided in the event descriptions. These checks indicated that our workflow effectively and correctly spatially placed the events. Finally, not all the events that we captured occurred in specific physical location. These events, as well as others like petitions and boycotts that were held entirely online, were not geocoded.

Identifying Duplicate Events and Final Cleaning Steps

Since our data on events was drawn from multiple sources, a major concern was the possible presence of duplicate events in our main database. Once the events from all our disparate sources were assembled into a main database, this concern was corroborated, as we found that 15% of the events in our resulting database had come from at least two different sources. Given this pattern, we developed a workflow to identify duplicate events using the fine-grained spatial and temporal information that we assembled for each event. We geocoded all the events to the county-level, and then manually reviewed all events taking place in the same county on the same date. If the events were clearly of a different type (e.g., a meeting and a protest), we treated them as distinct. For clusters of events of the same type in the same location, we read the description of each event and its organizers (when known) to determine whether each event was unique. During this phase, we also compared date ranges to identify duplicates (e.g., events occurring in the same county in the same week). Using larger temporal windows did not increase the accuracy of the data.

TEA PARTY CHAPTERS

A central focus of our analyses in Chapters 3, 4, 6, 8, and 9 involved the thousands of local Tea Party organizations that spread across the country starting in 2009. The research design we built to sample organizations ultimately found evidence that a total of 3,587 Tea Party groups were active at some point between 2009 and 2014. Previous research on Tea Party groups typically used cross-sectional data drawn from a single extraction of the main umbrella groups (Banerjee 2013; Burghart and Zeskind 2010). Our evidence on the ebb and flow of organizational births and deaths indicates that this strategy very likely over-estimated the number of active groups at any particular point of time. In contrast, our research design for sampling Tea Party chapters is dynamic over time and place. It is therefore a substantial improvement over earlier efforts to estimate the spatial distribution and temporal trajectory of Tea Party chapters.

Sampling Tea Party Chapters

Local Tea Party chapters began to emerge in early 2009 following the founding of the small number of "test-marketed Astroturf" groups we described in Chapter 3 (see also Lo 2012). Aside from these groups, organizational building did not begin in earnest until after the April 15 Tax Day rallies in 2009, when the main Tea Party umbrella groups appeared online. The decentralized organizational structure of the Tea Party meant that a single comprehensive list of local chapters never existed. Our sampling strategy mimics our research design for events by drawing from multiple sources to create a single, more comprehensive database.

This research design involved using web crawlers to index the entire set of organizations appearing on the umbrella groups' websites. The web crawlers were run every 24 hours across our entire analytic period. This level of detail was crucial to producing more precise estimates of the emergence and disappearance of local chapters, as well as in identifying overall patterns of organizational growth during the main wave of Tea Party activity. After the primary harvesting of organizational listings each day, we ran a second computer program to parse the results and look for newly founded groups. If new groups were present, we downloaded the individual webpage for each group which we stored in a separate database. This strategy ensured that we had collected data on each group within 24 hours of its founding.

We monitored the performance of our web scrapers daily during the data collection phase by programming them to produce daily reports detailing error rates or other glitches that may have suggested changes in the source code of the target website or other issues that may have required an update to our programs. In cases where the reports pointed to atypical error rates and other problems, we manually reviewed the website data within 24 hours and made all necessary corrections. This step was essential to maintaining the integrity of our chapter time-series and gave us higher confidence in the granular estimates of organizational founding and decline.

Identifying Relevant Groups

Our web scrapers were built to capture all organizational listings appearing on the target websites without regard to their name, activity status, or other criteria. One consequence of this decision was that this data collection strategy produced a sample of local chapters that included many groups that did not appear to be affiliated with the Tea Party insurgency. Some of the local groups' lists were created to help elect specific politicians, promote conservative causes beyond the Tea Party's issues, or otherwise advance claims that we deemed to be outside the scope of our analysis. Such groups were particularly present on the websites for FreedomWorks and the Patriot Action Network, where non-Tea Party groups were more commonly listed.

We filtered non-Tea Party groups out of the sample using a multipronged approach that considered all groups whose name contained the string "tea party" to be members of the Tea Party movement. Since many Tea Party groups were also affiliated with Glenn Beck's 9/12 movement or referred to themselves as patriots, we extracted all cases that contained either "9/12" or "patriot" and manually reviewed their description to determine relevance. Last, for the remaining groups, we began by reviewing the name of each group to determine whether it appeared affiliated with the Tea Party movement. In cases where we could make a clear determination of relevance, we coded the group accordingly. In more ambiguous cases, we reviewed the group's description as a final arbiter of relevance. These steps were quite labor intensive, but nevertheless were necessary to avoid including groups in our sample that were unrelated to the Tea Party.

Consolidating Duplicate Groups

During data collection, we grew suspicious of duplicate Tea Party groups within and between the listings of the main umbrella groups and on Meetup.

We adjusted our scrapers to create multiple unique identification codes for each group, using their name, founding date, and unique web address to more effectively track changes to the online presence of individual groups. This extra effort was vindicated, as many groups appeared again and again, several up to eight times across and within our different data sources. Finally, the umbrella groups carried out multiple redesigns during our analysis period, in the process changing the unique URL for each group.

We designed our web scrapers to identify and download all group listings, allowing us to identify and account for duplicate cases more effectively during our analysis using the full, non-unique, set of groups. As noted above, we collected the dedicated webpage for each group within 24 hours of its appearance. To supplement this step, we also completed subsequent downloads of all known groups every three months for the duration of data collection. This allowed us to coarsely trace the membership size of each group.

Once data collection was complete, we sorted each group by its state (as indicated online) and name. Next, we manually reviewed the name of each group to identify and consolidate duplicates. During this process, we found several groups with minor spelling variants that were consolidated, as well as groups appearing across multiple umbrella groups. Overall, we found that 11% of listed chapters appeared at least twice. Duplicates were excluded to create our final sample of groups.

Geocoding Chapter Location

The Tea Party groups were geocoded to their county and congressional district using the Google Geocoding API, which provided a location description on their individual webpages that were available for all umbrella groups. Similar to its handling of events, groups on FreedomWorks published geographical coordinates for all groups, which we used to identify their location. In most cases, geocoding chapters was a straightforward process because their activities took place in a relatively contained location, such as a single city or county. This allowed us to easily link each chapter to its county of operation or its congressional district. For approximately 100 groups, placement was more complicated because they were multicounty coalitions of Tea Party activists or otherwise did not mobilize in a single area. These groups were reviewed individually to determine the most appropriate specific location based on their membership, activities, and any other clarifying information. In all our statistical analyses, we conducted a separate analysis that included a flag for multi-area organizations as a robustness check. The flag was not statistically significant at $p<0.05$ (two-tailed) in these tests. We concluded, therefore, that the small number of multicounty chapters did not have a substantive impact on our many analyses. Finally, we randomly sampled geocoded chapters to ensure the integrity of our results. These checks indicated that the geocoding process was working as expected.

Estimating Chapter Size

The organizational listings available on the websites for each Tea Party umbrella group contained lists of members affiliated with each group. As a component of our data collection workflow for groups, we collected membership counts each time we scraped the groups. Since we collected data on each group upon identification, as well as every three months subsequently, the estimates were regularly updated.

It was theoretically possible to create dynamic counts of group membership with this research design. However, extrapolating chapter size from online listings will inevitably create noisy and frankly questionable estimates of actual membership counts. There is almost certainly a gap between the number of actual members of a local group at any specific point in time and the online listings of membership. Based on our several years of monitoring the Tea Party umbrella groups, it was clear that group memberships rarely declined, but only grew. The membership counts also remained online even for groups that had long since ceased any discernible form of mobilization. We suggest that the online listings, therefore, have a high upward bias and do not represent actual membership counts at any specific point in time, most likely only peak membership.

IRS FILING STATUS FOR TEA PARTY GROUPS

We built a separate workflow to identify all groups that engaged in some capacity with the Internal Revenue Service (IRS) to supplement the website data on Tea Party organizations. IRS scrutiny of Tea Party groups resulted in a significant backlash starting in 2013, making information on the filing patterns of the groups a valuable addition to our existing databases. Any social movement organization can petition the IRS to secure a non-taxable status, typically registering as either 501(c)(3) or 501(c)(4) within the US tax code. Such groups do not pay any federal tax and in return accept certain restrictions on their activities (e.g., explicitly political activities and lobbying). When approved, 501(c) groups are required to file annual returns with the IRS, using Form 990 (or Form 990-EZ). The information included in these forms provides useful details concerning the resources of a filing group for each filing year.

We searched for 990 forms submitted by Tea Party groups using three different sources. In all cases, we used the search string "tea party" to identify candidate groups. Alternatives such as "patriot" yielded an exorbitant number of false positives that significantly increased the amount of dross. We began searching the Tax Exempt Organization Check that is maintained by the IRS (https://apps.irs.gov/app/eos). This tool contains information on all 501(c) organizations that filed a Form 990 since 2007. Next, we searched for organizations listed by the National Center on Charitable Statistics that is maintained by the Urban Institute (https://nccsweb.urban.org). This database contains listings of organizations that had filed hard copies of Form 990 during our data collection period. Finally, we used Guidestar, a commercial database that contains information on nonprofit and charitable organizations including 990 filings. After combining the information available in these databases, we identified a total of 133 Tea Party groups that engaged with the IRS in at least some capacity. We coded whether each of these groups had their 501(c) petition approved, and whenever possible, collected and coded the information available in their annual filings of Form 990s. These data provide the basis of our analyses in Chapter 4.

Our research designs to capture the universe of local Tea Party groups and events were, we believed, well-suited to those tasks; however during data collection it became clear that a more focused workflow was required to sample the Tax Day rallies. These events were sometimes listed on a dedicated section of an umbrella group's website, making Tax Day rallies more difficult to identify with our workflows for chapter and event identification. We modified our approach to build a triangulated research design specifically aimed at identifying as many Tea Party rallies as possible. This method was updated annually each year between 2009 and 2014. Our final accounting of all rallies relies on two primary sources. First, we included listings of rallies on various Tea Party websites and Google's Search API. Second, we utilized two sources of media attention to the Tax Day rallies.

Website Listings of Tax Day Rallies

Starting in 2009, we exhaustively downloaded the websites used to organize the Tax Day rallies. The specific websites activists built each year varied as the Tea Party evolved and different organizing hubs appeared and disappeared online. After 2009, as each Tax Day approached we searched broadly for any event listings we could locate on the internet, aimed at maximizing the breadth of our data collection. Once identified, we exhaustively downloaded the raw HTML, images, and other information (e.g., press kits made available to activists). Once we collected this information, research assistants combed through the HTML files to identify events along with their location and other information listed by the organizers.

The 2009 Tax Day rallies were organized on a single website (taxdayteaparty.com). By 2010, we expanded our search grid to include the websites for FreedomWorks, Tea Party groups on Meetup, and the Tea Party Patriots. Importantly, in 2010, the taxdayteaparty.com website was no longer used as an organizing hub and did not contain any event listings. In 2011, we sampled from the 1776 Tea Party, Americans for Prosperity, FreedomWorks, Meetup, Patriot Action Network, Tea Party Nation, and Tea Party Patriots. We also supplemented this by using the Google Search API to identify any other events. In 2012, we expanded our list further to include all prior groups and the Tea Party Express, and also added Tea Party Perspective in 2013. For our final year of data collection in 2014, we collected website data from each of the aforementioned groups that remained active.

After we had completed processing the events to create our initial list, we geocoded the events with the Google Maps API. Though much of our analysis was conducted at the county-level, we always compiled the most fine-grained information available for geocoding purposes. We generated street addresses for each event using the textual descriptions available online, and used the addresses to capture the coordinates for each event. When the Google Maps API did not return coordinates (e.g., due to typographical errors in the address in the online listings), we manually corrected each case.

Newspaper Coverage of Tax Day Rallies

To ensure that we had a secondary source of information on the Tax Day rallies, we also used a sample of events listed in two databases of newspapers. This step also allowed us to code the characteristics of each protest event using the newspaper coverage. The newspaper data came from two sources: first, we used 452 newspapers from the Access World News database. Second, we use the LexisNexis database, which had another 785 newspapers. Both sources are full-text searchable archives of local, state, and national newspapers. Researchers have consistently found that using a single source to collect a national sample of social movement mobilization may introduce a significant geographic bias (Myers and Caniglia 2004; Ortiz et al. 2005; Rafail et al. 2019), so our use of 1,287 separate sources helped to minimize any such biases since we included hundreds of newspapers published in every state and the District of Columbia. Our wider net increased the total number of events that we identified and coded.

To identify articles about the Tax Day rallies in Access World News and LexisNexis, we used the search string '"tea party" or "tea parties" between April 1 and April 22 each year. We used a two-step design to process the candidate articles. First, we identified all articles appearing to be pertinent, which were then downloaded to a centralized database. Second, once we had assembled our complete set of articles, we trained a team of research assistants to code the information using a standardized codebook. We trained them to code basic information about each event, including where and when it occurred, and more detailed information about the size, claims, activities, and organizational sponsors of each gathering. Throughout the coding process we conducted regular reliability checks to ensure that we had a minimum of 90% agreement on all variables (though agreement was generally above 95%). Once new events were identified, they were also geocoded using the procedure described above.

Our coding process also involved manually linking the events covered in newspapers to the website listings of Tax Day rallies. We began by creating an event-level database from the online lists that contained the address, city, county, and state for each gathering. When the research assistants identified a Tax Day rally in the newspaper coverage, they were trained to first look for the event in the existing database, and then add new cases as they came up. After this primary coding was completed, we made a second pass through the database to identify and remove potential duplicates. To do so, we sorted by county and state to identify areas where multiple events occurred in close proximity. These events were then screened to ensure that each event was unique, and duplicates were deleted from subsequent analyses.

BLOG POSTS FROM TEA PARTY UMBRELLA GROUPS

The blog posts that we used in several chapters were drawn from the Tea Party umbrella groups, each of which had a blogging platform. These platforms adopted used a bridge blogging format (Karpf 2008), as any individual or group with an account could post content on the site. Our data collection strategy involved running web crawlers to identify posts and to save the HTML of each post in a database. The content of these posts was then used for analysis along with basic metadata on the title, author, and date of publication. We also collected the comments attached to each of the blog posts, but we did not use this material for our analyses in this book. These crawlers were run on the first of each month to identify and save to a database all new posts. For posts that we had already saved, our web crawlers also looked for new comments on the original post and stored that information as well. In cases where new comments were posted, we downloaded the updated listing while retaining all prior downloads in case the original post had been altered.

Our priorities during data collection were comprehensiveness, excising advertisements, and minimizing noise. We applied several filters to the blog data. These included eliminating posts not containing any written content (e.g., those containing only embedded videos), submissions appearing to be spam or unrelated self-promotions, and those with other irrelevant content. We processed each post to strip away the HTML, JavaScript, and other markup embedded in our source documents, leaving only the raw text for subsequent analysis. Our impressions from our several years of observing posting patterns was that few, if any, posts were removed for content reasons as even clear cases of spam remained accessible for several years. Accordingly, our sample of blogs is as close to a census of posted content as was possible.

TWITTER DATA ON THE IRS SCANDAL

To capture real-time reactions to the IRS scandal described and analyzed in Chapter 5, our research design used contemporaneous data collection with

Twitter's Search API. We sampled from what Rafail (2018a) calls a topic-restricted semi-bounded population, in that we restricted our data collection to posts on the IRS scandal, but did not restrict the accounts in our data collection workflow. Prior studies have shown that the Search API can defensibly capture topics that are being actively discussed on Twitter, especially when other APIs (e.g., the Streaming API) would not return adequate coverage (Driscoll and Walker 2014; Morstatter et al. 2013).

We built a computer program that interfaced with the Twitter Search API that ran constantly between May 20, 2013, and June 5, 2013. This period coincides with the emergence of the IRS scandal as a major news focus and while Tea Party activists organized a coordinated set of protests in response. We used the terms #dcintervention, #irs*, irs, Internal Revenue Service, #tcot, #teaparty, and Tea Party to query the Search API. We iterated over each term for the duration of our data collection to maximize the number of tweets captured in our sample. The search terms were based on either specific hashtags promoted by Tea Party groups, such as the Tea Party Patriot's amplification of the #dcintervention hashtag for the protests, or other hashtags and terms that emerged as relevant during the course of data collection.

This data collection strategy appears to have captured a census of all tweets about the IRS scandal during our analytic period, or at a minimum a defensible approximation of nearly all the tweets of interest. Our sampling strategy returned a cumulative 12,195,119 tweets, of which 814,812 were unique. The high number of duplicate tweets is evidence that our search terms exhausted the conversations based upon our search terms. The Twitter API allows up to 1,000 tweets per search request, and based on our real-time monitoring, none of our search terms exceeded this threshold during data collection.

After collecting the full database of Twitter content, we manually reviewed a random sample of 1,000 tweets to gauge the prevalence of content included that was unrelated to the IRS scandal. After experimenting with several combinations to filter out irrelevant tweets returned by our broad search terms, we retained only the tweets containing any combination of the strings "irs," "internal revenue service," "monitoring," or "scandal." Based on our random sample, selecting on these strings correctly classified the relevant tweets in 98% of cases. We used the filtered set of tweets in Chapter 5.

OUR WEB SURVEY OF SURVIVING TEA PARTY ORGANIZATIONS

During our core data collection of Tea Party events and organizations, it became clear that supplemental information about chapters would be helpful and could only be obtained by contacting surviving Tea Party groups. To do so, we designed a web survey for Tea Party chapters that remained active in 2015. Surveying local Tea Party organizations posed a unique challenge. As mentioned earlier, there exists no single, comprehensive list of local Tea

Party organizations, let alone one that included contact information. To collect contact information for Tea Party organizations we first began with a list of Tea Parties generated from the main umbrella groups as well as searches of websites hosting Tax Days, based on our web scrapers. Next, we searched websites, event listings, and social media sites to look for contact information for either the highest ranking official within each local Tea Party organization or its contact information. When multiple email addresses were identified, we used the email that specified the highest-ranking group officer. In addition to searching current online documents, we used the *Wayback Machine* to locate information for local Tea Party groups that no longer maintained active websites.

Through this triangulated effort we were able to identify a total of 653 organizational email addresses, though as we outlined in Chapter 6, based on their activity patterns, many of these groups had clearly long ceased operations. This is reflected in our response rates. Of the 653 email addresses to which we sent survey invitations, nearly 15% of messages were immediately returned as undeliverable. Given the precipitous decline of Tea Party activism by late 2014, we believe that many more of these 653 email accounts were no longer being actively monitored even if the email accounts themselves remained active. Of the 556 deliverable email addresses, we know that at least 211 were monitored as a recipient clicked on the survey link. After numerous follow-up messages were sent to each address, we ultimately received a total of 99 fully, or mostly, completed surveys. Since it is unclear exactly how many of the 556 email addresses were monitored, it is difficult to calculate an accurate response rate.

Our questionnaire included up to 118 questions, though we extensively used skips and contingent questions to minimize respondent burden. Our questions focused on each aspect of the group's activities, including their membership size, monetary and fiscal resources, whether they had applied for a 501(c) status with the IRS, and annual expenses. While constructing our questionnaire, we put particular emphasis on asking open-ended questions about each group's activities, relationship to the Republican Party, and overall approach to staging protest events. The open-ended questions were qualitatively coded, which provided useful information that complemented our quantitative data. Organizations that completed the survey received a summary report documenting the main findings.

The completed surveys came from across the US. Respondents were most prevalent in Texas and Illinois. Most respondents (89%) indicated that their Tea Party remained active, though this is likely an artifact of our survey design. Most of the groups were early riser Tea Party organizations, as over 55% were founded in 2009. Another 33% of groups were formed in 2010. The majority of respondents (70%) indicated that they, personally, had been involved in the founding of their group and the majority indicated that they continued to play a leadership role.

CABLE NEWS COVERAGE OF THE TEA PARTY

Our data on cable news coverage of the Tea Party included all references to the insurgency appearing on CNN, Fox News, and MSNBC between 2009 and 2014. We also included coverage from Fox Business News, as it also devoted extensive airtime to the Tea Party. The coverage itself came from the transcripts of each show on the networks contained in the Access World News archives. We used keyword searches of the transcripts for each network during our analytic period, using the string '"tea party" or "tea parties" to identify pertinent content. Tests on this search string indicated its high efficiency at filtering out irrelevant content while retaining coverage of the insurgency. We downloaded the HTML source for each transcript that mentioned the Tea Party, which we then used in our analysis. We also collected basic metadata on each case, including the name of the show and the date it was aired.

An immediate limitation with the keyword searches was that they returned the full transcript of each broadcast even if the show only mentioned the Tea Party in passing. To account for this, we narrowed the textual information to contain what we called mentions of the Tea Party. Mentions were operationally defined as the three sentences before and after any sentence that referenced the Tea Party. We experimented by using variable numbers of sentences before and after each reference to the Tea Party and found that three sentences adequately captured the context of most references while excluding irrelevant information. Thus, an individual broadcast analyzed could sometimes have multiple mentions of the Tea Party.

QUALITATIVE INTERVIEWS OF TEA PARTY LEADERS

A final component of our research design included qualitative interviews from 34 Tea Party leaders. The interviews were completed by Michael Heaney as a component of a project he carried out with Fabio Rojas (Heaney and Rojas 2011, 2015). Heaney provided us with the full-text transcripts of each interview. We thank Dr. Heaney for sharing this data with us – it was very useful in several chapters and in helping us develop our ecological arguments about the Tea Party. The research design for completing the interviews is described by Heaney and Rojas, to which we refer the reader. We adopted a summative coding approach (Hsieh and Shannon 2005) to the transcripts. We began coding the interviews by first carefully reading and annotating themes in their entirety to identify major themes. Next, we re-read the documents to refine our core codes and create subcategories that we used for analysis.

CONCLUSION

The research designs and workflows that we have discussed are replicable for investigating a wide variety of social movements, insurgencies, and other forms of contentious political action. We hope that the dense details we provide here provide the basis of a customizable template for capturing the main activities and groups for other movements beyond the Tea Party. Scholars have concluded that relying exclusively on mass media accounts of social movement mobilization may obfuscate the claims, rhetoric, and activities of activists (McAdam et al. 2005). We agree, and argue that using triangulated samples of organizations, events, and claims as we have done for the Tea Party can significantly improve the depth and scope of evidence generated to understand the trajectory of other insurgencies and social movements.

At the same time, the web data that we collected is certainly not a panacea. The web scrapers and other automated tools we used enabled us to collect large amounts of data quickly and quite efficiently. But in all cases, the resulting databases required extensive post-processing, manual adjustments, and other corrections. Using web data without the extensive post-processing would have created significant overestimation of the Tea Party's size and activities. Future work using such techniques must pay particular attention to issues of data quality rather than assuming that information gathered from online resources, once captured, is immediately ready for analysis.

References

Abbott, Andrew. 1995. "Sequence Analysis: New Methods for Old Ideas." *Annual Review of Sociology* 21: 93–113.

Airstrup, Joseph A. 2011. "Racism, Resentment, and Regionalism: The South and the Nation in the 2008 Presidential Election." *American Review of Politics* 32: 131–154. doi: 10.15763/issn.2374-7781.2011.32.0.131-154.

Almeida, Paul. 2010. "Social Movement Partyism: Collective Action and Oppositional Political Parties," pp. 170–196 in *Strategic Alliances: Coalition Building and Social Movements*, edited by N. Van Dyke and H. J. McCammon. Minneapolis, MN: University of Minnesota Press.

   2019. "The Role of Threat in Collective Action," pp. 43–62 in *Wiley-Blackwell Companion to Social Movements*, edited by D. Snow, S. Soule, H. Kriesi, and H. McCammon. Oxford: Wiley-Blackwell.

Almeida, Paul, and Nella Van Dyke. 2014. "Social Movement Partyism and the Tea Party's Rapid Mobilization," pp. 55–72 in *Understanding the Tea Party Movement*, edited by N. Van Dyke and D. S. Meyer. Burlington, VT: Ashgate Publishing Company.

Amenta, Edwin, Neal Caren, Elizabeth Chiarello, and Yang Su. 2010. "The Political Consequences of Social Movements." *Annual Review of Sociology* 36: 287–307.

Anderson, Sarah E., Daniel M. Butler, and Laurel Harbridge-Yong. 2020. *Rejecting Compromise: Legislators' Fear of Primary Voters*. Cambridge: Cambridge University Press.

Andrews, Kenneth T. 1997. "The Impacts of Social Movements on the Political Process: The Civil Rights Movement and Black Electoral Politics in Mississippi." *American Sociological Review* 62(5): 800–819. doi: 10.2307/2657361.

   2001. "Social Movements and Policy Implementation: The Mississippi Civil Rights Movement and the War on Poverty, 1965 to 1971." *American Sociological Review* 66(1): 71–95. doi: 10.2307/2657394.

Andrews, Kenneth T., and Michael Biggs. 2006. "The Dynamics of Protest Diffusion: Movement Organizations, Social Networks, and News Media in the 1960 Sit-Ins." *American Sociological Review* 71(5): 752–777.

Andrews, Kenneth T., and Neal Caren. 2010. "Making the News: Movement Organizations, Media Attention, and the Public Agenda." *American Sociological Review* 75(6): 841–866. doi: https://doi.org/10.1177/0003122410386689.

Andrews, Kenneth T., Marshall Ganz, Matthew Baggetta, Hahrie Han, and Chaeyoon Lim. 2010. "Leadership, Membership, and Voice: Civic Associations That Work." *American Journal of Sociology* 115(4): 1191–1242. doi: 10.1086/649060.

Anonymous. 2012. "Tea Party Express Endorses Ted Cruz for Senate in Waco." *Waco Tribune.* Retrieved April 12, 2021 (https://wacotrib.com/blogs/waco_politics_report/tea-party-express-endorses-ted-cruz-for-senate-in-waco/article_522b2244-d22f-5aed-bb4d-587c900c92c9.html).

2016. "Tea Party Patriots Citizens Fund PAC | Tea Party Patriots Citizens Fund Endorses Senator Ted Cruz for President." Retrieved March 3, 2022 (https://web.archive.org/web/20160309104618/https://www.teapartypatriotscitizensfund.com/find-out-who-tppcf-just-endorsed-for-president).

Arceneaux, Kevin, and Stephen P. Nicholson. 2012. "Who Wants to Have a Tea Party? The Who, What, and Why of the Tea Party Movement." *PS: Political Science & Politics* 45(4): 700–710. doi: 10.1017/S1049096512000741.

Association of Religion Data Archives. 2018. "Religious Congregations and Membership Study, 2000 (Counties File)." doi: 10.17605/OSF.IO/AV9KG.

Bader, Hans. 2009. "How ACORN Destroyed the Housing Market." *Competitive Enterprise Institute.* Retrieved December 30, 2019 (https://cei.org/blog/how-acorn-destroyed-the-housing-market).

Baldassarri, Delia, and Andrew Gelman. 2008. "Partisans without Constraint: Political Polarization and Trends in American Public Opinion." *American Journal of Sociology* 114(2): 408–446. doi: 10.1086/590649.

Balz, Daniel J., and Ronald Brownstein. 1996. *Storming the Gates: Protest Politics and the Republican Revival.* Boston, MA: Little, Brown.

Banerjee, Tarun. 2013. "Media, Movements, and Mobilization: Tea Party Protests in the United States, 2009–2010." *Research in Social Movements, Conflicts and Change* 36: 39–75.

Barreto, Matt A., Betsy L. Cooper, Benjamin Gonzalez, Christopher S. Parker, and Christopher Towler. 2011. "The Tea Party in the Age of Obama: Mainstream Conservatism or Out-Group Anxiety?" *Political Power and Social Theory* 22: 105–137.

Bauder, David. 2002. "Fox News Overtakes CNN in Ratings." Retrieved March 6, 2020 (www.ourmidland.com/news/article/Fox-News-Overtakes-CNN-in-Ratings-7076902.php).

Baum, Joel A. C., and Jitendra V. Singh. 1994a. "Organizational Niches and the Dynamics of Organizational Founding." *Organization Science* 5(4): 483–501. doi: 10.1287/orsc.5.4.483.

1994b. "Organizational Niches and the Dynamics of Organizational Mortality." *American Journal of Sociology* 100(2): 346–380.

Benford, Robert D. 1993. "Frame Disputes within the Nuclear Disarmament Movement." *Social Forces* 71(3): 677–701. doi: 10.1093/sf/71.3.677.

1997. "An Insider's Critique of the Social Movement Framing Perspective." *Sociological Inquiry* 67(4): 409–430.

Benford, Robert D., and David A. Snow. 2000. "Framing Processes and Social Movements: An Overview and Assessment." *Annual Review of Sociology* 26: 611–639.

Benkirane, Reda. 2012. "The Alchemy of Revolution: The Role of Social Networks and New Media in the Arab Spring." GCSP Policy Paper 2012/7. Geneva: Geneva Centre for Security Policy.

Benkler, Yochai, Robert Faris, and Hal Roberts. 2018. *Network Propaganda: Manipulation, Disinformation, and Radicalization in American Politics*. New York, NY: Oxford University Press.

Bennett, Kevin J., Matthew Yuen, and Francisco Blanco-Silva. 2018. "Geographic Differences in Recovery after the Great Recession." *Journal of Rural Studies* 59: 111–117. doi: 10.1016/j.jrurstud.2018.02.008.

Berry, Jeffrey M. 2003. *A Voice for Nonprofits*. Washington, DC: Brookings Institution Press.

2017. "Tea Party Decline." Paper presented at the *American Political Science Association Annual Meeting*, August 31–September 3, 2017, San Francisco, CA.

Beyerlein, Kraig, Peter Ryan, Aliyah Abu-Hazeem, and Amity Pauley. 2018. "The 2017 Women's March: A National Study of Solidarity Events." *Mobilization: An International Quarterly* 23(4): 425–449. doi: 10.17813/1086-671X-23-4-425.

Blee, Kathleen M., and Ashley Currier. 2006. "How Local Social Movement Groups Handle a Presidential Election." *Qualitative Sociology* 29(3): 261. doi: 10.1007/s11133-006-9025-x.

Blei, David M., Andrew Y. Ng, and Michael I. Jordan. 2003. "Latent Dirichlet Allocation." *Journal of Machine Learning Research* 3: 993–1022.

Blum, Rachel M. 2020. *How the Tea Party Captured the GOP: Insurgent Factions in American Politics*. Chicago, IL: University of Chicago Press.

Bojar, Abel, Theresa Gessler, Swen Hutter, and Hanspeter Kriesi, eds. 2021. *Contentious Episodes in the Age of Austerity: Studying the Dynamics of Government–Challenger Interactions*. New York, NY: Cambridge University Press.

Boykoff, Jules. 2007. "Surveillance, Spatial Compression, and Scale: The FBI and Martin Luther King Jr." *Antipode* 39(4): 729–756.

Braunstein, Ruth, and Malaena Taylor. 2017. "Is the Tea Party a 'Religious' Movement? Religiosity in the Tea Party versus the Religious Right." *Sociology of Religion* 78(1): 33–59. doi: 10.1093/socrel/srw056.

Bremer, Björn, Swen Hutter, and Hanspeter Kriesi. 2020. "Dynamics of Protest and Electoral Politics in the Great Recession." *European Journal of Political Research* 59(4): 842–866. doi: 10.1111/1475-6765.12375.

Brock, David, Ari Rabin-Havt, and Media Matters for America. 2012. *The Fox Effect: How Roger Ailes Turned a Network into a Propaganda Machine*. New York, NY: Anchor Books.

Brody, David. 2012. *The Teavangelicals: The Inside Story of How the Evangelicals and the Tea Party Are Taking Back America*. Grand Rapids, MI: Zondervan.

Brown, Heath. 2015. *The Tea Party Divided: The Hidden Diversity of a Maturing Movement*. Santa Barbara, CA: Praeger.

Bureau of Labor Statistics. 2012. *The Recession of 2007–2009*. Washington, DC.

Burghart, Devin, and Leonard Zeskind. 2010. *Tea Party Nationalism: A Critical Examination of the Tea Party Movement and the Size, Scope, and Focus of Its*

National Factions. Kansas City, MO: Institute for Research and Education on Human Rights.

2015. *The Tea Party Movement in 2015*. Kansas City, MO: Institute for Research and Education on Human Rights.

Calhoun, Craig. 2013. "Occupy Wall Street in Perspective." *British Journal of Sociology* 64(1): 26–38.

Campbell, Andrea Louise. 2013. "Tax Attitudes in the Obama Era." *Tax Law Review* 67(4): 647–668.

Caren, Neal, Sarah Gaby, and Catherine Herrold. 2017. "Economic Breakdown and Collective Action." *Social Problems* 64(1): 133–155. doi: 10.1093/socpro/spw030.

Cassino, Dan, Peter Woolley, and Krista N. Jenkins. 2012. *What You Know Depends on What You Watch: Current Events Knowledge across Popular News Sources*. Teaneck, NJ: Fairleigh Dickinson University.

Cho, Wendy K. Tam, James G. Gimpel, and Daron R. Shaw. 2012. "The Tea Party Movement and the Geography of Collective Action." *Quarterly Journal of Political Science* 7(2): 105–33. doi: 10.1561/100.00011051.

CNN and Opinion Research Corporation. 2010. *CNN/ORC Poll*. Atlanta, GA: CNN.

Committee on Finance. 2015. *The Internal Revenue Service's Processing of 501(c)(3) and 501(c)(4) Applications for Tax-Exempt Status Submitted by "Political Advocacy" Organizations from 2010–2013*, pp. 114–119. Washington, DC: United States Senate.

Congressional Budget Office. 2012. *Estimated Impact of the American Recovery and Reinvestment Act on Employment and Economic Output from October 2011 through December 2011*. Washington, DC: Congressional Budget Office.

2018. *The Budget and Economic Outlook: 2018 to 2028*. Washington, DC.

Conservapedia. 2019. "Rick Santelli." Retrieved July 1, 2019 (www.conservapedia.com/Rick_Santelli#cite_note-4).

Corn, David. 2021. "Sponsors of the Pre-Attack Rally Have Taken Down Their Websites. Don't Forget Who They Were." *Mother Jones*. Retrieved September 30, 2022 (www.motherjones.com/politics/2021/01/sponsors-of-the-pre-attack-rally-have-taken-down-their-websites-dont-forget-who-they-were).

Cornwell, Benjamin. 2015. *Social Sequence Analysis: Methods and Applications*. New York, NY: Cambridge University Press.

Courser, Zachary. 2012. "The Tea 'Party' as a Conservative Social Movement." *Society* 49(1): 43–53. doi: 10.1007/s12115-011-9501-0.

Cress, Daniel M., and David A. Snow. 2000. "The Outcomes of Homeless Mobilization: The Influence of Organization, Disruption, Political Mediation, and Framing." *American Journal of Sociology* 105(4): 1063–1104.

Cunningham, David. 2004. *There's Something Happening Here: The New Left, the Klan, and FBI Counterintelligence*. Berkeley, CA: University of California Press.

Cunningham, David, and Benjamin T. Phillips. 2007. "Contexts for Mobilization: Spatial Settings and Klan Presence in North Carolina, 1964–1966." *American Journal of Sociology* 113(3): 781–814.

Cunningham, Maurice T. 2021. "Boardroom Progressives or Rich People's Movement?" pp. 41–62 in *Dark Money and the Politics of School Privatization*, edited by M. T. Cunningham. Cham, CH: Springer International Publishing.

Cynamon, Barry Z., and Steven M. Fazzari. 2016. "Inequality, the Great Recession and Slow Recovery." *Cambridge Journal of Economics* 40(2): 373–399. doi: 10.1093/cje/bev016.

Davenport, Christian. 2015. *How Social Movements Die: Repression and Demobilization of the Republic of New Africa.* New York, NY: Cambridge University Press.

DiMaggio, Anthony R. 2011. *The Rise of the Tea Party: Political Discontent and Corporate Media in the Age of Obama.* New York, NY: New York University Press.

DiMaggio, Paul J., Manish Nag, and David Blei. 2013. "Exploiting Affinities between Topic Modeling and the Sociological Perspective on Culture: Application to Newspaper Coverage of US Government Arts Funding." *Poetics* 41(6): 570–606.

DiMaggio, Paul J., and Walter W. Powell. 1983. "The Iron Cage Revisited: Institutional Isomorphism and Collective Rationality in Organizational Fields." *American Sociological Review* 48(2): 147–160. doi: 10.2307/2095101.

Driscoll, Kevin, and Shawn Walker. 2014. "Working within a Black Box: Transparency in the Collection and Production of Big Twitter Data." *International Journal of Communication* 8(1): 1745–1764.

Dupont, Cédric, and Florence Passy. 2011. "The Arab Spring or How to Explain Those Revolutionary Episodes?" *Swiss Political Science Review* 17(4): 447–451. doi: 10.1111/j.1662-6370.2011.02037.x.

Dwyer, Caitlin E., Daniel Stevens, John L. Sullivan, and Barbara Allen. 2009. "Racism, Sexism, and Candidate Evaluations in the 2008 US Presidential Election." *Analyses of Social Issues and Public Policy* 9(1): 223–40. doi: 10.1111/j.1530-2415.2009.01187.x.

Earl, Jennifer. 2005. "'You Can Beat the Rap, But You Can't Beat the Ride:' Bringing Arrests Back into Research on Repression." *Research in Social Movements, Conflicts and Change* 26: 101–139.

Earl, Jennifer, Andrew Martin, John D. McCarthy, and Sarah A. Soule. 2004. "The Use of Newspaper Data in the Study of Collective Action." *Annual Review of Sociology* 30(1): 65–80. doi: https://doi.org/10.1146/annurev.soc.30.012703.110603.

Edsall, Thomas Byrne, and Mary D. Edsall. 1992. *Chain Reaction: The Impact of Race, Rights, and Taxes on American Politics.* New York, NY: W. W. Norton & Company.

Edwards, Bob, and Sam Marullo. 1995. "Organizational Mortality in a Declining Social Movement: The Demise of Peace Movement Organizations in the End of the Cold War Era." *American Sociological Review* 60(6): 908–927. doi: 10.2307/2096432.

Edwards, Bob, and John D. McCarthy. 2004. "Strategy Matters: The Contingent Value of Social Capital in the Survival of Local Social Movement Organizations." *Social Forces* 83(2): 621–651.

Ehrhardt, George. 2020. "Local Leaders in National Social Movements: The Tea Party." *Social Movement Studies* 19(4): 373–390. doi: 10.1080/14742837.2019.1681955.

Enders, Adam M., and Jamil S. Scott. 2019. "The Increasing Racialization of American Electoral Politics, 1988–2016." *American Politics Research* 47(2): 275–303. doi: 10.1177/1532673X18755654.

Fallin, Amanda, Rachel Grana, and Stanton A. Glantz. 2014. "'To Quarterback behind the Scenes, Third-Party Efforts': The Tobacco Industry and the Tea Party." *Tobacco Control* 23(4): 322–331.

Fassiotto, Magali, and Sarah A. Soule. 2017. "Loud and Clear: The Effect of Protest Signals on Congressional Attention." *Mobilization: An International Quarterly* 22 (1): 17–38. doi: 10.17813/1086-671X-22-1-17.

Fetner, Tina, and Brayden G. King. 2014. "Three-Layer Movements, Resources, and the Tea Party," pp. 35–54 in *Understanding the Tea Party Movement*, edited by N. Van Dyke and D. S. Meyer. Burlington, VT: Ashgate Publishing Company.

Fiorina, Morris P., and Samuel J. Abrams. 2008. "Political Polarization in the American Public." *Annual Review of Political Science* 11: 563–588.

Fisher, Patrick. 2015. "The Tea Party and the Demographic and Ideological Gaps within the Republican Party." *Geopolitics, History, and International Relations* 7 (2): 13–31.

Freeman, John, and Michael T. Hannan. 1983. "Niche Width and the Dynamics of Organizational Populations." *American Journal of Sociology* 88(6): 1116–1145. doi: 10.1086/227797.

Gaby, Sarah, and Neal Caren. 2016. "The Rise of Inequality: How Social Movements Shape Discursive Fields." *Mobilization: An International Quarterly* 21(4): 413–429.

Gale, William G., and Brennan Kelly. 2004. "The 'No New Taxes' Pledge." *Tax Notes* 104: 197–209.

Gallup. 2018. "Gallup Daily: Obama Job Approval." Retrieved July 19, 2022 (https://news.gallup.com/poll/113980/Gallup-Daily-Obama-Job-Approval.aspx).

  2019. "Most Important Problem." Retrieved January 7, 2019 (https://news.gallup.com/poll/1675/most-important-problem.aspx).

Gamson, William A. 1975. *The Strategy of Social Protest*. Homewood, IL: The Dorsey Press.

Gardner, Amy. 2010. "Gauging the Scope of the Tea Party Movement in America." *Washington Post*, October 24. Retrieved March 14, 2021 (www.washingtonpost.com/wp-dyn/content/article/2010/10/23/AR2010102304000.html).

Garrison, Joey. 2015. "Ted Cruz Expands Tennessee Leadership Team." *The Tennessean*. Retrieved March 3, 2022 (www.tennessean.com/story/news/2015/10/22/ted-cruz-expands-tennessee-leadership-team/74386434).

Gelman, Andrew, and Gary King. 1990. "Estimating Incumbency Advantage without Bias." *American Journal of Political Science* 34(4): 1142–1164. doi: 10.2307/2111475.

Gerlach, Luther P. 2001. "The Structure of Social Movements: Environmental Activism and Its Opponents," in *Networks and Netwars: The Future of Terror, Crime, and Militancy*, edited by J. Arquilla and D. Ronfeldt. Santa Monica, CA: National Defense Research Institute: RAND.

Gerlach, Luther P., and Virginia H. Hine. 1970. *People, Power, Change; Movements of Social Transformation [by] Luther P. Gerlach and Virginia M. Hine*. Indianapolis, IN: Bobbs-Merrill Company.

Gervais, Bryan T., and Irwin L. Morris. 2012. "Reading the Tea Leaves: Understanding Tea Party Caucus Membership in the US House of Representatives." *PS: Political Science & Politics* 45(2): 245–250.

  2018. *Reactionary Republicanism: How the Tea Party in the House Paved the Way for Trump's Victory*. New York, NY: Oxford University Press.

Gilens, Martin. 1995. "Racial Attitudes and Opposition to Welfare." *The Journal of Politics* 57(4): 994–1014. doi: 10.2307/2960399.

1996. "'Race Coding' and White Opposition to Welfare." *The American Political Science Review* 90(3): 593–604. doi: 10.2307/2082611.

1999. *Why Americans Hate Welfare: Race, Media, and the Politics of Antipoverty Policy.* Chicago, IL: University of Chicago Press.

Gillham, Patrick F., Nathan C. Lindstedt, Bob Edwards, and Erik W. Johnson. 2019. "The Mobilizing Effects of Economic Threats and Resources on the Formation of Local Occupy Wall Street Protest Groups in 2011." *Sociological Perspectives* 62(4): 433–454. doi: 10.1177/0731121418817249.

Gillion, Daniel Q. 2020. *The Loud Minority: Why Protests Matter in American Democracy.* Princeton, NJ: Princeton University Press.

Gillion, Daniel Q., and Sarah A. Soule. 2018. "The Impact of Protest on Elections in the United States." *Social Science Quarterly* 99(5): 1649–1664. doi: 10.1111/ssqu.12527.

Gitlin, Todd. 1980. *The Whole World Is Watching: Mass Media in the Making and Unmaking of the New Left.* Berkeley, CA: University of California Press.

Giugni, Marco. 1998. "Was It Worth the Effort? The Outcomes and Consequences of Social Movements." *Annual Review of Sociology* 24(1): 371–393.

Giugni, Marco, and Maria T. Grasso. 2016. *Austerity and Protest: Popular Contention in Times of Economic Crisis.* New York, NY: Routledge.

Goldstone, Jack A. 2003. "Introduction: Bridging Institutionalized and Noninstitutionalized Politics" pp. 1–24 in *States, Parties, and Social Movements,* edited by J. A. Goldstone. New York, NY: Cambridge University Press.

2004. "More Social Movements or Fewer? Beyond Political Opportunity Structures to Relational Fields." *Theory and Society* 33(3): 333–365. doi: 10.1023/B: RYSO.0000038611.01350.30.

Gould-Wartofsky, Michael A. 2015. *The Occupiers: The Making of the 99 Percent Movement.* New York, NY: Oxford University Press.

Green, Matthew. 2019. *Legislative Hardball: The House Freedom Caucus and the Power of Threat-Making in Congress.* New York, NY: Cambridge University Press.

Gross, Neil, Thomas Medvetz, and Rupert Russell. 2011. "The Contemporary American Conservative Movement." *Annual Review of Sociology* 37: 325–354.

Grossmann, Matt, and Daniel Thaler. 2018. "Mass–Elite Divides in Aversion to Social Change and Support for Donald Trump." *American Politics Research* 46(5): 753–784. doi: 10.1177/1532673X18772280.

Grusky, David B., Christopher Wimmer, and Bruce Western. 2011. "The Consequences of the Great Recession," pp. 3–20 in *The Great Recession,* edited by D. B. Grusky, B. Western, and C. Wimmer. New York, NY: Russell Sage Foundation.

Hackney, Philip. 2014. "Should the IRS Never Target Taxpayers – An Examination of the IRS Tea Party Affair Symposium: Money in Politics: The Good, the Bad, and the Ugly." *Valparaiso University Law Review* 49(2): 453–504.

Hall, Matthew, Kyle Crowder, and Amy Spring. 2015. "Variations in Housing Foreclosures by Race and Place, 2005–2012." *The Annals of the American Academy of Political and Social Science* 660(1): 217–237. doi: 10.1177/0002716215576907.

Haltinner, Kristin. 2016. "Individual Responsibility, Culture, or State Organized Enslavement? How Tea Party Activists Frame Racial Inequality." *Sociological Perspectives* 59(2): 395–418. doi: 10.1177/0731121415593275.

2018. "Right-Wing Ideologies and Ideological Diversity in the Tea Party." *The Sociological Quarterly* 59(3): 449–470. doi: 10.1080/00380253.2018.1479196.

Hannan, Michael T., Glenn R. Carroll, and László Pólos. 2003. "The Organizational Niche." *Sociological Theory* 21(4): 309–340. doi: 10.1046/j.1467-9558.2003.00192.x.

Hannan, Michael T., and John Freeman. 1977. "The Population Ecology of Organizations." *American Journal of Sociology* 82(5): 929–964.

Heaney, Michael T., and Fabio Rojas. 2011. "The Partisan Dynamics of Contention: Demobilization of the Antiwar Movement in the United States, 2007–2009." *Mobilization: An International Quarterly* 16(1): 45–64. doi: 10.17813/maiq.16.1.y8327n3nk0740677.

2015. *Party in the Street: The Antiwar Movement and the Democratic Party after 9/11*. New York, NY: Cambridge University Press.

Heffington, Colton, Brandon Beomseob Park, and Laron K. Williams. 2019. "The 'Most Important Problem' Dataset (MIPD): A New Dataset on American Issue Importance." *Conflict Management and Peace Science* 36(3): 312–335. doi: 10.1177/0738894217691463.

Helppie McFall, Brooke. 2011. "Crash and Wait? The Impact of the Great Recession on the Retirement Plans of Older Americans." *American Economic Review* 101(3): 40–44. doi: 10.1257/aer.101.3.40.

Henke, Joseph T. 1986. "Financing Public Schools in California: The Aftermath of Serrano v. Priest and Proposition 13." *University of San Francisco Law Review* 21(1): 1–40.

Hertel-Fernandez, Alexander. 2019. *State Capture: How Conservative Activists, Big Businesses, and Wealthy Donors Reshaped the American States – and the Nation*. New York, NY: Oxford University Press.

Hetzel, Robert L. 2012. *The Great Recession: Market Failure or Policy Failure?* New York, NY: Cambridge University Press.

Hilgartner, Stephen, and Charles L. Bosk. 1988. "The Rise and Fall of Social Problems: A Public Arenas Model." *American Journal of Sociology* 94(1): 53–78. doi: 10.1086/228951.

Hochschild, Arlie Russell. 2016. *Strangers in Their Own Land: Anger and Mourning on the American Right*. New York, NY: The New Press.

Hosmer, David W., Stanley Lemeshow, and Susanne May. 2008. *Applied Survival Analysis: Regression Modeling of Time-to-Event Data*. 2nd ed. Hoboken, NJ: John Wiley & Sons.

Hsieh, Hsiu-Fang, and Sarah E. Shannon. 2005. "Three Approaches to Qualitative Content Analysis." *Qualitative Health Research* 15(9): 1277–1288. doi: 10.1177/1049732305276687.

Hughey, Matthew W. 2012. "Show Me Your Papers! Obama's Birth and the Whiteness of Belonging." *Qualitative Sociology* 35(2): 163–181. doi: 10.1007/s11133-012-9224-6.

Hutter, Swen. 2014. "Protest Event Analysis and Its Offspring," pp. 335–367 in *Methodological Practices in Social Movement Research*, edited by D. Della Porta. Oxford, UK: Oxford University Press.

Hyclak, Thomas J., Chad D. Meyerhoefer, and Larry W. Taylor. 2015. "Older Americans' Health and the Great Recession." *Review of Economics of the Household* 13(2): 413–436. doi: 10.1007/s11150-013-9197-6.

Jamieson, Kathleen Hall, and Joseph N. Cappella. 2008. *Echo Chamber: Rush Limbaugh and the Conservative Media Establishment.* New York, NY: Oxford University Press.

Jardina, Ashley, and Michael Traugott. 2019. "The Genesis of the Birther Rumor: Partisanship, Racial Attitudes, and Political Knowledge." *Journal of Race, Ethnicity, and Politics* 4(1): 60–80. doi: 10.1017/rep.2018.25.

Johnson, Erik W., Jon Agnone, and John D. McCarthy. 2010. "Movement Organizations, Synergistic Tactics and Environmental Public Policy." *Social Forces* 88(5): 2267–2292.

Kahneman, Daniel, and Amos Tversky. 1979. "Prospect Theory: An Analysis of Decision under Risk." *Econometrica* 47(2): 263–291. doi: 10.2307/1914185.

Kahng, Lily. 2013. "The IRS Tea Part Controversy and Administrative Discretion." *Cornell Law Review Online* 99–100: 41–55.

Kalton, Graham, and Dallas W. Anderson. 1986. "Sampling Rare Populations." *Journal of the Royal Statistical Society: Series A (General)* 149(1): 65–82. doi: 10.2307/2981886.

Kamisar, Ben. 2016. "Tea Party Leader: Trump a Wolf in Sheep's Clothing." *TheHill.* Retrieved June 2, 2021 (https://thehill.com/blogs/ballot-box/gop-primaries/271814-tea-party-leader-trump-a-wolf-in-sheeps-clothing).

Kaplan, Abraham. 1998. *The Conduct of Inquiry: Methodology for Behavioural Science.* New York, NY: Routledge.

Karpf, David. 2008. "Understanding Blogspace." *Journal of Information Technology & Politics* 5(4): 369–385.

Kibbe, Matt. 2018. "The Tea Party Is Officially Dead. It Was Killed by Partisan Politics." *Reason.Com.* Retrieved February 26, 2021 (https://reason.com/2018/02/11/the-tea-party-is-dead-long-live-liberty).

King, Brayden G., Keith G. Bentele, and Sarah A. Soule. 2007. "Protest and Policymaking: Explaining Fluctuation in Congressional Attention to Rights Issues, 1960–1986." *Social Forces* 86(1): 137–163.

Klandermans, Bert. 1997. *The Social Psychology of Protest.* Cambridge, MA: Blackwell Publishers.

Koopmans, Ruud, and Jan Willem Duyvendak. 1995. "The Political Construction of the Nuclear Energy Issue and Its Impact on the Mobilization of Anti-Nuclear Movements in Western Europe." *Social Problems* 42(2): 235–251. doi: 10.2307/3096903.

Koopmans, Ruud, and Dieter Rucht. 2002. "Protest Event Analysis," pp. 231–259 in *Methods of Social Movement Research,* edited by B. Klandermans and S. Staggenborg. Minneapolis, MN: University of Minnesota Press.

Kriesi, Hanspeter. 2016. "Mobilization of Protest in an Age of Austerity," pp. 62–90 in *Street Politics in the Age of Austerity: From the Indignados to Occupy,* edited by M. Ancelovici, P. Dufour, and H. Nez. Amsterdam: Amsterdam University Press.

Langman, Lauren, and George Lundskow. 2012. "Down the Rabid Hole to a Tea Party." *Critical Sociology* 38(4): 589–597. doi: 10.1177/0896920512437055.

Lawrence, Eric, Todd Donovan, and Shaun Bowler. 2013. "The Adoption of Direct Primaries in the United States." *Party Politics* 19(1): 3–18. doi: 10.1177/1354068810393264.

Leonard, Christopher. 2020. *Kochland: The Secret History of Koch Industries and Corporate Power in America.* New York, NY: Simon & Schuster.

Licari, Peter R. 2020. "Sharp as a Fox: Are Foxnews.Com Visitors Less Politically Knowledgeable?" *American Politics Research* 48(6): 792–806. doi: 10.1177/1532673X20915222.

Lindsay, D. Michael. 2007. *Faith in the Halls of Power: How Evangelicals Joined the American Elite.* New York, NY: Oxford University Press.

———. 2008. "Evangelicals in the Power Elite: Elite Cohesion Advancing a Movement." *American Sociological Review* 73(1): 60–82.

Liu, Bing. 2015. *Sentiment Analysis: Mining Opinions, Sentiments, and Emotions.* New York, NY: Cambridge University Press.

Lo, Clarence Y. H. 2012. "Astroturf versus Grass Roots: Scenes from Early Tea Party Mobilization," pp. 98–129 in *Steep: The Precipitous Rise of the Tea Party*, edited by L. Rosenthal and C. Trost. Berkeley, CA: University of California Press.

Lowndes, Joseph. 2012. "The Past and Future of Race in the Tea Party Movement," pp. 152–170 in *Steep: The Precipitous Rise of the Tea Party*, edited by L. Rosenthal and C. Trost. Berkeley, CA: University of California Press.

MacLeod, Laurie, Darrel Montero, and Alan Speer. 1999. "America's Changing Attitudes toward Welfare and Welfare Recipients, 1938–1995." *Journal of Sociology and Social Welfare* 26(2): 175–186.

MacWilliams, Matthew C. 2016. "Who Decides When The Party Doesn't? Authoritarian Voters and the Rise of Donald Trump." *PS: Political Science & Politics* 49(4): 716–721. doi: 10.1017/S1049096516001463.

Madestam, Andreas, Daniel Shoag, Stan Veuger, and David Yanagizawa-Drott. 2013. "Do Political Protests Matter? Evidence from the Tea Party Movement." *The Quarterly Journal of Economics* 128(4): 1633–1685.

Manza, Jeff, and Ned Crowley. 2017. "Working Class Hero? Interrogating the Social Bases of the Rise of Donald Trump." *The Forum* 15(1): 3–28. doi: 10.1515/for-2017-0002.

———. 2018. "Ethnonationalism and the Rise of Donald Trump." *Contexts* 17(1): 28–33. doi: 10.1177/1536504218766548.

Margolis, Michele F. 2020. "Who Wants to Make America Great Again? Understanding Evangelical Support for Donald Trump." *Politics and Religion* 13(1): 89–118. doi: 10.1017/S1755048319000208.

Martin, Andrew W., Patrick Rafail, and John D. McCarthy. 2017. "What a Story?" *Social Forces* 96(2): 779–802. doi: 10.1093/sf/sox057.

Martin, Isaac. 2013. *Rich People's Movements: Grassroots Campaigns to Untax the One Percent.* New York, NY: Oxford University Press.

Martin, Jenny Beth. 2016. "The Tea Party Movement Is Alive and Well – And We Saw Trump Coming." *POLITICO.* Retrieved July 9, 2021 (www.politico.com/magazine/story/2016/11/the-tea-party-movement-is-alive-and-well-and-we-saw-trump-coming-214469).

———. 2020. "Email: Where Do You Stand?" Sent to subscribers of the Tea Party Patriots Email Listserve, April 18, 2020.

Marx, Gary T. 1974. "Thoughts on a Neglected Category of Social Movement Participant: The Agent Provocateur and the Informant." *The American Journal of Sociology* 80(2): 402–442.

Massey, Douglas, and Nancy A. Denton. 2003. *American Apartheid: Segregation and the Making of the Underclass.* Cambridge, MA: Harvard University Press.

Maxwell, Angie, and T. Wayne Parent. 2012. "The Obama Trigger: Presidential Approval and Tea Party Membership." *Social Science Quarterly* 93(5): 1384–1401. doi: 10.1111/j.1540-6237.2012.00907.x.

Maxwell, Angie, and Todd Shields. 2019. *The Long Southern Strategy: How Chasing White Voters in the South Changed American Politics.* New York, NY: Oxford University Press.

Mayer, Jane. 2016. *Dark Money: The Hidden History of the Billionaires behind the Rise of the Radical Right.* New York, NY: Penguin Random House.

McAdam, Doug. 1983. "Tactical Innovation and the Pace of Insurgency." *American Sociological Review* 48(6): 735–754.

1990. *Freedom Summer.* New York, NY: Oxford University Press.

1999. *Political Process and the Development of Black Insurgency, 1930–1970.* 2nd ed. Chicago, IL: University of Chicago Press.

McAdam, Doug, and Karina Kloos. 2014. *Deeply Divided: Racial Politics and Social Movements in Post-War America.* New York, NY: Oxford University Press.

McAdam, Doug, Robert J. Sampson, Simon Weffer, and Heather MacIndoe. 2005. "'There Will Be Fighting in the Streets': The Distorting Lens of Social Movement Theory." *Mobilization* 10(1): 1–18.

McAdam, Doug, and Sidney Tarrow. 2010. "Ballots and Barricades: On the Reciprocal Relationship between Elections and Social Movements." *Perspectives on Politics* 8 (2): 529–542. doi: 10.1017/S1537592710001234.

2013. "Social Movements and Elections: Toward a Broader Understanding of the Political Context of Contention," pp. 325–346 in *The Future of Social Movement Research: Dynamics, Mechanisms, and Processes,* edited by J. van Stekelenburg, C. Roggeband, and B. Klandermans. Minneapolis, MN: University of Minnesota Press.

McCarthy, John D. 1987. "Pro-Life and Pro-Choice Mobilization: Infrastructure Deficits and New Technologies," pp. 48–66 in *Social Movements in an Organizational Society,* edited by M. N. Zald and J. D. McCarthy. New Brunswick, NJ: Transaction Publishers.

1996. "Constraints and Opportunities in Adopting, Adapting, and Inventing," pp. 141–151 in *Comparative Perspectives on Social Movements: Political Opportunities, Mobilizing Structures, and Cultural Framings,* edited by D. McAdam, J. D. McCarthy, and M. N. Zald. New York, NY: Cambridge University Press.

2005. "Persistence and Change among Nationally Federated Social Movements," pp. 193–225 in *Social Movements and Organization Theory,* edited by G. Davis, M. N. Zald, R. Scott, and D. McAdam. New York, NY: Cambridge University Press.

2013. "Social Movement Organization (SMO)," pp. 1195–1197 in *The Wiley-Blackwell Encyclopedia of Social and Political Movements,* edited by D. Snow, D. Della Porta, B. Klandermans, and D. McAdam. Oxford: Wiley-Blackwell.

2019. "Toward a Strategy for Integrating the Study of Social Movement and Populist Party Mobilisation," pp. 147–169 in *Populism and the Crisis of Democracy: Volume 1: Concepts and Theory,* edited by G. Fitzi, J. Mackert, and B. S. Turner. New York, NY: Routledge.

McCarthy, John D., David W. Britt, and Mark Wolfson. 1991. "The Channeling of Social Movements in the Modern American State." *Social Movements, Conflict, and Change* 13: 45–76.

230

References

McCarthy, John D., and Clark McPhail. 1998. "Policing Protest: The Evolving Dynamics of Encounters between Collective Actors and Police in the United States," pp. 336–351 in *Eingerwilligkeit und Rationaitat SzoialerProzesse*, edited by J. Gerhards and R. Hitzer. Wiesbaden: Westdeutscher Velag.

2006. "Places of Protest: The Public Forum in Principle and Practice." *Mobilization: An International Quarterly* 11(2): 229–247. doi: 10.17813/maiq.11.2.45054350171u704q.

McCarthy, John D., Clark McPhail, and Jackie Smith. 1996. "Images of Protest: Dimensions of Selection Bias in Media Coverage of Washington Demonstrations, 1982 and 1991." *American Sociological Review* 61(3): 478–499. doi: 10.2307/2096360.

McCarthy, John D., Larissa Titarenko, Clark McPhail, Patrick Rafail, and Boguslaw Augustyn. 2008. "Assessing Stability in the Patterns of Selection Bias in Newspaper Coverage of Protest During the Transition from Communism in Belarus." *Mobilization: An International Quarterly* 13(2): 127–146. doi: 10.17813/maiq.13.2.u45461350302663v.

McCarthy, John D., and Edward T. Walker. 2004. "Alternative Organizational Repertoires of Poor People's Social Movement Organizations." *Nonprofit and Voluntary Sector Quarterly* 33(3 (Supplement): 97S–119S. doi: 10.1177/0899764004266200.

McCarthy, John D., and Mark Wolfson. 1996. "Resource Mobilization by Local Social Movement Organizations: Agency, Strategy, and Organization in the Movement against Drinking and Driving." *American Sociological Review* 61(6): 1070–1088. doi: 10.2307/2096309.

McCarthy, John D., and Mayer N. Zald. 1977. "Resource Mobilization and Social Movements: A Partial Theory." *American Journal of Sociology* 82(6): 1212–1241.

2002. "The Enduring Vitality of the Resource Mobilization Theory of Social Movements," pp. 533–565 in *Handbook of Sociological Theory*, edited by J. H. Turner. New York, NY: Kluwer Academic/Plenum.

McCarty, Nolan. 2016. "In Defense of DW-NOMINATE." *Studies in American Political Development* 30(2): 172–184. doi: 10.1017/S0898588X16000110.

McGhee, Eric, Seth Masket, Boris Shor, Steven Rogers, and Nolan McCarty. 2014. "A Primary Cause of Partisanship? Nomination Systems and Legislator Ideology." *American Journal of Political Science* 58(2): 337–351.

McNitt, Andrew D. 2014. "The Tea Party Movement and the 2012 House Election." *PS: Political Science & Politics* 47(4): 799–805. doi: 10.1017/S1049096514001073.

McVeigh, Rory. 1999. "Structural Incentives for Conservative Mobilization: Power Devaluation and the Rise of the Ku Klux Klan, 1915–1925." *Social Forces* 77(4): 1461–1496. doi: 10.2307/3005883.

2001. "Power Devaluation, the Ku Klux Klan, and the Democratic National Convention of 1924." *Sociological Forum* 16(1): 1–30. doi: 10.1023/A:1007655818083.

2009. *The Rise of the Ku Klux Klan: Right-Wing Movements and National Politics.* Minneapolis, MN: University of Minnesota Press.

McVeigh, Rory, Kraig Beyerlein, Burrel Vann, and Priyamvada Trivedi. 2014. "Educational Segregation, Tea Party Organizations, and Battles over Distributive

Justice." *American Sociological Review* 79(4): 630–652. doi: 10.1177/0003122414534065.

McVeigh, Rory, and Kevin Estep. 2019. *The Politics of Losing: Trump, the Klan, and the Mainstreaming of Resentment*. New York, NY: Columbia University Press.

McVeigh, Rory, Daniel J. Myers, and David Sikkink. 2004. "Corn, Klansmen, and Coolidge: Structure and Framing in Social Movements." *Social Forces* 83(2): 653–690. doi: 10.1353/sof.2005.0019.

Meckler, Mark, and Jenny Beth Martin. 2012. *Tea Party Patriots: The Second American Revolution*. New York, NY: Henry Holt and Company.

Medzihorsky, Juraj, Levente Littvay, and Erin K. Jenne. 2014. "Has the Tea Party Era Radicalized the Republican Party? Evidence from Text Analysis of the 2008 and 2012 Republican Primary Debates." *PS: Political Science & Politics* 47(4): 806–812. doi: 10.1017/S1049096514001085.

Meirick, Patrick C. 2013. "Motivated Misperception? Party, Education, Partisan News, and Belief in 'Death Panels.'" *Journalism & Mass Communication Quarterly* 90(1): 39–57. doi: 10.1177/1077699012468696.

Meyer, David S., and Sidney Tarrow. 1998. "A Movement Society: Contentious Politics for a New Century," pp. 3–32 in *The Social Movement Society: Contentious Politics for a New Century*, edited by D. S. Meyer and S. Tarrow. Lanham, MD: Rowman & Littlefield.

Mohammad, Saif M. 2018. "Word Affect Intensities," pp. 1–10 in *Proceedings of the 11th edition of the Language Resources and Evaluation Conference*. Miyazaki, Japan: Association for Computational Linguistics.

Morgan, Stephen L. 2018. "Status Threat, Material Interests, and the 2016 Presidential Vote." *Socius* 4: 2378023118788217. doi: 10.1177/2378023118788217.

Morgan, Stephen L., and Jiwon Lee. 2017. "The White Working Class and Voter Turnout in US Presidential Elections, 2004 to 2016." *Sociological Science* 4(27): 656–685. doi: 10.15195/v4.a27.

2018. "Trump Voters and the White Working Class." *Sociological Science* 5(10): 234–245. doi: 10.15195/v5.a10.

Morris, Aldon D. 1986. *The Origins of the Civil Rights Movement: Black Communities Organizing for Change*. New York, NY: Free Press.

Morstatter, Fred, Jürgen Pfeffer, Huan Liu, and Kathleen M. Carley. 2013. "Is the Sample Good Enough? Comparing Data from Twitter's Streaming API with Twitter's Firehose." *ArXiv*: 1306.5204 [cs.SI]. doi: https://doi.org/10.48550/arXiv.1306.5204.

Mort, Sébastien. 2012. "Tailoring Dissent on the Airwaves: The Role of Conservative Talk Radio in the Right-Wing Resurgence of 2010." *New Political Science* 34(4): 485–505. doi: 10.1080/07393148.2012.729739.

Mueller, Jennifer. 2014. "Defending Nuance in an Era of Tea Party Politics: An Argument for the Continued Use of Standards to Evaluate the Campaign Activities of 501(C)(4) Organizations." *George Mason Law Review* 22(1): 103–158.

Munnell, Alicia H., and Matthew S. Rutledge. 2013. "The Effects of the Great Recession on the Retirement Security of Older Workers." *The Annals of the American Academy of Political and Social Science* 650(1): 124–142. doi: 10.1177/0002716213499535.

Munson, Ziad W. 2010. *The Making of Pro-Life Activists: How Social Movement Mobilization Works*. Chicago, IL: University of Chicago Press.

Murphy, Kevin P. 2012. *Machine Learning: A Probabilistic Perspective*. Cambridge, MA: MIT Press.

Mutz, Diana C. 2018. "Status Threat, Not Economic Hardship, Explains the 2016 Presidential Vote." *Proceedings of the National Academy of Sciences* 115 (19): E4330–4339. doi: 10.1073/pnas.1718155115.

Myers, Daniel J. 2000. "The Diffusion of Collective Violence: Infectiousness, Susceptibility, and Mass Media Networks." *American Journal of Sociology* 106 (1): 173–208.

Myers, Daniel J., and Beth Schaefer Caniglia. 2004. "All the Rioting That's Fit to Print: Selection Effects in National Newspaper Coverage of Civil Disorders, 1968–1969." *American Sociological Review* 69(4): 519–543. doi: https://doi.org/10.1177/000312240406900403.

Nesbit, Jeff. 2016. *Poison Tea: How Big Oil and Big Tobacco Invented the Tea Party and Captured the GOP*. New York, NY: Macmillan.

Newport, Frank. 2009. *Obama Signs Stimulus into Law with Majority Support*. Princeton, NJ: Gallup.

Nokken, Timothy P., and Keith T. Poole. 2004. "Congressional Party Defection in American History." *Legislative Studies Quarterly* 29(4): 545–568.

Nummi, Jozie, Carly Jennings, and Joe Feagin. 2019. "#BlackLivesMatter: Innovative Black Resistance." *Sociological Forum* 34(S1): 1042–1064. doi: 10.1111/socf.12540.

Oberschall, Anthony. 1993. *Social Movements: Ideologies, Interests, and Identities*. New Brunswick, NJ: Transaction Publishers.

O'Harrow Jr., Robert. 2021. "Rallies Ahead of Capitol Riot Were Planned by Established Washington Insiders." *Washington Post*, January 17. Retrieved September 28,2022 (www.washingtonpost.com/investigations/capitol-rally-organizers-before-riots/2021/01/16/c5b40250-552d-11eb-a931-5b162d0d033d_story.html).

Ohlemacher, Stephen. 2013. "IRS Apologizes for Targeting Tea Party Groups." *AP NEWS*. Retrieved June 8, 2020 (https://apnews.com/article/9d2d5e28d661455da834aee66f54353a).

Oliver, J. Eric, and Wendy M. Rahn. 2016. "Rise of the Trumpenvolk: Populism in the 2016 Election." *The Annals of the American Academy of Political and Social Science* 667(1): 189–206. doi: 10.1177/0002716216662639.

Oliver, Pamela. 2021. "Introduction: Black Lives Matter in Context." *Mobilization: An International Quarterly* 26(4): 391–399. doi: 10.17813/1086-671X-26-4-391.

Oliver, Pamela, and Hank Johnston. 2000. "What a Good Idea! Ideologies and Frames in Social Movement Research." *Mobilization: An International Quarterly* 5(1): 37–54.

Oliver, Pamela E., and Gregory M. Maney. 2000. "Political Processes and Local Newspaper Coverage of Protest Events: From Selection Bias to Triadic Interactions." *American Journal of Sociology* 106(2): 463–505. doi: https://doi.org/10.1086/316964.

Olson, Mancur. 1965. *The Logic of Collective Action: Public Goods and the Theory of Groups*. Cambridge, MA: Harvard University Press.

Olzak, Susan, and Sarah A. Soule. 2009. "Cross-Cutting Influences of Environmental Protest and Legislation." *Social Forces* 88(1): 201–225.

Opelka, Mike. 2012. "Is Obama Using the IRS to Silence Opposition Voices?" *TheBlaze*. Retrieved June 8, 2020 (www.theblaze.com/news/2012/02/14/is-obama-using-the-irs-to-silence-opposition-voices).

Ortiz, David G., Daniel J. Myers, Eugene. N. Walls, and Maria E. D. Diaz. 2005. "Where Do We Stand with Newspaper Data?" *Mobilization: An International Quarterly* 10(3): 397–419. doi: 10.17813/maiq.10.3.8360r760k3277t42.

Owens, Peter B., David Cunningham, and Geoff Ward. 2015. "Threat, Competition, and Mobilizing Structures: Motivational and Organizational Contingencies of the Civil Rights-Era Ku Klux Klan." *Social Problems* 62(4): 572–604. doi: 10.1093/socpro/spv016.

Parker, Christopher S., and Matt A. Barreto. 2014. *Change They Can't Believe In: The Tea Party and Reactionary Politics in America*. Princeton, NJ: Princeton University Press.

Parker, Christopher S., Mark Q. Sawyer, and Christopher Towler. 2009. "A BLACK MAN IN THE WHITE HOUSE?: The Role of Racism and Patriotism in the 2008 Presidential Election." *Du Bois Review: Social Science Research on Race* 6 (1): 193–217. doi: 10.1017/S1742058X09090031.

Parkin, William S., Joshua D. Freilich, and Steven M. Chermak. 2015. "Tea Party Mobilization and Power Devaluation." *Sociological Spectrum* 35(4): 329–348. doi: 10.1080/02732173.2015.1043680.

Patenaude, Willis. 2019. "Modern American Populism: Analyzing the Economics behind the 'Silent Majority,' the Tea Party, and Trumpism." *American Journal of Economics and Sociology* 78(3): 787–834. doi: https://doi.org/10.1111/ajes.12281.

Perrin, Andrew J., Steven J. Tepper, Neal Caren, and Sally Morris. 2014. "Political and Cultural Dimensions of Tea Party Support, 2009–2012." *The Sociological Quarterly* 55(4): 625–652. doi: 10.1111/tsq.12069.

Pettinicchio, David. 2017. "Elites, Policy, and Social Movements." *Research in Political Sociology* 24: 155–190.

Pew Research Center. 2004. "Cable and Internet Loom Large in Fragmented Political News Universe." Retrieved April 5, 2020 (www.pewresearch.org/politics/2004/01/11/cable-and-internet-loom-large-in-fragmented-political-news-universe).

Pinto, Edward. 2009. "Acorn and the Housing Bubble." *Wall Street Journal*, November 13.

Piston, Spencer. 2010. "How Explicit Racial Prejudice Hurt Obama in the 2008 Election." *Political Behavior* 32(4): 431–451. doi: 10.1007/s11109-010-9108-y.

Piven, Frances Fox, and Richard Cloward. 1977. *Poor People's Movements: Why They Succeed, How They Fail*. New York, NY: Random House.

Polletta, Francesca. 2004. *Freedom Is an Endless Meeting: Democracy in American Social Movements*. Chicago, IL: University of Chicago Press.

Polletta, Francesca, and James M. Jasper. 2001. "Collective Identity and Social Movements." *Annual Review of Sociology* 27: 283–305.

della Porta, Donatella. 2015. *Social Movements in Times of Austerity: Bringing Capitalism Back into Protest Analysis*. New York, NY: Polity Press.

della Porta, Donatella, and Mario Diani. 2020. *Social Movements: An Introduction*. 3rd ed. Hoboken, NJ: John Wiley & Sons.

Pressman, Jeremy, Erica Chenoweth, Tommy Leung, L. Nathan Perkins, and Jay Ulfelder. 2022. "Protests under Trump, 2017–2021." *Mobilization: An International Quarterly* 27(1): 13–26. doi: 10.17813/1086-671X-27-1-13.

Rafail, Patrick. 2010. "Is There an Asymmetry in Protest Control? Comparing Protest Policing in Montreal, Toronto, and Vancouver." *Mobilization* 15(4): 405–422.

    2014. "What Makes Protest Dangerous? Ideology, Contentious Tactics, and Covert Surveillance." *Research in Social Movements, Conflict, and Change* 37: 235–263.

    2018a. "Nonprobability Sampling and Twitter: Strategies for Semibounded and Bounded Populations." *Social Science Computer Review* 36(2): 195–211. doi: 10.1177/0894439317709431.

    2018b. "Protest in the City: Urban Spatial Restructuring and Dissent in New York, 1960–2006." *Urban Studies* 55(1): 244–260.

Rafail, Patrick, and John D. McCarthy. 2018. "Making the Tea Party Republican: Media Bias and Framing in Newspapers and Cable News." *Social Currents* 5(5): 421–437. doi: 10.1177/2329496518759129.

Rafail, Patrick, John D. McCarthy, and Samuel Sullivan. 2019. "Local Receptivity Climates and the Dynamics of Media Attention to Protest." *Mobilization: An International Quarterly* 24(1): 1–18. doi: 10.17813/1086-671X-24-1-1.

Rafail, Patrick, Sarah A. Soule, and John D. McCarthy. 2012. "Describing and Accounting for the Trends in US Protest Policing, 1960–1995." *Journal of Conflict Resolution* 56(4): 736–65.

Ratliff, Kate A., Liz Redford, John Conway, and Colin Tucker Smith. 2019. "Engendering Support: Hostile Sexism Predicts Voting for Donald Trump over Hillary Clinton in the 2016 US Presidential Election." *Group Processes & Intergroup Relations* 22(4): 578–593. doi: 10.1177/1368430217741203.

Reuters. 2017. "Justice Department Settles with Conservative Groups over IRS Scrutiny." *Reuters*, October 26. Retrieved March 18, 2021 (www.reuters.com/article/us-usa-tax-conservative-idUSKBN1CV1TY).

Rohlinger, Deana A., and Leslie Bunnage. 2017. "Did the Tea Party Movement Fuel the Trump-Train? The Role of Social Media in Activist Persistence and Political Change in the 21st Century." *Social Media + Society* 3(2): 2056305117706786. doi: 10.1177/2056305117706786.

Rojecki, Andrew. 2016. *America and the Politics of Insecurity.* Baltimore, MD: Johns Hopkins University Press.

Rothwell, Jonathan T., and Pablo Diego-Rosell. 2016. "Explaining Nationalist Political Views: The Case of Donald Trump." SSRN Scholarly Paper. ID 2822059. Rochester, NY: Social Science Research Network. doi: 10.2139/ssrn.2822059.

Rubin, Ruth Bloch. 2017. *Building the Bloc: Intraparty Organization in the US Congress.* New York, NY: Cambridge University Press.

Rucker, Philip. 2009. "S.C. Senator Is a Voice of Reform Opposition." *NBC News.* Retrieved August 30, 2022 (www.nbcnews.com/id/wbna32181674).

Sale, Kirkpatrick. 1973. *SDS: The Rise and Development of the Students for a Democratic Society.* New York, NY: Random House.

Schlozman, Daniel. 2015. *When Movements Anchor Parties: Electoral Alignments in American History.* Princeton, NJ: Princeton University Press.

Schradie, Jen. 2019. *The Revolution That Wasn't: How Digital Activism Favors Conservatives.* Cambridge, MA: Harvard University Press.

Settels, Jason. 2021. "Changes in City-Level Foreclosure Rates and Home Prices through the Great Recession and Depressive Symptoms among Older Americans." *Society and Mental Health* 11(1): 1–19. doi: 10.1177/2156869319895568.

Sewell, William H. Jr. 1992. "A Theory of Structure: Duality, Agency, and Transformation." *American Journal of Sociology* 98(1): 1–29.

Shah, Archit. 2009. "Emergency Economic Stabilization Act of 2008." *Harvard Journal on Legislation* 46(2): 569–584.

Sherman, Lawrence W. 2018. "Reducing Fatal Police Shootings as System Crashes: Research, Theory, and Practice." *Annual Review of Criminology* 1: 421–449.

Simmons, Erica. 2014. "Grievances Do Matter in Mobilization." *Theory and Society* 43 (5): 513–546.

Skocpol, Theda. 2003. *Diminished Democracy: From Membership to Management in American Civic Life.* Norman, OK: University of Oklahoma Press.

    2020. "The Elite and Popular Roots of Contemporary Republican Extremism," pp. 3–27 in *Upending American Politics: Polarizing Parties, Ideological Elites, and Citizen Activists from the Tea Party to the Anti-Trump Resistance*, edited by T. Skocpol and C. Tervo. New York, NY: Oxford University Press.

Skocpol, Theda, and Morris P. Fiorina. 1999. "Advocates without Members: The Recent Transformation of American Civic Life," pp. 461–509 in *Civic Engagement in American Democracy*, edited by T. Skocpol and M. P. Fiorina. Washington, DC: Brookings Institute Press.

Skocpol, Theda, Marshall Ganz, and Ziad Munson. 2000. "A Nation of Organizers: The Institutional Origins of Civic Voluntarism in the United States." *American Political Science Review* 94(3): 527–546. doi: 10.2307/2585829.

Skocpol, Theda, and Alexander Hertel-Fernandez. 2016. "The Koch Network and Republican Party Extremism." *Perspectives on Politics* 14(3): 681–699. doi: 10.1017/S1537592716001122.

Skocpol, Theda, and Vanessa Williamson. 2011. *The Tea Party and the Remaking of Republican Conservatism.* New York, NY: Oxford University Press.

Smelser, Neil J. 1962. *Theory of Collective Behavior.* New York, NY: The Free Press.

Smith, David Horton. 1997. "The Rest of the Nonprofit Sector: Grassroots Associations as the Dark Matter Ignored in Prevailing 'Flat Earth' Maps of the Sector." *Nonprofit and Voluntary Sector Quarterly* 26(2): 114–131.

Smith, Jackie, John D. McCarthy, Clark McPhail, and Boguslaw Augustyn. 2001. "From Protest to Agenda Building: Description Bias in Media Coverage of Protest Events in Washington, D.C." *Social Forces* 79(4): 1397–1423. doi: 10.1353/sof.2001.0053.

Snow, David A. 2004. "Framing Processes, Ideology, and Discursive Fields," pp. 380–412 in *The Blackwell Companion to Social Movements*, edited by D. A. Snow, S. A. Soule, and H. Kriesi. Hoboken, NJ: John Wiley & Sons.

Snow, David, Daniel Cress, Liam Downey, and Andrew Jones. 1998. "Disrupting the 'Quotidian': Reconceptualizing the Relationship between Breakdown and the Emergence of Collective Action." *Mobilization: An International Quarterly* 3(1): 1–22.

Snow, David A., E. Burke Rochford, Steven K. Worden, and Robert D. Benford. 1986. "Frame Alignment Processes, Micromobilization, and Movement Participation." *American Sociological Review* 51(4): 464–481. doi: 10.2307/2095581.

Snow, David A., and Sarah A. Soule. 2010. *A Primer on Social Movements*. New York, NY: W. W. Norton.

Snyder, David. 1979. "Collective Violence Processes: Implications for Disaggregated Theory and Research." *Research in Social Movements, Conflicts and Change* 2(3): 35–61.

Street, Paul, and Anthony R. DiMaggio. 2015. *Crashing the Tea Party: Mass Media and the Campaign to Remake American Politics*. New York, NY: Routledge.

Svitek, Patrick. 2015. "Cruz Taps Fleming as Campaign's Texas Tea Party Chairwoman." *The Texas Tribune*. Retrieved March 3, 2022 (www.texastribune.org/2015/07/28/cruz-taps-fleming-texas-tea-party-chairwoman).

Swank, Eric. 2020. "Gender, Religion, and Pro-Life Activism." *Politics and Religion* 13 (2): 361–384. doi: 10.1017/S1755048319000531.

Tarrow, Sidney. 2021. *Movements and Parties: Critical Connections in American Political Development*. New York, NY: Cambridge University Press.

Tarrow, Sidney G. 2011. *Power in Movement: Social Movements and Contentious Politics*. 3rd ed. New York, NY: Cambridge University Press.

Taylor, John B. 2014. "The Role of Policy in the Great Recession and the Weak Recovery." *American Economic Review* 104(5): 61–66. doi: 10.1257/aer.104.5.61.

Thiede, Brian C., and Shannon M. Monnat. 2016. "The Great Recession and America's Geography of Unemployment." *Demographic Research* 35: 891–928. doi: 10.4054/DemRes.2016.35.30.

Tilly, Charles. 1978. *From Mobilization to Revolution*. New York, NY: McGraw-Hill.
1986. *The Contentious French*. Cambridge, MA: Harvard University Press.
2006. *Regimes and Repertoires*. Chicago, IL: University of Chicago Press.

Treasury Inspector General for Tax Administration. 2017. *Review of Selected Criteria Used to Identify Tax-Exempt Applications for Review*. Report no: 2017-10-054. Washington, DC: Department of the Treasury.

Vann, Burrel, Jr. 2021. "Persuasive Action and Ideological Polarization in Congress." *Social Problems* 68(4): 809–830. doi: 10.1093/socpro/spab023.

Vogel, Kenneth P. 2009. "Tea Partiers Turn on Each Other." *POLITICO*. Retrieved June 29, 2022 (www.politico.com/story/2009/11/tea-partiers-turn-on-each-other-029744).

Vornovitsky, Marina, Alfred Gottschalck, and Adam Smith. 2011. *Distribution of Household Wealth in the US: 2000 to 2011*. Washington, DC: US Census Bureau.

Walgrave, Stefaan, and Rens Vliegenthart. 2012. "The Complex Agenda-Setting Power of Protest: Demonstrations, Media, Parliament, Government, and Legislation in Belgium, 1993–2000." *Mobilization: An International Quarterly* 17(2): 129–156. doi: 10.17813/maiq.17.2.pw053m281356572h.

Walker, Edward T. 2014. *Grassroots for Hire: Public Affairs Consultants in American Democracy*. New York, NY: Cambridge University Press.

Walker, Edward T., Andrew W. Martin, and John D. McCarthy. 2008. "Confronting the State, the Corporation, and the Academy: The Influence of Institutional Targets on Social Movement Repertoires." *American Journal of Sociology* 114(1): 35–76.

Walker, Edward T., and John D. McCarthy. 2010. "Legitimacy, Strategy, and Resources in the Survival of Community-Based Organizations." *Social Problems* 57(3): 315–340. doi: 10.1525/sp.2010.57.3.315.

Walsh, Edward J. 1981. "Resource Mobilization and Citizen Protest in Communities around Three Mile Island." *Social Problems* 29(1): 1–21. doi: 10.2307/800074.

Weisman, Jonathan. 2012. "Scrutiny of Political Nonprofits Sets Off Claim of Harassment." *The New York Times*, March 7. Retrieved March 8, 2021 (www .nytimes.com/2012/03/07/us/politics/irs-scrutiny-of-political-groups-stirs-harass ment-claim.html).

    2013. "I.R.S. Scrutiny Went beyond the Political." *The New York Times*, July 5. Retrieved March 8, 2021 (www.nytimes.com/2013/07/05/us/politics/irs-scrutiny-went-beyond-the-political.html).

Westermeyer, William H. 2016. "Local Tea Party Groups and the Vibrancy of the Movement." *PoLAR: Political and Legal Anthropology Review* 39(S1): 121–138.

    2019. *Back to America: Identity, Political Culture, and the Tea Party Movement*. Lincoln, NE: University of Nebraska Press.

    2022. "Stigmatized Identity Motivating Right Wing Populism: How the Tea Party Learned to Love Donald Trump," pp. 21–39 in *The Anthropology of Donald Trump: Culture and the Exceptional Moment*, edited by J. D. Eller. New York, NY: Routledge.

Wetts, Rachel, and Robb Willer. 2018. "Privilege on the Precipice: Perceived Racial Status Threats Lead White Americans to Oppose Welfare Programs." *Social Forces* 97(2): 793–822. doi: 10.1093/sf/soy046.

Williamson, Vanessa, Theda Skocpol, and John Coggin. 2011. "The Tea Party and the Remaking of Republican Conservatism." *Perspectives on Politics* 9(01): 25–43. doi: 10.1017/S153759271000407X.

Womick, Jake, Tobias Rothmund, Flavio Azevedo, Laura A. King, and John T. Jost. 2019. "Group-Based Dominance and Authoritarian Aggression Predict Support for Donald Trump in the 2016 US Presidential Election." *Social Psychological and Personality Science* 10(5): 643–652. doi: 10.1177/1948550618778290.

Woodly, Deva R. 2021. *Reckoning: Black Lives Matter and the Democratic Necessity of Social Movements*. New York, NY: Oxford University Press.

Wouters, Ruud, and Stefaan Walgrave. 2017. "Demonstrating Power: How Protest Persuades Political Representatives." *American Sociological Review* 82(2): 361–383. doi: 10.1177/0003122417690325.

Zald, Mayer N., and John D. McCarthy. 1980. "Social Movement Industries: Competition and Cooperation among Movement Organizations." *Research in Social Movements, Conflict, and Change* 3: 1–20.

Zernike, Kate. 2010. *Boiling Mad: Inside Tea Party America*. New York, NY: Times Books.

Zoorob, Michael, and Theda Skocpol. 2020. "The Overlooked Organizational Basis of Trump's 2016 Victory," pp. 79–100 in *Upending American Politics: Polarizing Parties, Ideological Elites, and Citizen Activists from the Tea Party to the Anti-Trump Resistance*, edited by T. Skocpol and C. Tervo. New York, NY: Oxford University Press.

Index

ACORN. *See* Association of Community Organizations for Reform Now
activists, in Tea Party movement, 65–72. *See also* early activists; *specific groups*
  demographics for, 68, 69–70
  sample size for, 68
  January 6 insurrection and, 195–196
  membership trends for, 67
  political views of, 69
  Republican Party and
    as distinct identity, 71
    distrust of, 70–72
    transactional nature of relationship between, 71, 72
  self-reported, 66
  size estimation for, 72–75
    comparisons with other social movements, 75
    with survey data, 73
    at Tax Day rallies, 72, 91, 92
    through website listings, 74–75
  supporters compared to, 65–66
  surveys for, 66–67
    American National Election Survey, 75
    on self-reported activism, 66
    at Tax Day rallies, 72, 91, 92
    theoretical approach to, 64–65
    during 2010 Republican primaries, 154–157
Affordable Care Act. *See* Patient Protection and Affordable Care Act
AFP. *See* Americans for Prosperity
Age of Austerity, 198
American Family Association, 60–61
American Liberty Alliance, 4, 43

American National Election Survey (ANES), 31–32, 75
American Recovery and Investment Act, US (2009), 34, 36, 43
Americans for Prosperity (AFP), 4, 18, 21, 27, 47, 60–61. *See also* FreedomWorks
  chapter activity, 53, 118
  as grassroots coalition, 27
  Koch family involvement in, 27–28
Americans for Tax Reform (ATR), 21
  Norquist and, 22–23, 131
  Taxpayer Protection Pledge, 22–23
ANES. *See* American National Election Survey
Arab Spring protests, 18
Armey, Dick, 47
Aryan Nations, 64
Association of Community Organizations for Reform Now (ACORN), 33–34
Astroturf movement, Tea Party as, 5, 11
  test-marketed groups, 42–44
ATR. *See* Americans for Tax Reform

Bachman, Michelle, 5–6, 146, 162. *See also* Tea Party Caucus
Beck, Glenn, 45, 59–61
Biden, Joe, 194
birth and emergence, of insurgency. *See also* fragility of Tea Party insurgency; political legacy; Tax Day rallies; trajectory
  amplification of messaging, 44–46
    by Fox News, 44–46
    through media attention, 45

Emergency Economic Stabilization Act, 34
Patient Protection and Affordable Care Act, 109, 149
  attempted repeal of, 191–192
Tax Cuts and Jobs Act, 1–2, 191–192

Van Susteren, Greta, 44

White Christian conservatives. *See also* racial resentment
  decline in social power for, 115
  mobilization potential of, 19
  power devaluation for, 115
  Religious Congregations and Membership Study, 53

response to election of Obama, 20
  status threats to, 172
  Trumpism and, 172
White racial attitudes. *See also* racial resentment
  ethnonationalism and, 173–174
  on government spending, 32
  racial resentment, 31–32
White racism. *See also* racial resentment
  ethnonationalism and, 173–174
  toward Obama, 4, 7–8, 19, 20, 21
  racial resentment and, 31–32
  patriotism and, 32
  perceived loss of social power and, 8
White working class, perceived material threats to, 172–173

Printed by Printforce, United Kingdom